Executive's Guide to
Information Technology

Executive's Guide to Information Technology

Shrinking the IT Gap

James Cox

JOHN WILEY & SONS, INC.

New York • Chichester • Weinheim • Brisbane • Singapore • Toronto

Library of Congress Cataloging-in-Publication Data:

Cox, James (James J.)
    Executive's guide to information technology : shrinking the IT gap
  / James Cox.
        p.   cm.
    Includes bibliographical references.
    ISBN 0-471-35668-9 (cloth : alk. paper)
    1. Information technology.   I. Title.
    T58.5.C693   1999
    658.4'038—dc21   99-29007

Printed in the United States of America.

10 9 8 7 6 5 4 3 2 1

For Justin, age five, and Brady, age two, my grandsons—and for all the children of their generation who will live and work in a future that the readers of this book are building today

"Order and simplification are the first steps toward the mastery of a subject—the actual enemy is the unknown."

THOMAS MANN, *The Magic Mountain*

Contents

Preface

This book has been written for business executives, chief executive officers (CEOs), chief operating officers (COOs), chief financial officers (CFOs), line-of-business senior vice presidents (VPs), and anyone aspiring to those positions. It is for nontechnical business executives who must now manage information assets and directly influence decisions about the technologies that support information in business and public service organizations. This is not a technical book for technologists. It is a book about information technologies for business executives.

During almost 25 years in the computer industry, I have participated in several thousands of business meetings with both technical and nontechnical executives. In many of those meetings, I have drawn diagrams and models to explain, in general and nontechnical terms, how information technologies work in business organizations, what hardware and software components are involved, and how these components interrelate to form viable business systems.

These explanations have been mostly for *nontechnical* executives. At the end, many of these business executives usually say something like "Why the hell didn't anyone explain it that clearly before?" Surprisingly, many *technical* managers—chief information officers (CIOs), VPs of information systems, and so on—follow these same discussions with keen interest and even enthusiasm. In fact, even high-tech executives in charge of business and marketing in several very large computer companies listened with new awareness and interest.

But the models with which we worked in the 1980s and early 1990s began changing rapidly and radically with the commercialization of the Internet and the emergence of the World Wide Web in the mid-1990s. And at the same time, interactive business websites, electronic and Internet/Web commerce, and applications like integrated supply chain management, along with the rapid rise of a global economy–based on networked information all began infusing themselves into the boardroom agendas of the world's largest corporations.

In 1998 I became intrigued by A. T. Kearney's report, *Strategic Information Technology and the CEO Agenda,* which is discussed in Chapter 2, and the report's finding that top-level business executives, although they know significantly more about information technologies than they did two years earlier, express very little improvement in their comfort level with information technology (IT) issues. The chief reason why many business executives are not comfortable is that often explanations of IT are overly complicated. These explanations usually focus on individual components and how these components work, rather than on how the components interrelate and work together as a whole. For years, I have been an advocate of understanding whole systems as systems and not as a collection of parts, even when, during the 1960s and 1970s, forsaking the analysis of components as a way of understanding the whole was looked on as a kind of heresy.

When the Internet and Web tsunami started in the early 1990s, I began constructing integrated models of information technologies that illustrated how these technologies formed an infrastructure that in turn supported the practical business uses of information in an inter-networked economy—all the while, keeping the discussion focused on top-level executives in business and public service organizations. I tested these models with technologists to make certain that there was nothing out-and-out wrong or misleading and that nothing important was overlooked. I also tested the models with business practitioners and academicians for interest level and accessibility.

This book is about technology, and it needs to be comprehensive. But at the same time, it needs to avoid technological convolution and obfuscation. There is more to information technologies and their roles in business and public service organizations than intricate explanations of how the parts work. In order to sense where IT may be headed, we need to know something about its evolution. We also need to have a feel for the business dynamics of the IT industry itself and for the commercial contexts within which IT now plays such a prominent role. Although some more technically predisposed readers may quibble about a lack of in-depth technological minutiae, the contents are actually comprehensive. I hope I have managed to balance the technology content with business context in which information technologies need to be understood.

AIM OF THIS BOOK

As a business executive's guide, this book is aimed simply at three things: First, I want to give top-level business executives a firmer grip on the governance, direction, and management of what has become two of their most valuable assets, information and the technologies that support it.

Second, I hope to supply business executives with a coherent and trustworthy frame of reference that will, in turn, lay a foundation for more effective working relationships among business executives and technology managers.

Third, I want to help nontechnical executives ask better questions about the IT issues they may confront and to understand better some of the answers they may get from technical managers or advisors. Sometimes people hesitate to ask questions for fear that they might appear stupid. I hope this book will give nontechnical executives more confidence in asking key questions about IT issues. At the very least, an executive can always preface his or her question by saying "Let me ask a stupid question." This book should help executives better understand the answers they may get, even to supposedly "stupid" questions, and will help them ask the next, more penetrating question.

I want to cover all the major bases, but most of all I want to equip the top-level executives with a comprehensive model that clearly depicts the relationships among all the components that make up an information technology infrastructure. By understanding a general, macrocosmic model of this IT infrastructure, executives will gain a better grasp of the evolving roles information technologies play in their own organizations. And, even more important, nontechnical executives will develop a greater comfort level in dealing with IT business issues in general. This fundamental understanding of the complete IT infrastructure model will in turn yield a keener comprehension of the component technologies that are typically the focus of IT management and governance and of the strategic and tactical business decisions that surround them.

By way of analogy, think of building a house. Our chief concerns might be its functional viability, its aesthetic appeal, its costs, its resale value. But we may be called on for decisions about various grades of lumber, concrete, plumbing, electrical wiring, and the like. While we may not choose to get involved with every decision, we should understand which decisions deserve our attention, for we may be living in the house a long, long time. In a similar way, the IT infrastructure our organizations build today must be "lived in" tomorrow, and these IT infrastructures will, to a very large extent, determine the kind of tomorrow our organization will either enjoy or suffer through.

OUR "ROAD AHEAD"

Chapter 1 sets the stage by showing just how the executive's role and responsibilities have been impacted by the rapid rise of information and IT as the critical resource and asset in virtually all organizations. I also want to discuss some methodologies and explain, to an extent, why most commentators have so far failed to provide a comprehensive—and comprehensible—model through which business professionals and nontechnical managers can understand and, thereby, manage their own information assets and IT investments.

Chapters 3, 4, and 5 are absolutely crucial to an understanding of the IT infrastructure. In these chapters I build a generic, macrocosmic IT infrastructure model that can be understood quickly and easily. I also briefly discuss each of the component technologies that compose the model as both a roadmap and an introduction to the remaining chapters. The rest of the chapters, in turn, expand on the component technologies that make up the IT infrastructure, concentrating not so much on *how* the technologies work but on *what* they do for organization, what they deliver to business, and what roles they play in the macrocosmic IT infrastructure.

At the end, I peek into possible future IT directions and offer some observations and suggestions about using this material in governing and managing an organization's information technology strategies, capabilities, and assets. If readers decide to skip around after the key chapters on the IT infrastructure (Chapters 3, 4, and 5), I urge them to at least read the concluding chapters (13 and 14) before putting this book aside.

SUGGESTIONS ON HOW TO READ THIS BOOK

I personally cannot recall having read a business book from cover to cover, as I would read a novel. With a business book, I usually try to get a flavor for it in the first few chapters, then poke about to find what is of interest to me and what I can adopt and employ in my own work.

I encourage readers to do the same here. The next chapter is brief but lays out some critical information that will prove useful in the chapters that follow. Again, Chapters 3, 4, and 5 describing the IT infrastructure model are absolutely pivotal. Readers who do not understand these chapters will have wasted the time and money invested in this book.

Two of the "component" sections are also crucial for any sound comprehension of the IT infrastructure—the sections on networking and on information management systems (IMSs). Although many components compose the IT infrastructure, IMSs constitute the very core of it. IMSs manage the raw materials, the information itself—how it is stored, how it is retrieved, how we know it is secure and accurate as it virtually floats in the ether of networks around the globe. IMS is the *information* in information technologies. IMS is the cornerstone. That's why the topic is called *information* technology.

And although networking, in one form or another, has been around for several decades, only since the mid-1990s, with the swift commercial adaptation of the Internet and related phenomena like the World Wide Web, search engines, and electronic and Internet commerce, has networking moved to center stage. The foundations of the Internet were laid in the late 1960s, but today's Internet is a part of hundreds of millions of lives every day and will soon be as pervasive as the telephone and television.

It is not a stretch of the imagination to predict that the Internet and its related technologies will, in the not-too-distant future, be considered alongside language, mathematics, and movable type as one of humankind's premier inventions. So a familiarity with some of the fundamentals of IT networking is crucial.

An understanding of the first four chapters will give executives a much greater comfort level with IT issues, which in turn will enable them to better govern and manage their organizations' information assets and the technology investments that support those assets. By studying *all* of the remaining chapters, most readers will be able to hold forth on almost any IT issue with almost any IT specialist, understanding not only the particulars of any given IT issue but relating those particulars to both the tactical business decisions at hand and the strategic directions of the larger organization.

Finally, this is a reference book that should be used to refresh and reset readers' bearings before participating in almost any new business meeting on IT issues. Readers who are about to go into a meeting on, for example, decision support (what some people now call "business intelligence systems") should take a few minutes to review the section on decision support and business intelligence applications. And keep in mind that regardless of what IT issue is up for discussion, at the core of that issue (and of virtually every other IT issue) is both networking and information management.

As a business executive's guide, this book also should encourage further investigations of component technologies and IT infrastructures as they apply to an organization's needs and specific business decisions. IS professionals, whether company employees or contractors and consultants, should provide excellent resources for additional information and insights. And if an IS professional questions the accuracy or applicability of the IT infrastructure model I am about to build, simply ask him or her to make alterations or to draw a specific version of the IT infrastructure. That should provide a starting point for some very interesting business discussions.

Executive's Guide to
Information Technology

CHAPTER 1

Introduction: Shrinking the Gap

The winds and waves are always on the side of the ablest navigator.
—EDWARD GIBBON, *History of the Decline and Fall of the Roman Empire*

NAVIGATING THE SPHERES OF INFORMATION TECHNOLOGY

There is an old and often told story about a high-ranking admiral who every morning would open his private safe, take out a single index card, look at it for a moment, and then place it back in the safe. The admiral's staff officers and even his personal aide never knew what was on that card until, after a long and successful career, the admiral had retired. While inspecting the flag officer's sea cabin prior to the arrival of a new admiral, one of the staff officers found the card still inside the safe. On it were four neatly printed words: "Port left. Starboard right."

Just as this admiral set his bearings each morning with a simple but crucial frame of reference, this book provides top-level business executives with an appropriate model that will help them navigate one of the most intricate and vital spheres of modern commerce—information technology (IT). And although what follows may be a bit more involved than the admiral's simple formula, the model is easily comprehended and will serve as a reliable frame of reference for nontechnical, top-level executives who must navigate the depths and shoals of today's global economy.

The book also aims to give senior executives and business managers a firmer grasp of their own organizations' IT capabilities and the IT issues surrounding them. This will allow executives to consolidate their information assets with the ongoing business processes of expanding competitive value for both customers and constituents. Increased customer value, that is, the value that a customer *receives* and *perceives* from a business engagement, ultimately not only improves a firm's competitive position and its profitability but also increases its shareholders' wealth. During the last quarter of the twentieth century, the focus on improving quality and increasing customer value has perhaps been the crowning contributions of the industrial era. And as Tom Peters and other commentators are constantly pointing out, top-notch quality is a given—it is the ante required just to get into the game. Improved customer value, both received and perceived, is the only real way to sustain profits, growth, and shareholder wealth. And since senior executive compensation normally is interlaced tightly with both improved profitability and increased shareholder wealth, and since IT is intertwined with both, a better grasp of IT issues by top-line executives positively impacts not just the organization's bottom line but also most executives' personal net worth.

SHRINKING THE GAP

This book's audience consists of top-level executives and senior managers in business and in public service organizations as well as anyone who aspires to these types of positions. The book is built on a broadly accepted premise that information is, at the end of the twentieth century, the most valuable asset of virtually any modern organization. Of the many assets with which an organization's top executives are entrusted, information and its supporting technologies have now become the most crucial resources for the creation of value and wealth.

Over the past half decade a persistent theme among professional periodicals, books, conferences, and seminars aimed at information systems (IS) executives has been this urgent need for IS management to better align IT with business and larger organizational priorities—to shrink the gap, as it were, between what IS professionals and their IS organizations do and what top-level executives establish as the priorities of their business or public service organizations. There is plenty of discussion among IS professionals about how they can become more business savvy and bring IT to bear on real business issues and larger organizational needs, presumably as these are set forth by top executives. Some discussion about why this effort should be a two-way street also is beginning, determining why business executives need to become more familiar and comfortable with IT issues so that they can better communicate business priorities to their IS staffs.

The *first gap* this book aims to shrink is the one between top executives, who need a better comprehension of and comfort level with IT and the issues surrounding IT, and IS executives, who need to better understand business issues and how to work more effectively with business management to achieve larger organizational goals. Unlike other books, this book places the onus on top executives in business and public service organizations to do their part and meet the IS professionals partway.

First, top-level executives need to define their business and organizational priorities within the context of longer-term organizational strategies and with fairly specific missions and objectives. Then, together with IS executives, top executives should determine how IT fits into that larger picture. They should not just assume that IS executives can do this on their own. An old adage contends we are not truly businesspeople unless we have done one of two things, and preferably both of them: We have either had to make payroll for our company, that is, we have made certain that there is money in the company bank account when our employees try to cash their paychecks, or we have carried a sales bag and our ability to feed and shelter our families depended directly on our ability to earn commissions on what we sell. Business school is not a substitute for either experience, unless, of course, the worker relied on tips from waiting tables to pay his or her way through school. Most IS professionals, unless they have been part of the team heading a technology start-up company, have not had and are not likely to have either of these core business experiences. To its credit, IBM in years past required that anyone desiring to move up into executive ranks had to have carried successfully an IBM bag in a sales territory; this experience ensured that, regardless of their professional backgrounds, IBM executives had a keen appreciation for front-line business and customer values.

Today top executives need to define business priorities as these relate specifically to IT and communicate those priorities to their IS professionals. This book will help executives to begin shrinking that gap between their organization's business priorities and their IS organization's

IT endeavors. That effort requires both a comprehension of and a comfort with information technologies and the surrounding issues, and that is what this book offers to nontechnical executives.

But there is *a second gap,* one that is perhaps even more important for business executives to bridge—shrinking the gap between the emergence of new information technologies and the innovative use of new IT capabilities in the creation of new value for customers and constituents. Let us imagine for a moment that it is 1994 and we are Jeff Bezos, the founder of Amazon.com. We understand what the commercialization of the Internet and the World Wide Web can mean for commerce. We devise a business plan, focusing on retail book sales. Why books? Because most people know what book they want to buy when they go into a bookstore, or they browse on their own through titles and topics. There is not much real selling going on, at least from the retailer, the bookstore itself. Mostly it is customer selection and a payment transaction.

Thus it is a rather straightforward retail transaction, which we know how to automate. With the Internet and the Web, we could replicate the buying and browsing experience in hyperspace, so to speak. And we could even personalize the book-buying experience by tracking purchases and matching these to recommendations, thereby expanding sales beyond the customer's original planned purchase, something book retailers count on. Finally, we could reduce inventory costs by networking with distributors and innovating a few wholesale arrangements and delivery capabilities.

And so Amazon.com is born and transforms at least one sector of the retail industry while influencing a number of others. This book cites other examples of how businesses have been transformed by the Internet, the Web, and other networked information technologies. But the text returns again and again to Amazon.com, not because there are no other fine business websites—there are plenty. Rather, Amazon.com is focused because it is not an extension of an existing business but a fully blown Web-enabled business, and Jeff Bezos and company do an outstanding job of providing a retail experience for customers that offers new customer value and is engaging, efficient, and uncommonly reliable. Another reason is because it is very easy for readers to go to Amazon.com and see for themselves what we are talking about.

So Jeff, who knows technology but had never been in retailing before, takes an array of networked information technologies and builds a business that in less than five years makes him an on-paper billionaire. He did not buy an off-the-shelf business application as a way of creating new customer value. He created a new and different type of business that delivers new value to customers and creates new wealth for Amazon.com's shareholders and himself. (AMZN traded from a low of around $10 to a high of $199 and seems settled in at around $100 to $110 per share.)

Unfortunately, most top executives confine their business innovation to what technology providers give them. By doing so these executives are condemned to waiting for intermediaries to devise new ways of using emerging technologies. These technology solution providers sell technology bundles that may reduce costs by automating previously manual processes but that usually bring neither new value for their customers nor any real competitive advantage in the executives' industries and markets. In addition, the technology suppliers are selling the same solutions to our competitors. Implementing SAP financial software is not a competitive advantage when everyone else has SAP financial software or something very like it.

Let us draw two pictures. They will be oversimplifications, of course, but they are useful in illustrating this second gap. First, let us look at how emerging technologies usually find their way into businesses, starting with emergence of new hardware and software technologies and ending with the business uses of those new technologies. (See Exhibit 1.1.)

In the evolution of new information technologies in particular, the development of new hardware almost invariably precedes the evolution of

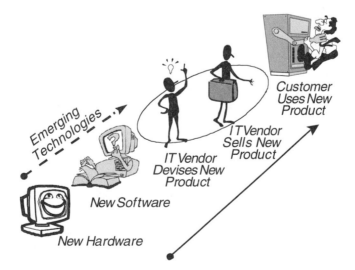

Exhibit 1.1   Common Migration of Technology to Business

new software. In turn, new software capabilities precede commercial adoption and use of the new technologies, both hardware and software. The thing to notice especially in Exhibit 1.1 is that technology vendors assume the responsibility of figuring out how businesses can use these new and emerging technologies. The vendors then build and bundle those technologies, and finally sell them on their merits and business benefits, as the vendors have defined these merits and benefits, to businesses.

What is wrong with that? For one thing, this process usually entails no real competitive advantage for businesses. But perhaps even more important, there is a huge gap between the availability of new and emerging information technologies and the actual adoption and application of those technologies by business and public service organizations to create new value for customers and constituents.

Which brings us back to the second kind of gap that needs shrinking, that between technology availability and the use of new technologies in the creation of new customer value. The shrinking of this gap will be even more challenging, more demanding for top-level executives than that of shrinking the gap between business executives and IS management. And those businesses and public service organizations whose executives can shrink this second crucial gap will lead the field and pull quickly ahead of their competitors, forging new customer value and even transforming their industries while expanding their shareholders' wealth. (See Exhibit 1.2.)

Executives themselves must be keenly aware of the emergence of new networked information technologies and continually must innovate strategies and direct tactics that adopt these new technologies in creating customer value well ahead of their competitors. If the gap between the emergence of a new set of information technologies and the useful business application of those technologies is five or six years, and the organization, because of executive leadership and involvement, can shrink that gap to two years, imagine the kind of competitive lead that organization could have. And this use of technology, although soon copied by competitors, would not be off-the-shelf and for sale, unless the organization itself chose to sell it.

In his widely read book, *Crossing the Chasm,* Geoff Moore sets up a model for high-tech companies that takes us through several stages of the "technology adoption life cycle." It moves from innovator (the very earliest technical users), to early adopters (the first real business users), to early majority (more cautious but still advanced business users), to late majority (who use only widely accepted technologies, and then somewhat

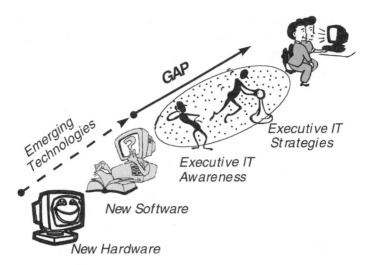

Exhibit 1.2 Creating New Customer Values through Executive IT Strategies

reluctantly), to laggards (who use technologies only when they are buried inside other products).[1]

Moore directs his insights strictly to high-tech providers and focuses on the critical chasm between early adopters and the early majority. While early adopters do not necessarily lead to an early majority, the latter almost always leads to a later majority. Early and late majorities spell market dominance for high-tech providers who can cross the chasm from early adopters to early majority.

This book is not intended for high-tech providers or their marketing professionals, as *Crossing the Chasm* is. Here we are talking to business and public service executives and their organizations. And the gap we talk about shrinking here could almost be seen as a mirror image of Moore's model. But in this context, top business executives are urged to move their awareness closer to the innovator and early-adopter cycles, so they can shrink the gap between the emergence of new information technologies and their organizations' use of those technologies in the creation of new customer value. The more that business executives can shrink that gap, the better able their organizations are to survive and thrive into the next century in a networked information economy.

The world's leading organizations are now engaged and competing in a global knowledge-based economy, and most of the leaders of those companies are thoroughly committed to the governance of information and its supporting technologies. Yet even for a dedicated IS professional, staying on top of rapidly developing technologies and keeping current with technology's evolving roles are time-consuming and ongoing endeavors. This book will give nontechnical business executives a sort of Rosetta stone that will help make sense of what often seems to be a chaotic cluster of esoteric components.

I cannot wave a magic wand or provide an injection of structured DNA that will make executives permanently "technology literate." Nor is the effort required to stay on top of constantly advancing technologies likely to diminish soon. But executives can make that effort more efficient and more effective.

This book offers one central statement: *Senior executives and business managers today can manage and lead their organizations toward success only if they understand two things:*

1. How to use information as a fundamental resource in fulfilling their organizational missions
2. How to manage information assets and the investments in their organizations' IT infrastructure and its supporting technologies and services

To accomplish this, executives must develop a comprehensive understanding of their organization's information technology infrastructure and cultivate a firm grasp of its components, how these components interrelate, and how they can be used to achieve the goals and fulfill the mission of the organization, whether large or small, commercial or public sector.

"Technophobia" is no longer a tolerable trait in any senior executive or business manager. From financial markets and services to the modern military, from health care to transportation, from retail sales to public services, in virtually every industry, every profession, and every walk of life, information is not just a vital asset—it is *the* vital asset.

Information technology infrastructures—information and its supporting technologies and services—also represent the single largest capital expenditures in large organizations today. IT-related expenditures account for more than 50 percent of all capital spending in the United States and for more than one-third of the nation's economic growth.[2] Individual organizations and large economies that fall behind this curve are finding it increasingly difficult to catch up to their competitors and to improve or even sustain their own business and economic conditions.

Suddenly, at the turn of the twenty-first century, top-level executives are responsible for strategic directions and even key tactical decisions that earlier were the sole province of technology managers in the MIS or IT department. Heretofore, fiscal supervision from the chief financial officer provided the sole link in most organizations between IS functions and top-level executive management.

The IT infrastructure and the information assets it provides and supports are too crucial to an organization's general success or failure to remain remote from the guidance of top-level executives. Nor is the decentralization of IS responsibility into lines of business and functional divisions a viable long-term alternative to the informed and prudent governance of board-level executives. Lines-of-business executives and operational managers need a broad range of technologies to fulfill their missions and to deliver their contributions to the larger organization. However, fragmentation of corporate or organizational IT infrastructures into lines of business frequently squanders both IT budgets and information resources; it also can severely weaken a business's ability to compete in a global knowledge-based economy.

A poorly planned, fragmented IT infrastructure will also diminish a public sector organization's ability to deliver services among a rapidly changing mix of constituencies. Think for a moment of changing demands that are likely to be made on healthcare, social security, education, defense, law enforcement, and just about every other public service sector during the next ten years, not just in the United States but in virtually every nation, state, province, city, and town around the world. And every demand, every change will in some fundamental way be directly linked to the capabilities and capacities, or lack thereof, of a public service organization's IT infrastructure.

IT infrastructures are now as important for almost every one of us as are roads, bridges, railways, airports, water and sewage systems, and the supply of electricity and the telephone systems that are the immediate predecessors of the IT infrastructures. And law enforcement, emergency services, and healthcare in much of the world are critically dependent on IT infrastructures. Anyone not affected by IT infrastructures is quite literally in a very isolated minority.

In commercial and public sector organizations alike, IT issues are now a compelling priority on the boardroom agendas. Peter Weill and Marianne Broadbent point out in their book *Leveraging the New Infrastructure* that "Senior managers clearly cannot afford to delegate or abdicate to technical personnel critical decisions about the new [IT] infrastructure."[3] But are top-level executives fully prepared to take up this new responsibility for IT governance and direction?

The fundamental management problem is that the generation of executives currently occupying mahogany row, although generally well versed in Drucker, Porter, Peters, Handy, Naisbitt, and others, usually have little acquaintance with information technology beyond Excel or Lotus 1-2-3 spreadsheets and email, if that. And although many in the upcoming generation of executives hold MBA degrees, are experienced with personal computers, and can access the Internet and World Wide Web, these future top executives display little understanding of technologies that comprise the "new infrastructure." It would be almost as if the next generation of civil engineers knew how to drive their own personal automobiles but knew very little about building roads and bridges, while the generation of civil engineers preceding them still relied mostly on chauffeurs to drive their cars.

A lack of knowledge and understanding of IT issues on the part of senior executives and business managers can—and does—lead to disastrous consequences. Clayton Christensen unveils some of these disasters in his book, *The Innovator's Dilemma,* and throughout this book are provided some cautionary tales of anonymous but real-life IT infrastructure missteps caused by inadequate executive governance of information technologies.[4]

Much has been said and written about the need for IS executives to become better versed in and adept at business issues, so that they might better align IT efforts with business priorities. And the best and brightest among IS professionals are doing just that.

But at the dawn of the twenty-first century, current top-level executives and the new generation of aspiring executives need to assume responsibility for understanding the IT infrastructure and meet the IS professionals at least partway. No longer can top-level managers afford to govern vital information assets and manage critical IT investments by throwing darts in self-imposed darkness. It is time some lights were turned on.

NOTES

1. Geoffrey A. Moore, *Crossing the Chasm: Marketing and Selling High-Tech Products to Mainstream Customers* (New York: HarperBusiness, 1991).

2. Tom Davenport with Larry Prusak, *Information Ecology: Mastering the Information and Knowledge Environment* (New York: Oxford University Press, 1997), p. 6.

3. Peter Weill and Marianne Broadbent, *Leveraging the New Infrastructure: How Market Leaders Capitalize on Information Technology* (Boston: Harvard Business School Press, 1998), p. 8.

4. Clayton M. Christensen, *The Innovator's Dilemma: When New Technologies Cause Great Firms to Fail Technology* (Boston: Harvard Business School Press, 1997).

CHAPTER 2

Another Brave New World

Oh brave new world,
That it has such people in it.
WILLIAM SHAKESPEARE, *The Tempest,* Act V

A NEW EXECUTIVE PHENOMENON

The core of this book deals with an immediate and very real set of business and economic phenomena that are rapidly altering the roles and behaviors of executives in every industry and in almost every organization around the world. Top-line business executives, in addition to their various traditional responsibilities, must now engage directly in the governance of information resources and the information technologies supporting those resources.

A. T. Kearney, the management consulting arm of EDS, surveyed 213 chief executive officers (CEOs) from large companies worldwide. Kearney's report, released in June 1998, finds for the first time that IT and data management "are top-of-mind [issues for] CEOs and business executives across industries and around the globe." Their most prominent finding: "Information Technology and its surrounding issues are firmly—and probably permanently—entrenched in the boardrooms of today's major corporations. No longer strictly the realm of the technicians, IT is now a leading concern of top decision-makers and is therefore increasingly a number one priority on the CEO agenda."[1]

Executives today fully understand that information is a critical asset—if not *the* most valuable asset—in the creation of value and wealth for almost all business organizations. At the end of the twentieth century, the "intangible" assets of information itself and of the knowledge workers who use information as their raw material have superseded the industrial era asset triumvirate of land, labor, and capital.[2]

CEOs and business executives everywhere instinctively recognize their responsibilities in governing information and knowledge resources. These executives know they must manage information and its supporting technologies as they would any other asset entrusted to them by their boards of directors, shareholders, and customers and constituents.

The Kearney report goes on to disclose two apparently conflicting phenomena. First, top-level business executives are "devoting an increasing amount of time to improving their technology awareness." According to Kearney's survey, CEOs spend an average of 22 percent of their total business time "trying to keep abreast of technologies that might affect their companies." For most CEOs that could be 10 to 12 hours or more every week.

Second, and herein lies the paradox, even though these executives are claiming a better working knowledge of technology than they had two years earlier, "they express little if any improvement in their comfort level in dealing with technology issues." It seems somewhat like a case of "the faster I go, the farther behind I get."

There is no question that creation of value and wealth in both local and global economies now hinges on the effective management of information and knowledge and on the prudent governance of information resources and technologies. Yet few top-level executives feel comfortable governing and managing these vital economic resources.

As reported in *Computerworld,* James Champy, coauthor with Michael Hammer of *Reengineering the Corporation,* provides a more personalized boardroom experience which underscores the Kearney report's findings[3]:

> Recently, I sat in on a skull session of a very famous company's top management team. Just one item loomed on the agenda: the future of the business. Oddly, the meeting had been called by the company's IT executive, of all people.
>
> As I looked at the folks from research, marketing, logistics, sales, finance, human resources and legal, I thought: "Shouldn't the CEO have scheduled this gathering?" With the CEO hanging on his every word, the IT guy smoothly opened the discussion on digitally enabled global channels and commerce.[4]

The executives of this "very famous" company seem fortunate in that they apparently have an IT executive who can "smoothly" (by which I infer "coherently") lead a business discussion and explain the technologies involved to nontechnical business managers. We also should assume that this IT executive knows what he is talking about.

Unfortunately, many top-level executives feel that they possess few trustworthy frames of reference to help them verify their IT managers' assertions and contentions or that would equip them to ask cogent questions of IT executives, or at least to ask questions that penetrate beyond "How much will this cost?" or "What is the return on investment?"

Perhaps the chief barrier to understanding information technology is its daunting complexity. But simply because a subject is complex does not mean it must of necessity be complicated. The purpose of this book is to render the complexities of information technologies in uncomplicated terms. To achieve that, this book builds an easily comprehended model of the information technology infrastructure. But before doing that, it will be helpful to understand a bit of methodology, which, in turn, will reveal why most commentators have not yet offered, to paraphrase Thomas Mann, "order and simplification" toward mastery of this complex subject.

OF "INFOSTRUCTURES" AND INFRASTRUCTURES

Don Tapscott, author of *The Digital Economy,* among several others, refers to this phenomenon as the "infostructure."[5] And the term "infrastructure" in relation to information technology is getting bandied about more and more. Even the President of the United States receives elaborate executive briefings on the key roles of information technologies as they relate to the "national infrastructure."[6]

This book talks about an *information technology infrastructure (IT infrastructure),* not as if it were some mythical beast. It is defined in terms that make sense to business executives who must govern and manage information assets.

The IT infrastructure has attracted growing attention over the past few years. Peter Weill and Marianne Broadbent's *Leveraging the New Infrastructure* provides an excellent and detailed discussion of how business managers can grapple with today's single largest capital investment—information technologies—and turn it into an asset that "generates measurable value."

Weill and Broadbent define their infrastructure as "a firm's total investment in computing and communications technology," including all services and related expenses. And their definition is both appropriate and useful in the context of measuring and managing IT as a capital asset. And if, after reading this book, readers want more in-depth management guidance, Weill and Broadbent's book is the best available.

Here the concern is not so much total capital expense or investment leverage but understanding the various technology components and their roles and their interrelationships within the context of an IT infrastructure model. In order to make sound decisions about leveraging capital investment, some knowledge about the things in which the capital is being invested is needed.

In the IT context, the organization's total IT expense could be less than $1 million over three years, or its monthly IT communications bill alone could be ten times that. The IT infrastructure model to be built will be both pertinent and consistent for either scenario.

More and more discussions about IT infrastructures are taking place as we move into the twenty-first century. Governments of developed and emerging nations are beginning to realize that countries that build and maintain superior IT infrastructures will produce economies and societies that will thrive and prevail. The economies and even the societies and cultures of countries that cannot or do not build and maintain adequate IT infrastructures are likely to struggle and decline.

And it is the same with business organizations. Those businesses whose management teams build and maintain robust, dependable, and flexible IT infrastructures will advance and prosper. Those that do not will decline and eventually dissolve.

"PARTS IS PARTS"

Modern science has shown that we are not likely to understand complex dynamic systems by focusing on the parts. And a central problem in comprehending something like an IT infrastructure lies in fundamental, formal thought processes that have prevailed in Europe and the Americas for 2,500 years, processes instilled by years of rote learning and convention. *What are those thought processes? People tend first to examine and try to understand the individual "parts" as a means of perceiving the "whole."*

This is Western civilization's Cartesian and Newtonian heritage. Its roots lie in the Eleatic school of Greek philosophy in the fifth century B.C.; the beliefs travel in a relatively straight line from Democritus and the Greek atomists through Aristotle to Descartes and Newton. The penultimate manifestation of the belief that understanding all or just some of the "parts" can lead to a comprehension of the "whole" can be found in the Neilson television ratings and in the ubiquitous political and news polls.

That is not to say that this mental practice of focusing on components is not useful and productive. Such analytical thinking has resulted in much of what we enjoy today as the fruits of progress in our professional and our personal lives. But it also limits our cognition, and those limitations can have dire long-term results. Witness, for example, a global ecosystem that seems teetering on the brink of disruption, chiefly as a result of all this progress—and of our sometimes self-limiting cognitive capabilities.

Modern science began moving beyond this mental construct almost a century ago. With the introduction of quantum mechanics and the new physics and the advent of complex systems thinking, chaos theory, complementarity, fractals, emergent computation, autopoiesis, Gaia theory, organismic biology, and a host of other revolutionary directions of inquiry, science began pursuing an understanding of the "whole" not through a mechanistic analysis of constituent parts but through observations of the dynamic relationships among various entities and phenomena that make up the universe and life—in other words, the ultimate "whole."

Not to worry. Gravity still works, at least in the dimensions of our day-to-day existence, so far as we know these. But modern science has shown that we are not likely to understand complex dynamic systems by focusing on the parts. Perceiving the intricate webs of relationships will begin leading us to a comprehension of the whole.

In fact, management systems theory adopts as its fundamental precept the view that a system is not merely a sum of constituent parts, and in order to be successful, the system cannot be managed simply as discrete, compartmentalized units but as a "whole" system. The fundamental precepts of business process management focus on managing the "process," not just the tasks that make it up. And managing the parts does not necessarily result in effective management of the whole. In fact, that may be the singular misconception under which humans have labored since the dawn of the Industrial Revolution. It now seems clear that during our hunter-gatherer and agrarian epochs, humankind, being more intimately involved with the natural environment, focused much more on the "whole"—the larger cycles of nature—than on individual parts or events.

With a subject like IT infrastructures in particular, as with technology in general, mental habits of attempting to understand the "parts" in order to comprehend the "whole" hinder us from achieving even a comfort level with the "parts" themselves. For one thing, there are simply just too many components. IT infrastructures seem to approach what modern science calls *complex systems,* that is, forms of matter that tend to organize themselves into increasingly intricate relationships with a greater variety of components. A system is complex in that "a great many independent agents are interacting with each other in a great many ways."[7] Like most scientists, even highly talented information technologists can only truly know that set of components in which they specialize. But that knowledge seems almost never to lead to a comprehension of the "whole."

Indeed, technicians may be the least likely to perceive the whole. As Gary Zukav says about technicians (whom he distinguishes from scientists) in his book on the New Physics, "Because their noses often are buried in the bark of a particular tree, it is difficult to speak meaningfully to them of forests."[8]

Here the focus is on seeing the forest. While attention is paid to many of the different types of trees that make it up, we are especially interested in finding the paths that will lead us through the forest. The focus is not on a particular type of bark.

Keep in mind the discussion of "parts" versus "whole." Business executives have always needed to see the "big picture." Now that IT is a vital part of that big picture, executives must maintain a similarly broad vision when governing and managing IT. Maintaining this broad vision requires a disciplined effort. It is easy to become sidetracked by the complexities of component technologies, which leads executives into the quagmire of complication and away from the "order and simplification" required for leadership and governance.

Since the aim is an understanding of a "whole," the next chapter builds a comprehensive model of the entire IT infrastructure and begins to draw the relationships among the technologies that compose that infrastructure, the "whole." As mentioned earlier, an understanding of the next chapter is vital.

NOTES

1. A.T. Kearney, *Strategic Information Technology and the CEO Agenda,* (June 1998).

2. See Peter Drucker, *Post-Capitalist Society* (New York: HarperBusiness, 1993); Charles Handy, *The Age of Paradox* (New York: Harvard Business School Press, 1994); Tom Stewart, *Intellectual Capital: The New Wealth of Organizations* (New York: Bantam Doubleday Dell, 1997); among others.

3. James Champy and Michael Hammer, *Reengineering the Corporation: A Manifesto for Business Revolution* (New York: HarperBusiness, 1993).

4. *Computerworld,* July 27, 1998, p. 72; http://www.computerworld.com/home /print.nsf/all/9807275CDA

5. Don Tapscott, *The Digital Economy: Promise and Peril in the Age of Networked Intelligence* (New York: McGraw-Hill, 1996).

6. http://www.hpcc.gov/talks/case-9Dec97/

7. M. Mitchell Waldrop, *Complexity: The Emerging Science at the Edge of Chaos* (New York: Touchstone/Simon & Schuster, 1992/1993), p. 11.

8. Gary Zukav, *The Dancing Wu Li Masters: An Overview of the New Physics* (New York: William Morrow & Co., 1979), p. 10.

CHAPTER 3

Building the New Information Technology Infrastructure Model

*Synergy means behavior of whole
systems unpredicted by the behavior of their parts.*
—BUCKMINSTER FULLER, 1966

LEGACY INFORMATION TECHNOLOGY MODELS

The model built here is not without precedent. Since the early 1980s people working within the information technology (IT) business have been using similar models to explain the relationships among a number of technology components. Before that time almost all explanations of commercial computing technologies were confined to a particular hardware vendor's worldview. All platform components (hardware and operating systems) were either acquired from a single hardware vendor or had to conform to a particular vendor's specifications, frequently referred to as application programming interfaces (APIs). For the technology vendors, it was the golden age of proprietary systems.

Technology providers tend to favor proprietary systems over open systems (these are systems that are made publicly available and all third parties have the opportunity to understand, modify, and enhance them). Why? The answer goes back at least as far as the bitter rivalry between George Westinghouse and Thomas Edison over different models of

21

delivering electricity, AC versus DC. It was all about customer lock-in then, and it is all about customer lock-in now.

Thus IBM's model did not look like Digital's model, which did not look like Data General's or Burroughs's or Wang's, and on and on. Even if a company developed a business application in a computer language that conformed to specific standards, such as "standard" COBOL or BASIC, a business application developed for one hardware vendor's system would not work on another vendor's hardware. Technology vendors frequently called this "differentiation." Regardless of vendor rhetoric, proprietary technology means "customer lock-in." (Even the term "open system" is subject to rhetorical abuse by high-tech marketers.)

Things began changing for business computing in the late 1970s because of events that began occurring over a decade earlier. As a direct effect of the Cold War and the space race in the 1960s, key elements of U.S. scientific and research communities developed a compelling need to share information and applications. Therefore they began, out of necessity, to migrate toward "open systems," including an operating system from Bell Labs (now Lucent Technologies) called Unix and new computer language called C. Also during the 1960s, the scientific and research communities concentrated chiefly among universities and defense and aerospace companies, the need arose to share information among geographically remote computer installations. That need generated an open networking concept, initially funded by the U.S. Defense Advanced Research Project Agency (DARPA) and later called the ARPAnet. It was the forerunner of today's Internet, which itself was funded by the U.S. National Science Foundation and was first called NSFnet.

Where science leads, so shall business follow sooner or later, at least sometimes. During the first few years of the 1980s, several pivotal phenomena impacted commercial computing. First, IBM developed an open system for the personal computer based on off-the-shelf, 16-bit hardware and software technologies, principally the Intel processor and a DOS operating system provided by a then-tiny Seattle-based company called Microsoft. In effect, IBM put the nascent, 8-bit hobbyist computer on commodity-based steroids, shifted the PC industry into warp speed, and forever changed the way the world does business, while inadvertently making Bill Gates the world's wealthiest individual and creating tens of thousands of multimillionaires (and a few other billionaires) in Gates's wake. IBM's role in creating both the PC industry and the proliferation of entrepreneurial wealth that accompanied it should silence those critics who feel that large American corporations lack a sense of largess.

During the first couple of years of the 1980s, Wang Laboratories was perhaps best positioned among all computer companies to dominate the personal computer market. Wang contended with Digital for the number-two global market position behind IBM for all commercial computer systems and held absolute dominance in office automation. Digital chairman Ken Olson openly scoffed at the personal computer. IBM legitimized the concept, built an open system with commodity components, but refused to cannibalize its corporate market by selling the PC through its massive global sales force. Wang had the global sales and support capabilities, the customer base in large commercial and government organizations, and the expertise in desktop applications where the PC would find its first and largest markets (word processing and spreadsheets), but the company fumbled badly by building a completely proprietary—and thus incompatible—personal computer. The three tall office towers of Wang's headquarters that dominate the Lowell, Massachusetts, skyline, filled and bustling in 1980, were almost vacant a decade later. Wang's inherent mentality of building proprietary and closed systems prevented the company from participating in the PC revolution at a time when it could have very well been the dominant market leader for corporate PCs.

At just about the same time the PC phenomenon was taking place, the Unix operating system and the C programming language germinated at Bell Labs and relational database technologies from IBM and Oracle began supporting more and more larger commercial and government applications. And customers, at first slowly then with rapidly growing momentum, began preferring open systems based on Unix and relational databases over proprietary minicomputer technologies. It would not be long before a new generation of commercial applications running on open systems technologies would begin usurping the traditional domains of mainframe computers.

When all this began happening, a need developed for new ways of explaining how the various open systems technologies fit together. Sometimes called the "technology stack" or, mostly among vendor marketing types, the "solution stack," these models have provided useful contexts for understanding the gap between business problems and possible technology solutions. These models also allowed technology vendors to position their products—or "solutions"—inside the stack and in relation with other technology components.

The high-tech use of a stack model is based on the seven-layer ISO telecommunications stack that, in fact, created the foundation for the consistent, standards-based global telecommunications people enjoy today. Following the ISO model, the legacy open-systems technology stack started at the bottom with hardware and proceeded upward through operating systems, relational database, tools and middleware, to applications, and, at the top, user interfaces or graphical user interfaces (GUIs), mostly commonly today are Microsoft's Windows and Apple's Macintosh. (See Exhibit 3.1.)

The use of this stack model is not confined to technology vendors. High-tech analysts and commentators find technology stack useful to understand the investment potential of diverse technology stocks and to position the various strengths and shortcomings of competing technology providers. Geoff Moore, Paul Johnson, and Tom Kippola use a variation of the technology stack in their book, *The Gorilla Game.*[1] They separate technologies into enabling technologies and application software. Their enabling technologies include everything from hardware and operating systems to databases, networking, and tools—in other words, from Intel, Compaq, and Microsoft, to Oracle, Cisco, and Java. Applications software encompasses a broad range of enterprise applications— loosely called ERP (enterprise resource planning). These include "back-office" applications like manufacturing, distribution and supply

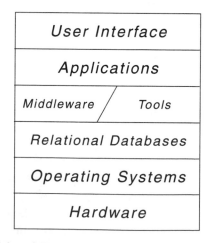

Exhibit 3.1   Traditional Technology Stack

chain management, and financial and human resource applications, currently supplied by software companies like SAP, PeopleSoft, Oracle, Baan, among others, and a broad range of more highly focused niche business and industry application providers. Most recently these ERP applications also encompass "front-office" applications, such as sales force automation and customer care from software vendors like Siebel, Epiphany, and Arum (now a part of Baan). And as businesses move into more Internet-centric endeavors, there has been a growing emphasis on and proliferation of "e-business" applications, including electronic commerce and one-to-one marketing applications.

Moore, Johnson, and Kippola further segment their enabling technologies layer into "systems software," "hardware," and "semiconductors," most of which can become commodities and thereby form self-proliferating standards—Intel processors, Microsoft Windows operating systems, even Oracle databases. And this model fits their purposes, which are aimed at discerning "hypergrowth markets" and detecting the emerging "gorillas" that represent the optimum investment opportunities in high-tech stocks. If Weill and Broadbent's *Leveraging the New Infrastructure* is recommended reading for managing a firm's value-producing IT assets, then *The Gorilla Game* might be mandatory reading for managing personal investments in high-tech stocks. In a broad sense, both books are about managing IT investments to achieve optimum returns on investment.

These books rely on a variation of the IT infrastructure model to explore their fundamental (yet very different) theses. This book is dedicated solely to describing IT infrastructure as an interlaced web of complementary technology components, so it is more specific about the components and their interrelations than either of the other two books are.

Put another way, if these three books were about automobiles, Weill and Broadbent would consider everything, from the price of the vehicle to the insurance, fuel, and upkeep—even the parking expense, driver training, and licensing—to illustrate how to realize increased business value for the total automotive investment.

Moore, Johnson, and Kippola, however, want to understand which of the component suppliers for automobiles will emerge as the dominant supplier of its component inside its competitive market, so that stock bets can be placed on the "gorilla" component supplier. Should someone invest in Michelin or Goodyear or both? And how does one know that automobile tires are a hypergrowth market in the first place?

In building the infrastructure model of this book, we want to know what the components are (engine, drive train, axle, steering, etc.), but we also want to have some idea of how they interrelate, of the differences among similar components, and what they all mean for what we may want to do with a car. Should we get a V8 or a V6? What do we get if we spend an extra $2,500 for the Nakamichi or Blaupunkt luxury CD sound system? Or do we just need basic, reliable transportation from point A to point B and back? Or should we skimp on the engine and brakes and spend more on a leather interior?

We must know what roles the components play and how they interrelate in order to make informed and prudent decisions, whether about acquiring an automobile or shaping strategies for an IT infrastructure.

NEW INFORMATION TECHNOLOGY INFRASTRUCTURE MODEL

One word of caution: Do not worry about completely comprehending this IT infrastructure model immediately. By the end of these first few chapters, readers should feel comfortable navigating the model. To gain a thorough comfort level, readers will need to read each chapter on the individual infrastructure components.

As mentioned in Chapter 1, this chapter provides a general understanding of how all the pieces fit into the "whole"—the IT infrastructure. Many readers will understand this in the context of their own organization's internal IT infrastructure, and that is an appropriate place to start.

The understanding of other readers will reach beyond organizational firewalls and encompass an overarching IT infrastructure, which blends components from the Internet and the World Wide Web and reaches out to suppliers' and customers' infrastructures. All these and more go into making up broader, more expansive, and shared IT infrastructures—like electronic commerce, healthcare, and shared scientific research, where the Internet finds its roots.

What makes information technology so radically different on the eve of the twenty-first century are not only the advances in the technologies themselves, although those advances are considerable and continual. The difference lies in the ways we are beginning to view and use the information, not just *in* but *among* business organizations. Peter Drucker points out that we are beginning now to concentrate on the "I"—the *information*—and less on the "T."[2]

For precisely these reasons, "information" is positioned at the center of the IT infrastructure model we are about to build. Ultimately, the technology exists solely to support the information and the knowledge workers. Information itself and knowledge workers, who use information as their raw material, are the core asset of all modern organizations. Also, technology is not a mere commodity or a contemporary form of magic.

In addition to shifting emphasis from the "T" to the "I" in IT, a radical open systems change has occurred in networking. In the legacy stack of the early and mid-1980s, networking was pretty much an afterthought, something added when it absolutely had to be added. Networking was delicate, limited, mostly proprietary, and sometimes diaphanous. During the early and mid-1990s all that changed with the rapid commercial adoption of the Internet, which has quickly elevated business IT to a new plateau.

And if anyone doubts that we have entered a new era of commerce, picture yourself as the CEO of the book retailer Barnes and Noble in 1994. Your competitive strategies would have focused on Borders and B. Dalton. You would not have envisioned that in less than three years a then-unknown company in Seattle, which would open a website and not one single retail storefront, would be your most fearsome competitor. And that happened because of the Internet, the World Wide Web, and browser technologies from Netscape and later by Microsoft—none of which was really commercially feasible before 1994 and all of which focus on *networked information.*

In the very short span of five years—fast even for technology—the world has moved from an era of "information systems" to an age of "networked information." That is much more than a simple semantic change. Information systems were generally stand-alone, transaction-oriented systems that automated previously manual tasks, like bookkeeping. *Networked information* provides the foundations for entirely new types of commerce and public service that involve increasingly intricate relationships and greater variety. Beginning to sound like one of modern science's *complex systems,* isn't it?

Networking now is the fundamental component of modern information systems. Although many components make up the IT infrastructure, without open, standards-based networking, an organization's IT infrastructure would be about as useful as an internal corporate phone system that does not connect to telephones outside the building. And if any doubt lingers concerning the centrality of networking, try to think of how many PCs are *not* connected to either local area networks or to the Internet or to its immediate offspring, intranets and extranets. Almost all PCs sold today contain modems and Internet software; Microsoft Windows literally cannot be purchased without the Internet Explorer browser. In fact, most first-time PC buyers list Internet access of some type as their number-one or number-two reason for purchasing a PC.

And most of these dramatic changes have happened since 1994.

BUILDING THE INFORMATION TECHNOLOGY INFRASTRUCTURE MODEL

The IT infrastructure model begins with information and networking, specifically Internet-harmonious networking. As we build the IT infrastructure model, information itself will be kept at the center, with networking the foundation for everything else, as illustrated in Exhibit 3.2. By adding the next two categories of IT infrastructure components, platforms and software infrastructure, we can begin to discuss the four basic areas of the model in more detail. (See Exhibit 3.3.)

Think of the underlying black star shape in Exhibit 3.3 as the platform technologies, consisting of both hardware and software, and the

Exhibit 3.2   Networking Foundations

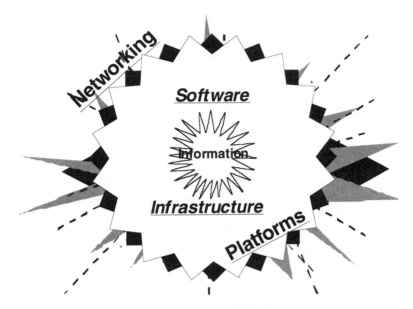

Exhibit 3.3   Major Components of the IT Infrastructure

overlapping white star shape as the software infrastructure, where information management systems (the data), enabling technologies, business applications, middleware, application servers, and systems and networking management can be found.

This general IT infrastructure model is built on four broad and interrelated areas:

1. *Information* is not just alphanumeric data. It includes graphical information, audio and video information, and may soon include aroma, taste, and tactile information. (In some virtual reality applications, mostly games, the tactile sensations are almost there!) The important point is never to forget that all of this is about information, which is why information occupies the central position in the model and why this is called an *information* technology infrastructure. The IT infrastructure, in turn, supports business and organizational activities that are dependent on information.

2. *Networking,* as mentioned, underlies the entire IT infrastructure. Networking provides not just the "glue" that holds everything together; it provides the very foundation of modern IT infrastructures both internally for organizations, such as PC local area

networks and companywide intranets, and externally, specifically the Internet and World Wide Web.

3. *Platforms* include hardware of all types, both clients and servers, and their operating systems, such as Microsoft Windows and Unix. Platforms contain and direct the electrical currents that, in turn, make everything happen. So why is the category of platforms not more fundamental than that of networking? In fact, platforms are just as basic. In past models (the legacy "technology stack"), platforms occupy one-third or more of the model. But today platforms have become mostly commodities. Batteries are very important in our daily lives, and Duracell and the Ever Ready bunny continue to slug it out on entertaining TV commercials. But batteries are commodities, so we do not pay as much attention to battery technologies, even though they are part of a fascinating field of electrical engineering.

4. *Software infrastructure* encompasses literally everything that is not networking technology or platform hardware or specifically networking software or operating systems. Exhibit 3.4 breaks the

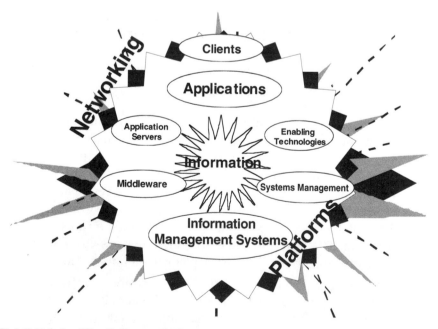

Exhibit 3.4   The Software Infrastructure

software infrastructure down further. The topic is discussed in depth in the following chapters.

Exhibit 3.4 expands the IT infrastructure model by adding client technologies to the platform layer and by filling in the components of the software infrastructure. Although client technologies are properly part of the platform technology group, they are discussed here because, for most users, client technologies provide access to the software infrastructure. The seven additions to the model can be defined as follows:

1. *Client technologies* are one of two key platform technologies, and as such are comprised of hardware, operating systems, and, most recently, browsers, which are users' way of interacting with the World Wide Web. Broadly, client technologies are what most users use to access the resources and services of the IT infrastructure. The technologies can include Windows and Macintosh PCs, cellular phones and smart beepers, and ATM machines.

2. *Applications* are, in the simplest terms, what information is input into and information or results are requested out of. Basically, applications process information and requests and return results through the client. Think of a bank's ATM machine as a client through which a user requests a withdrawal of cash from his or her account. The bank's application software processes the request, confirms and adjusts the information in the account, and dispenses cash, perhaps in local currency halfway around the world from the bank's physical location.

3. *Information management systems (IMSs)* are the information storehouse and contain software that manages the information as it goes into and comes out of the "data store." As such, IMS is critical to all other functions in the software infrastructure; without IMS, the software infrastructure does not function.

4. *Enabling technologies* are tools used to build applications. These can be sophisticated programming languages used to build, for example, the ATM bank applications, or a personal productivity tool like a spreadsheet (Lotus 1-2-3 or Microsoft Excel) with which users build a monthly budgeting application.

5. *Middleware* is mainly integration and monitoring technologies that coordinate and integrate applications and transactions among different applications or information resources. Although most

commonly used in very large mainframe environments, middleware is finding its way into Unix environments and into more traditionally simpler Microsoft Windows server applications.

6. *Application server technologies* are the newest components in the software infrastructure and, in the simplest sense, provide technologies that link business applications to the Internet. Some view application servers as extensions of middleware; however, they are sufficiently different to deserve separate classification.

7. *Systems management technologies* are also tools, used this time by system administrators to manage the software infrastructure technologies, the platform technologies, and the networking technologies, although some network professionals prefer to keep their networking administration roles separate from systems management.

The following chapter looks briefly at each of these interrelated areas and devises a picture that shows how, together, they compose the broader IT infrastructure. Later chapters look even more closely at the individual components and their relationship to "whole." Readers may decide to pick and choose among these later chapters, referring back to component sections as they may come up in day-to-day encounters with IT discussions and decisions.

NOTES

1. Geoffrey Moore, Paul Johnson, and Tom Kippola, *The Gorilla Game: An Investor's Guide to Picking Winners in High Technology* (New York: HarperBusiness, 1998).
2. Peter Drucker, "The Next Information Revolution," *Forbes ASAP* (September 1998).

CHAPTER 4

Understanding the New Information Technology Infrastructure Model I: Networking and Platform Technologies

. . . the web of life consists of networks within networks.
At each scale, under closer scrutiny, the nodes of the network
reveal themselves as smaller networks. We tend to arrange
these systems, all nesting within larger systems, in a hierarchical
scheme by placing the larger systems above the smaller ones
in pyramid fashion. But this is a human perception. In nature
there is no "above" or "below," and there are no hierarchies.
There are only networks nesting within other networks.

—FRITJOF CAPRA, *The Web of Life*

INFRASTRUCTURE FOUNDATIONS

This chapter takes a closer look at the vital underpinnings of the IT infrastructure, the networking and platform technologies. Chapter 5 focuses on the software infrastructure—the infrastructure within an infrastructure. Of all the advances in information technologies, the areas of networking technology and of the software infrastructure have

33

expanded and evolved dramatically since the early 1990s, especially since 1995. These areas encompass the largely invisible plumbing supporting the applications an organization uses in day-to-day transactions and management of its commercial activities.

The rapid advances in and proliferation of network technologies and software infrastructure technologies have substantially, and dramatically, changed the way we do business, both as business practitioners and as consumers in a global economy. However, the complicated, arcane nature of networking and platform technologies themselves makes them virtually unintelligible to almost everyone except computer scientists and electrical engineers. And even then, these technologies are usually the domain of dedicated specialists.

But nothing in the IT infrastructure takes place in a vacuum. In order to comprehend any component of the IT infrastructure, we must understand the "whole." And a basic understanding of both networking technologies and platform technologies is a prerequisite for approaching the software infrastructure where executive governance of strategies and keen management of tactical decisions are most likely to occur. So this chapter concentrates on the primary roles of networking and platform technologies, their fundamental categories, and some of the business considerations that attend networks and platforms.

NETWORKING TECHNOLOGIES

Most large organizations are now spending as much as one-third of their entire IT (and IT-related) budgets on networking—networking hardware, networking software, networking support and services. And that is not including the phone bills from AT&T, MCI, and other local or national telephone service providers.

Networking technologies may not be very interesting in and of themselves for network users, just as telephony technologies may not be interesting in and of themselves for telephone users. What matters to the person using a telephone is the conversation taking place, or at least the message that is transmitted, received, and stored. And the real focus of networking is not networks but information. Chapter 6 explains, very briefly, what all of this entails and goes over some of the key areas where executives might need to influence strategies and decisions. Here I expand our discussion so you can gain a familiarity with the types of networking environments executives encounter. (See Exhibit 4.1.)

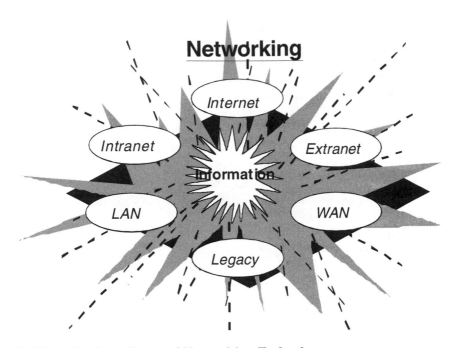

Exhibit 4.1   Some Types of Networking Technology

The Internet is not actually an entity in and of itself; it is a network of computer networks built on a foundation of open systems standards. The Internet is sort of overarching, conceptual "meta" network of hundreds of thousands of computer networks. Internet standards, particularly Transmission Control Protocol/Internet Protocol (TCP/IP), dictate how information sent out on the network is packaged, literally, how it may be routed to ensure its proper reception at the intended destination, and how the information is "unpackaged" and reassembled in a coherent and usable form. And all of this is completely independent of, and actually indifferent to, the types of platform technologies (hardware and operating systems) either hosting the information being sent or receiving the information for its new use.

Intranets and *extranets* evolved from the Internet in the mid to late 1990s with particularly significant impacts for commercial and public sector organizations. An *intranet* is a network inside an organization using Internet standards and technologies—the TCP/IP protocol, web technologies and browsers—built around common organizational interests and information needs. An intranet, by definition, is not intended to be accessed by users outside the organization. Intranets could be set up by departments or divisions or even by a workgroup within a department. In a real sense, intranets form the informational backbone of what is broadly called knowledge management and its forerunner, groupware.

An extranet also focuses on common interests and information needs but this time among two or more organizations, which together form a confederation of Internet-compliant networks. Extranets are normally designed for a specific set of purposes, for example, an extranet among an automobile manufacturer and its parts suppliers. As such, extranets may not just share information but may exchange transactions as well, which not only extends the reach of an extranet but also can intensify its commercial value.

In some ways, local area networks (LANs) and wide area networks (WANs) are the forerunners of intranets and extranets respectively. LANs are workgroup or departmental networks that originally began as ways to share among a group of PC users expensive devices, principally printers, and some common files. LANs then began evolving into limited client-server applications environments sharing departmental applications, like project management, or even some confined back-office transactional applications, like accounts receivable.

WANs developed from a need to share network users, information, and computing resources among workgroups, departments, and even divisions of an organization that extended beyond the physical limitations of LANs, which were usually confined to only a few hundred feet. LANs are local, within departments and workgroups; WANs are longer distance, among campus sites or geographically remote locations.

LANs and WANs are generally based on proprietary technologies, but chiefly because they both emerged during a period of "open" systems preferences, most offer more flexibility in integrating with other networks than do *legacy networks*. Beginning in the 1970s, mainframe and some minicomputers permitted the networking of users and resources among remote sites by using network models such as IBM's System Network Architecture or Digital's DecNet. These proprietary computer networks demanded conformity to the vendors' communications specifications. Although there was some conformity to international telecommunications standards, vendors could and did do pretty much anything they wanted to get their own computers to talk with each other.

Most WAN and LAN vendors probably wanted to have almost exclusively proprietary technologies as well (it is that "differentiation" thing again), but market demands for greater flexibility and interoperability during the mid-1980s steered LANs and WANs toward more open systems environments. That quasi-openness, in turn, allowed more LANs and WANs to interconnect through "bridge" technologies. All of this accelerated in 1984 when a new computer company arrived on the scene. In about ten years, Sun Microsystems would replace the once-stalwart Digital Equipment Company (DEC) to become one of the three major providers of enterprise-class computing platforms alongside IBM and Hewlett-Packard. Sun Microsystems based its platform on the "open" Unix operating system and loudly proclaimed that "the network is the computer," a courageous and portentous marketing slogan if there ever was one. And coming as this platform did from the open systems disciplines of Unix and C, Sun Microsystems engineers naturally looked to NSFnet and the emerging Internet technologies for their networking models.

Today intranets and extranets based on Internet standards and technologies are rapidly eclipsing LANs and WANs and replacing proprietary legacy networks. Internet technologies simply offer more flexibility, interoperability, and scaleability at lower costs. Unless an organization's networking experts can offer compelling arguments why new networks, in particular, need to be proprietary and not based on Internet standards and technologies, there is little justification for investing heavily in legacy and proprietary networking technologies. Secure server technologies are even overcoming crucial security issues surrounding electronic commerce on the Internet. If an organization already has proprietary networks in place, these will likely need to be maintained and perhaps even extended in the near term. But for new networking strategies, proprietary legacy network technologies are passé.

From networking we need to look at the next building block of the IT infrastructure, platform technologies. (See Exhibit 4.2.) And in the era of networked IT, platforms are generally divided into two types, clients and servers.

Both clients and servers depicted in Exhibit 4.2 are comprised of two basic technologies, hardware and operating systems technologies, which in combination are here called *platform technologies.* Just as the power generators, substations, water mains, and pipelines of a city's infrastructure provide the physical backbone that delivers electricity and running water to offices and homes, IT platform technologies provide the backbone for the IT infrastructure.

Nicholas Negroponte, author of *Being Digital,* neatly observed that it all begins with sand and electricity—the hardware.[1] Chapter 7 discusses hardware's varieties and permutations in more detail. But for now, keep

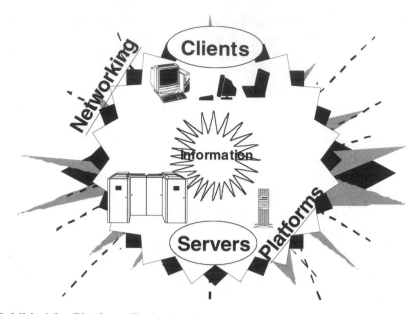

Exhibit 4.2   Platform Technologies

in mind that everything, from operating system, to the software infrastructure, to applications, to the client, happens primarily because electricity flows through increasingly intricate circuits microscopically
etched on silicon.

The earliest computational hardware consisted of mechanical trips
and switches. Then came vacuum tubes, then transistors, and now microprocessors. Chapter 7 briefly examines the kinds of microprocessor
technologies that will emerge in the near future.

Hardware is, by and large, a commodity component, which means it
can be incredibly inexpensive, but that does not necessarily mean that
decisions about hardware are "no-brainers." In fact, precisely because it
is so inexpensive, virtually anyone with budget authority of a few thousand dollars can acquire rather powerful hardware platforms, a fact that
foreshadows the integration problem discussed later in middleware.

And, contrary to Mr. Gates's protestations about how inexpensive his
company has made computing in general, the increases in the power and
capacity of hardware along with the concomitant decreases in hardware
prices actually have brought about the price-performance ratios in technology that users enjoy today.

As with everything depicted in the IT infrastructure model, hardware is a capital expenditure, which is either expensed or depreciated over time. And taxation authorities seem slow to understand that depreciation schedules are not in sync with the rapid rates of hardware evolution and obsolescence.

Nor is "hardware" limited to processing power. Storage technologies, networking and communications technologies, output and input devices, and more all fall in the category of hardware. Put simply, if it has a plug that draws current from an electrical outlet or if it needs a battery, it is hardware.

Otherwise, it is software. And even though operating systems are "software," they are discussed in virtually the same breath as hardware, because the two are so closely linked. The operating system (O/S) instructs the hardware how to direct the flow of electricity through its circuits, when to flow and where to flow, and when not to flow. That's why everything in computing is binary, 1s and 0s. Electricity is either flowing or not flowing.

Operating systems are also sort of like a primordial goo from which all other software evolves and on which all other software depends. The O/S presents the first level of real difficulty in building and managing IT infrastructures. The O/S chosen and used can limit not only what hardware and other software can be used but what can be done; how it can be done; when and where it can be done; how reliably, accurately, and securely it can be done; and with whom it can be done. The section on O/S navigates this trickiest of minefields, but notice that almost everything beginning with the O/S and going up the model is software. Obviously, all of this software requires hardware to do anything; software does not have plugs that draw electrical current.

But as with a home stereo or entertainment center, once the hardware is in place, users are more concerned with the software—music CDs, DVDs, cable or satellite receptions—than they are with the hardware. That is, until the hardware malfunctions. And just as users are most likely to spend more money over time on the software for home entertainment systems, users are likely over time to spend more on IT software and related expenses, such as support and upgrades, than on IT hardware itself. Most businesses have spent and are spending more, for example, on SAP's software licenses and on the consulting and support it takes to implement this class of large-scale business applications than they have spent on the commodity hardware platforms running the software.

This phenomenon can be expected to perpetuate as software capabilities increase and hardware becomes even more of a commodity. In fact, hardware is now being spoken of as "appliances." So perhaps we should think of an appliance like a refrigerator. Over the useful life of a refrigerator, a family will spend infinitely more on the food that goes into and comes out of it than on the refrigerator itself. However, GE does not make its refrigerators obsolete every eighteen months as the Wintel industry (combination of the Windows operating system running on Intel hardware) does with PCs.

CLIENT TECHNOLOGIES

The term "client" does not refer to "users." "Client" actually stands for "client devices," those devices through which users interact with an application and with the information infrastructure as a whole. For example, the client can be the Windows or Macintosh desktop or notebook. But clients can and do come in many shapes and sizes. A "dumb" computer terminal is a client device. The bank's ATM device and the cash machines in airports and hotel lobbies are client devices as well.

Look carefully at the retail client station at a point-of-sale retail environment. In a modern supermarket, for example, the checkout station is a group of interconnected client devices—a bar code reader, a scale, a cash register, a magnetic card reader for the bank or credit card—all connected to the store's computers, which recognize pricing, control inventory, and track purchases through a customer care program that identifies each customer and gives him or her promotional and volume discounts. Of course, supermarkets are doing all this not simply because they love us so much but because they want us to spend more of our money with them, not with their competitors. The sophistication of the combined client devices at the checkout station in concert with the networked applications on the store's back-office servers enhances customer services and improves their customer retention and competitive capabilities.

For people with satellite TV service, such as Direct TV, or digital cable from TCI, their television sets have evolved from a more or less straightforward viewing device into an interactive client, which allows users to scroll through menus and select programming and information about programs. Through the TV client device, users are accessing and interacting with both information and applications.

Clients will become more and more varied and more ubiquitous in the near future. Cellular phones now access the Internet and email. Network appliances and smart devices—from Palm Pilots to smart pagers—are already a part of our daily lives. NCR announced a microwave oven with a front panel that can access recipe databases on the Internet and can order groceries from Internet supermarkets, in addition to paying bills and doing banking.

Chapter 7 returns to this realm of the "variegated client" and looks at some ways it will affect future IT infrastructure decisions. For the present, think of the "client" as any device that might be used to access and interact with information and applications, both today and in a future even the MIT Media Lab can barely imagine.

SERVER TECHNOLOGIES

Server technologies can range from relatively simple file and print servers that cost a few thousand dollars and that allow a workgroup to share documents (files), groupware (Lotus Notes), and a printer, modems, scanners, in a local area network, to mainframe computers that cost tens of millions of dollars, like IBM's chess-playing Big Blue. But, in a generic sense, all servers fulfill a fundamentally identical role. They provide access to shared software and hardware for a community of users who, in turn, use networked client devices to interact with the hardware and software capabilities housed on the server.

So if all servers are fundamentally doing the same thing, why does one cost less than $3,000 and another cost $30 million? Broadly speaking, it is somewhat analogous to the difference between buying a six-seat, twin-propeller engine Cessna airplane and a Boeing 747-400 airliner. Each is designed for a different purpose, with a different workload in mind and different set of economies at play. In many ways, it would be almost as foolish to buy 80 to 100 six-seat Cessnas to fly 300 passengers from London to Bombay as it would to install departmental-size Wintel servers to support 1,000 employees using a transaction process application—say, airline ticketing and reservations—24 hours a day, seven days every week.

Having said that, I offer a major caveat: networking. Networking makes plausible just such a scenario with Intel-based servers. Upcoming advances in hardware technologies, principally from Intel but also in storage and interconnect technologies, make the networking and clustering of commodity servers not just likely but commercially viable. However, in order for this to become a widespread reality, an operating system needs to emerge that is capable of supporting reliable, high-performance networks and clusters of powerful commodity servers.

Just about now the Microsofties are jumping up and down in protest, crying "We have it! It's Windows NT, err, we mean Windows 2000!" And Unix aficionados are smugly pointing out that Unix on Intel is perfectly capable of doing that today. And the Unixers are right, but Unix lacks momentum in the Intel server markets and, just as important, carries a higher price tag in terms of the Unix professionals required to administer and maintain Unix servers.

Chapter 4 takes a closer look at both Unix and Windows 2000. For the moment, keep two things in mind. Windows 2000, especially the Data Server version intended to support enterprise environments, will not likely be fully released as a commercial product until sometime after the year 2000. As a completely new operating system, Windows 2000, and particularly the Data Server product, will need to go through several years of customer use and several revisions and fixes before it approaches the stability of enterprise server operating systems based on Unix. Unix operating systems, however, have been supporting mission-critical telecommunications, engineering, and scientific applications for over two decades and have been the unquestioned cost-effective alternatives to mainframe computers for business-critical applications since the mid-1980s.

Unix, however, although reliable, stable, and, most important, "open," has been implemented differently by almost every hardware manufacturer, which has hindered the proliferation of a single Unix standard. In addition, Unix has not been a market force in the Intel-based hardware arena. Until recently most Intel-based systems were generally not robust enough to take advantage of Unix's capabilities, and most Intel users simply did not need those capabilities. Santa Cruz Operations (SCO) has made a nice, if modest, living by selling its SCO Unix on Intel-based servers, especially from Compaq. But a large portion of this market was in Europe and Asia, where Intel-based Unix servers are used chiefly as lower-cost versions of minicomputers, like very low-cost IBM AS400s. The major exception to this is Sequent, which builds commercial, high-end Unix-based servers using symmetric configurations of dozens of commodity Intel processors.

Unix is also more sophisticated than the primary Intel-server operating systems, Windows NT 4.0 and Novell's Netware. In turn, Unix professionals are generally more highly educated (almost always with degrees in computer science), more experienced, and, consequently, more expensive. Taken together, commercial Unix servers from Sun Microsystems, IBM, Hewlett-Packard, Sequent, and others usually support business-critical enterprise applications and are not generally found in departmental or workgroup environments.

When it comes to servers, the cost of the platform—the hardware and operating system—is one thing. The cost of the people who manage and maintain the systems is another thing. Up until recently, lower-cost, less-experienced—albeit certified—people could be hired to manage and maintain Wintel desktops and servers. More expensive Unix professionals were harder to come by. It would seem logical to assume that in the future, companies would save money by implementing even more powerful Wintel enterprise servers and employing similarly lower-cost Wintel server managers. Wrong!

First, the upcoming generation information systems professionals will not simply be responsible for installing a new piece of software on a clerical worker's desktop or for fixing a printer problem on a local area network. They will be responsible for ensuring the stability and security of vital enterprise information systems, of the IT infrastructure itself. By way of analogy, we could compare a local transit bus driver with the pilot of a 747 airliner. In a broad sense, both are doing the same thing. They are moving people sitting in seats in a transport conveyance from point A to point B. Why do we pay the airline pilot four or five times more than we pay the bus driver? It has everything to do with education, experience, and increased responsibility.

Returning to our Unix-Wintel quandary, it is virtually certain that modern IT infrastructures, beginning now and going well into the next decade, will be a mixture of both Windows 2000 servers, mostly at the departmental and line-of-business levels, and Unix servers, at the large-enterprise and mission-critical levels. Thus both servers must function within the same IT infrastructure and among any number of IT infrastructures outside an organization's corporate boundaries, all in a sophisticated Internet-based web of computer networks.

In turn, the personnel responsible for the management, maintenance, security, and general well-being of the information systems will need to be more educated, more experienced, and more responsible—and therefore will be more expensive. Even if an organization opts for a "pure" Microsoft environment, the information systems professionals will not be less expensive than if it opted for a "pure" Unix environment. And very probably users would not want them to be less expensive. How would users feel about flying with an airline that prides itself on having the lowest-paid 747 pilots in the industry?

There are many benefits to this brave new world of Internet networked commercial computing. Do not be fooled by promises of consistently decreasing information systems costs. The hardware technologies pretty much continue to follow Moore's Law, that is, processing power will double every 18 months while processor prices continue to fall. Internet access to processing power will even accelerate that pace. Software prices may even fall, at least for software commodity components.

But as information requirements increase—and they will—and as commercial dependence on IT infrastructures becomes absolute—which it has—users will need more highly skilled, better trained, and more experienced information systems professionals. Currently some experts estimate that the United States alone has a shortage of up to a half-million programmers and IS professionals. No one should understand better the laws of supply and demand than top-level business executives, who also understand the dynamics governing the compensation of highly skilled professionals. So why do so many business executives readily listen to technology vendors who offer visions of increasingly lower costs of ownership? The people costs will continue to rise. This is not magic; this is sophisticated science.

TIERS AND TEARS OF CLIENTS AND SERVERS

One major factor influencing platform decisions is client-server architectures, that is, the division of work among clients and servers, which is also discussed in more detail in Chapter 11. The division of work among clients and servers can have two tiers, or *n* tiers. In a two-tiered environment, the client performs much of the "business logic" and all of the "presentation layer" work while the server supplies the information and also may support part of the "business logic." In an *n*-tiered environment, any number of servers are providing data, business logic (the application itself), networking, web access, and so on while the client is generally supporting the graphical user interface (GUI), a browser, and some local processor power.

Both two-tiered and *n*-tiered models are relatively recent phenomena, and I believe the two-tiered model, which requires a fully functional and usually high-end PC, may be relatively short-lived. Many technology observers believe that had information managers communicated better with network managers during the 1980s, the whole morass and high cost of two-tiered client-server technology might have been avoided in the first place. An entire generation of application technology evolution may be required to completely shed the shackles of virtually obsolete two-tiered client-server applications, which have been eclipsed by *n*-tier architectures. Both models use client and server platforms, but the *n*-tiered model, because it uses a greater number of specialized networked servers and because it encompasses a broader diversity of client platforms, offers more complex relationships and greater variety.

A major consideration in the platform technologies is the different types of work done by clients and servers—that is, what kinds of applications are used by businesses and by individuals within each organization, how demanding are those applications on processing power, storage, availability (up time), administration, and security? And how are these likely to increase, in the near term and over time?

For the present, two decision factors should be kept in mind: flexibility or adaptability and scaleability. Servers must have the flexibility to handle new types of clients as well as new types of software and networking technologies. Lacking this flexibility, a firm would fall prey to competitors who could take advantage of emerging business opportunities faster than it could.

The scaleability issue is just as important. If server platform technologies cannot expand to meet growing business requirements, users are disadvantaged in several ways. First, because most new business opportunities will in large part depend on networked information (i.e., the Internet and the Web), if a firm cannot scale to meet information and transaction demands quickly, customers will *immediately* go to a competitor who can meet those demands. "Immediately" is stressed because there is virtually no lag time in the networked information-based economy. Retail consumers and manufacturers acquiring parts or raw materials have very real choices, and they can exercise those choices with incredible speed.

Second, scaleability determines an organization's capability to respond to both growing demands and peaks of intense activity, whether it is a retailer responding to a holiday buying season or a nation's military organization responding to enemy aggression. So platform technologies need not only meet current and foreseen demands but also need to scale and meet possible growth and unforeseen peaks in demand, from internal users and customers and business partners alike.

Amazon.com provides an illustration of how top-level executive concerns about scaleability affect business viability and long-term company success. In planning for their company's web-based business, Amazon.com's executives chose to install large 64-bit Alpha-Turbo servers from Digital Equipment Corp. running Unix and Oracle—in effect, one of the most robust open systems servers combinations available. Their overwhelming success as a web-based business stems in large part from that decision. If less robust, less scaleable servers, such as the Microsoft NT 4.0 server, had been chosen, instead of becoming an almost instant force in the retail media industry, Amazon.com would have given its competitors, Barnes and Noble and Borders, ample opportunity to catch up and perhaps crush it. Because it had built scaleability into its business plan, Amazon.com did not need to convert from Wintel servers to gain scaleability or to wait for Microsoft to deliver NT 5.0 on 64-bit Intel servers. Jeff Bezos and his managers planned well and invested up front in robust, scaleable open systems servers and software, even though they had yet to sell their first book when they made that decision.

Networks and platforms are the foundations and structural frameworks of an organization's IT infrastructure. Both need to be planned as carefully as the foundation and structural steel of a skyscraper. Top-level executive oversight and strategic involvement determine to a great extent how stable, flexible, and scaleable an organization's IT infrastructure will be. But perhaps most of all, top-level management must realize themselves and convey to their staff and the levels of management involved that low acquisition cost is not a primary criterion. That would be like telling a construction company that is building our new office tower, "Whatever you do, get the cheapest steel, the cheapest glass, and the cheapest concrete you can find. And use the cheapest unskilled labor available."

This should remind us to always keep in mind that the hidden (and largest) cost of networking and platform technologies are people costs. And the price tags for educated, experienced, and capable personnel who can help build and maintain the networking and platform foundations of IT infrastructures are very likely to keep rising for a long time to come. Someday, in the distant future, when the grandchildren of readers occupy mahogany-row offices, they may enjoy an era of Lego-like technologies that plug together effortlessly, that require little or no management or maintenance. We are not there today, nor is technology likely to bring us to that point in the first half of the first decade of the twenty-first century. Be very skeptical about any easy promises or fast tracks to an IT nirvana.

The next chapter explores the almost invisible infrastructure within an infrastructure—the software infrastructure. To extend the skyscraper analogy, now that we have the foundation and structural framework, we will begin to build out the interior, the wiring, plumbing, and environmental systems. In short, we will now make it functional.

NOTE

1. Nicholas Negroponte, *Being Digital* (New York: Alfred A. Knopf, 1995).

CHAPTER 5

Understanding the New Information Technology Infrastructure Model II: Software Infrastructure

Still follow sense, of ev'ry art the soul,
parts answering parts shall slide into a whole.

—ALEXANDER POPE, *Epistles to Several Persons* (1731)

PURE SOFTWARE

Exhibit 5.1 illustrates the major components that make up the software infrastructure. This infrastructure within the larger IT infrastructure differs from the networking and platform components in that it is made up entirely of software; there are no real physical components in the software infrastructure. Since the parts have no empirical dimensions, organizations do not *buy* the components in the software infrastructure; companies license these software components for use, much as copyrighted material like music or writing would be licensed. Software elements need platform technologies in order to operate, but the parts of the software infrastructure usually are acquired separately from the platform technologies that run them and the networking technologies that support them.

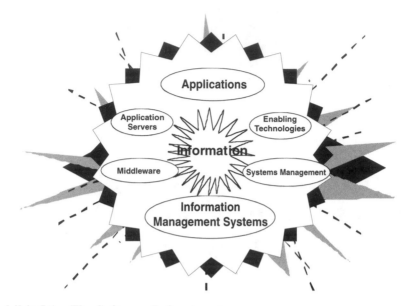

Exhibit 5.1   The Software Infrastructure

As mentioned earlier, somewhat different but basic IT infrastructure models have been used for some time in the IT industry. Commentators refer to IT infrastructures in a number of ways, sometime broadly, others more purposefully, and some with a focus on public policy[1]; many others refer to this IT infrastructure more vaguely, as if it were some sort of mythical beast lurking just outside our sight. But what has changed most dramatically in the 1990s, and especially since about 1995, is the portion here called the software infrastructure. These components recently have expanded in magnitude, complexity, and importance. Before 1994, not too many people even in technology companies and IT departments knew what a website was, much less what it might be used for, or that a client technology called a "browser" would be used to "surf" the Internet and access information contained in websites.

And most people probably thought the word "Mosaic" referred to an artform. Then Mosaic was reengineered and became Netscape Navigator, and then Microsoft followed and produced Internet Explorer to compete for this new and lucrative market. Microsoft immediately decided that bundling Internet Explorer with its desktop operating system, Windows 98, would ensure its dominance in this new technology and these new markets, all of which ignited one of the most significant antitrust actions in U.S. history.

Today tens of millions of businesspeople use browsers (mostly Netscape Navigator or Microsoft Internet Explorer) every hour of every day to locate and retrieve information on the Internet and to buy and sell everything from books and CDs to automobiles and real estate. Almost every company, from General Motors to a one-person home-based business, has its own unique website. Even some children have their own unique websites.

All of this is just one example of how technologies in the software infrastructure layer have expanded and have become not only more sophisticated but more vital to the entire IT infrastructure. It also shows how this software infrastructure is intimately related to client technologies and individual interactions with the IT infrastructure.

Keep in mind that most of this has happened since 1995. This networked nature of contemporary information environments and of global knowledge-based economy continues to drive the expansion and intricacy of the software infrastructure. Let us take a closer look at this infrastructure with an infrastructure, as it were, the generally invisible plumbing that makes all the rest of our model work.

INFORMATION MANAGEMENT SYSTEMS

Information management systems (IMSs) form the vital cornerstone of IT infrastructures because they house and manage the information itself. Although certain technology providers may downplay the importance of IMS, the capabilities and capacities of an IMS are fundamental to the viability of an organization's IT infrastructure. The basic database technologies, the rows and columns of relational databases, have become commodities. But the *data store* itself is only part of IMS.

IMS technologies can be furthered divided into databases, which actually contain and maintain information, and information management systems and tools, which work on the data, defining and manipulating it while ensuring its accuracy, integrity, security, transportability, and a host of other attributes, not the least of which includes backup and audit trails. Moreover, IMS providers today offer such a wide range of bundled attributes that viewing one IMS offering as pretty much the same as any other is a bit like thinking that a subcompact Ford Escort automobile is pretty much the same as a BMW 700 series sedan. True, they both have an engine and wheels, a transmission and brakes, doors, windows, an interior and seat belts, and they both get us from point A to point B. But that's where the similarities begin to fade.

Most databases in commercial use today are relational database management systems (RDBMSs). And most combine database and information management tools. For example, Oracle8i, Oracle Corporation's current RDBMS product, is roughly 50 percent database and 50 percent information management technologies, and now includes a host of Internet capabilities not found among competing products. Unfortunately, Oracle insists on calling this product a "database," which masks its extensive IMS features.

Other software companies may—and do—supply separate information management systems and tools for RDBMSs. This practice seems more common with large mainframe databases, principally IMS on IBM mainframes that usually supply data for legacy applications, most commonly COBOL applications. But today most RDBMS providers have integrated the information management technologies with their database products. Separate IMS tools are rarely necessary except where multiple types of databases and perhaps multiple applications require integration tools, which are discussed in the middleware section.

As mentioned, information management technologies—databases and tools—form the cornerstone of the IT infrastructure. Users can legitimately have a complete IT system without networking, without systems management, and with a bare minimum of enabling technology (e.g., a programming language or a spreadsheet). But without information, there is no "information" technology system, much less an IT infrastructure.

Take, for example, a business executive on an airplane who turns on his or her notebook PC and writes a memo or works on a spreadsheet—that person is using a complete, albeit simple, IT infrastructure. Hardware is drawing electrical current from the battery. Input and output hardware (keyboard, trackball, and display) exist. The hardware boots an operating system, which in turn responds to software commands and tells electricity where and when to flow—retrieving a requested file from a disk, for instance.

Enabling technology allows this business executive to create a document or devise and use a spreadsheet. And databases are supplying information to applications.

There is no networking. There is no separate systems management, no middleware or application server technologies, no real application technologies. Everything is all part of Windows or Microsoft Office. Yet a notebook PC contains a working IT infrastructure. However, without information already stored throughout the system (fonts, clip art, spell-checkers, spreadsheet templates and macros, names, addresses)—in other words, without data—the business executive has little more than an expensive platform for playing amusing games, and even then the game software itself would contain prestored information in its own IMS.

Of course, comparing this executive's notebook PC to the kind of IT infrastructure under discussion is a bit like comparing a personal automobile to the global air transportation system. But it provides a useful illustration. And just about a decade or so ago, that was pretty much what commercial IT installations looked like—hardware, O/S, data, limited enabling technology (e.g., COBOL), applications, user interface (dumb terminal). Not much real networking was going on; not too much systems management; and everything was preintegrated because users got it all from one vendor, principally IBM or Digital. These proprietary, host-based systems of the 1970s and 1980s are still very much with us today. And, of course, as they were proprietary, almost nobody's system worked with anyone else's systems.

Today most of that has changed. For our economies and our social structures to work at all, systems must work with all other systems. The digital economy—the digital culture—is networked. The networking of information and applications all makes work so much better, but it also makes it so much more complicated to govern and manage.

So everything we actually do in the software infrastructure, and especially the applications, centers on the IMS technologies that store, maintain, and manipulate the information. Now that organizations depend on networked information, IMS technologies—and their capabilities and limitations—and the networking technologies pretty much dictate what the IT infrastructure is capable of.

In short, once the IMS technologies and networking technologies are right, an organization's IT infrastructure is very likely to support anything that top-level executives want to do and everyone else needs to do. If either of the technologies is wrong, everyone in the organization, from the CEO to the file clerks, will be fighting a constant uphill battle against an inadequate IT infrastructure.

ENABLING TECHNOLOGIES

Spreadsheet programs like Lotus 1-2-3 and Excel are good examples of enabling technologies. These personal productivity tools allow users to create applications that in turn produce end results—in the case of spreadsheets, decision-making information. Likewise, other enabling technologies allow users to create documents (word processing) and presentations (e.g., PowerPoint).

In the broadest sense, think of enabling technologies as anything that specifically supports the development or delivery of an application. These can range from the personal productivity tools just mentioned (spreadsheets, word processing, presentation tools), to groupware (Lotus Notes), to workflow (OpenText), to document management (Documentum or PC Docs), all of which might be called "group productivity" tools.

Central among enabling technologies are application design and development tools, including third-generation programming languages (3GLs), like COBOL, and C and fourth-generation languages (4GLs), like PowerBuilder or the most ubiquitous of all, Microsoft's Visual Basic. The difference between 3GLs and 4GLs? Generally speaking, with 3GLs a programmer must write every line of program code one line at a time. With 4GLs programmers can use utilities and code generators that automatically compose entire sections of a program.

CASE tools—computer aided software engineering—are more complex and controversial. Sophisticated CASE environments allow programmers—more properly called "application designers"—to use a business scenario to design a business solution, then pass it by business management emendations and approval, make adjustments, and then allow the CASE software to generate the actual program code. In theory, all of this should work and make life so much better for business executives and IS professionals alike. So what is the weak link between theory and reality? Unfortunately, for the most part, it is the business executive. Generally, business executives have not taken the time and effort to understand their own business and its strategic requirements, especially in relation to information systems. Most executives' apparent inability, or reluctance, to envision real business and organizational strategies and to define specific and workable goals and objectives, especially as they relate to information resources and application requirements, prevents the promise of CASE from becoming reality. Too bad. CASE could be a real money-saver for almost all organizations and could help them respond more efficiently and effectively to rapidly changing realities. But it is probably too late for CASE, which has been rendered a neglected and debilitated enabling technology.

Rapidly increasing in importance are two closely related enabling technologies, *object management* and *object request brokers*. Users who have taken a pie chart or graph generated from spreadsheet information and inserted it into a word processing document or a presentation slide have used one of Microsoft's versions of object management, COM, or Compound Object Management.

Now think of different objects, such as printed text, graphics, videos, sound, all moving around the Internet from websites to the PC display. An object request broker manages those objects, and the broker is at the heart of application server technologies. Thus the technologies are interrelated, each depending on others to make up the IT infrastructure.

Sun Microsystems' much-publicized application development environment, Java, and its closely related cousins, Java Beans and Enterprise Java Beans, all of which were created specifically for web and Internet-based applications.

Java is teetering on the brink of becoming a mainstream development environment for business applications of all types and sizes. It has broad support among influential technology vendors, including IBM, Oracle, Netscape/AOL, Inprise, Computer Associates, and Sun Microsystems. Java allows developers to both build and deploy applications faster and at lower cost. That, in turn, means that businesses can respond to market and economic conditions better and faster, and cheaper.

As an added bonus, Java is built specifically to take advantage of object and web technologies. Finally, coming as it does from Sun Microsystems, Java is the most network-centric enabling technology yet devised. Networked information constitutes a large portion of Java's DNA.

Java suffered some early disappointments, including a history of delivering less than expected performance, particularly when compared with 3GLs and more mature 4GLs. But these types of technology problems improve with software revisions and with higher-performance and lower-priced hardware. The 1999 releases of Java seem to overcome previous performance hurdles. Moreover, the advent of 64-bit servers based on high-volume, commodity-priced Intel architectures will accelerate both the world of objects and the fortunes of Java. And after all, Java and the web-based applications it is intended for are both in their relative infancy. Applications built today should be built with next-generation platform technologies in mind, not just run on current platforms or just solve current business problems.

Most of us do expect that the business and organizational challenges we will face in two or three years will be a bit different from those we face today, do we not? Why then do we think those challenges will be met with yesterday's technologies which we are only now buying and implementing? Top-level executives are paid to look ahead, past the current quarter's results. They need also to take a longer-term, considered view of information technologies.

Microsoft views Java and its offspring as perhaps the most perilous threat to its ascendant position in software markets, including desktop operating systems. Early on Microsoft attempted to defuse and debilitate Java by introducing its own version, which had all of Java's functionality but ran only on Microsoft platform technologies. But so far, Sun has prevailed in the U.S. federal courts. The suitability of Java to the Internet and web applications and the fact that hundreds of thousands of application developers around the world are writing new business software using Java makes the alliance among Netscape, America Online, and Sun Microsystems the kind of threat to Microsoft's dominance that Microsoft, Apple, and Intel were in the 1980s to IBM's. The chief difference is that today Microsoft is fully aware of this threat.

Enabling technologies determine what sorts of business and organizational applications can be built, how fast they can be built, how expensive—or inexpensive—it is to build them, who can use them, and where, when, and how they can be used. When it comes to business, applications are the most visible components of the software infrastructure.

APPLICATION TECHNOLOGIES

One way to recognize an application is to look for anything that resembles a business form that contains fields of information or must be filled out. Anyone who has ordered a book from Amazon.com or from Barnes and Noble's or Borders Books' websites have worked with an information infrastructure that allowed access to specific information requested and with an application (order entry) that asked for information that completed and executed the order.

FedEx's "point-click-and-ship" promotions invite users to interact with a FedEx shipping, tracking, and billing application, which in turn puts users in touch with Fred Smith's, CEO, FedEx, global IT infrastructure and his tens of thousands of employees.

Business executives spend a good deal of decision-making effort on choosing applications that form the financial and operation backbone of their business. Most readers here will be familiar with SAP, PeopleSoft, Baan, Oracle Applications, and others, at least in name if not in detail.

But applications come in many shapes and sizes. The ATM an executive used to get cash on his last business trip to London or Hong Kong is a client device. It enabled him to interact with a relatively simple yet amazingly efficient networked application, which processed the request, checked the account balance at a bank half a world away, deducted funds from his account, and dispensed local currency to him, all in less time than it probably would take for him to cash a check at his own bank at home.

Most applications process transactions, such as an ATM transaction or an airline reservation and ticketing application. But more and more applications fulfill requests for information according to preset parameters and ad hoc queries. These decision support or business intelligence applications interact with a wide array of information resources, some of which may have been generated by transaction applications but others of which are increasingly found on the Internet and its companion intranets and extranets, both of which are discussed in more detail in Chapter 6.

Users might even build their own applications with, for example, a spreadsheet program like Lotus 1-2-3 or Microsoft's Excel. The spreadsheet program itself is not properly an application. It is an enabling technology that allows users to build an application. The business plan spreadsheet that is built, for example, is the application.

BACK-OFFICE AND FRONT-OFFICE APPLICATIONS

The terms "back office" and "front office" in the context of applications are pretty straightforward. Back office refers to those applications that are traditionally used only by employees of a company or internal members of an organization, and usually only by those individuals who are authorized to use the applications. Traditional back-office applications include financial applications, such as accounts receivable, payroll, general ledger, and the like; human resources applications, such as benefits and organizational charts; manufacturing applications, such as shop floor and quality assurance; and distribution applications, such as shipping or receiving.

The biggest change among these applications is their integration into the IT infrastructure, particularly the integration at the networked information level. Rather than each application maintaining its own unique database, smart companies are building common IMSs that support a broad range of applications. The current generation of back-office applications, such as SAP, Baan, PeopleSoft, and Oracle Applications, are all based on this concept. But the concept can go even further to include distributed and networked databases that replicate data among sites and among different applications, constantly updating and backing up each other's information store.

Information also can be shared by front-office applications, which are applications like sales force automation, call center management, marketing, and customer care, among others, that are closer to the customer or constituent. These front-office applications generally focus on some aspect of the connection between the customer and the business or the public service provider and the constituent.

The line gets a bit blurred the farther we go. Some technology providers talk about "middle-office" applications. These seem mostly to be applications that are shared among an organization's internal users and a defined set of outside users, say, among a business and its key suppliers. Others may refer applications that allow customers to interact directly with parts of a company's internal IT infrastructure; examples include, FedEx's "point-click-and-ship" application, the frequent flyer programs of most airlines, or even some electronic banking and credit card applications.

When it comes to electronic commerce, the lines become very blurry indeed. When we order a book from Amazon.com, for example, as a customer we are literally touching almost every part of Amazon.com's IT infrastructure—inventory, order entry, shipping, credit. Not that we can get our hands inside of those applications and muck about with vital data, but we are certainly doing, on our own as customers, a great many of the things that, just a short time ago, we would think of as "back-office" functions. We can expect this phenomenon to expand as both business and public service organizations become more web-enabled during the next few years.

These applications—where information is entered, usually into an electronic "business" form, and then processed by the internal system, and a result is returned to the user or to a designated recipient—are called *transaction processing applications.* An ATM machine is a perfect example of transaction processing, as is the supermarket checkout, the airline ticketing and check-in counter, even a home satellite TV or digital cable that allows users to punch up pay-per-view movies or sporting events. While most transaction processing applications are largely back-office applications, many have front-office extensions.

Decision support applications, now sometimes called "business intelligence" applications, often use the same data gathered by transaction processing applications, but here those data are used by business specialists and managers to determine how, when, and where to adjust or direct business activities. Perhaps a beer distributor would want to know when to order additional inventory from the supplier based on peak consumption periods from the previous year or from a pattern that has emerged over the years. Or an airline would want to know if it should add extra flights or substitute larger aircraft on certain routes during a peak holiday period based on historical transactional data.

Decision support applications most prominently include data warehousing and data marts. Although a relatively recent phenomena, these are having immediate impacts not only on business and organizational decisions but on customer behavior as well. When we return as an established customer to Amazon.com, for example, a data warehouse has tracked our more recent purchases and matched them to books or CDs we might be interested in. Of course, these systems tend not to be very smart yet. If we purchased a half-dozen or so Nancy Drew mystery books as Christmas gifts for our preteen niece, Amazon.com is likely to recommend more of the same to us for several months until we have purchased our normal quota of Tom Clancy novels and Tom Peters business books.

Decision support applications are becoming highly sophisticated and offer not only an excellent means of making knowledge workers more effective and efficient but also can extend the reach of an organization to its customers and constituents.

Some high-tech pundits believe that decision support applications may soon become give-away commodities, a notion principally fueled by Microsoft's no-charge inclusion of its Plato On-line Analytical Processing tools in its recent SQL Server 7.0 RDBMS product. Do not buy into this deception. Companies could give away decision support software from now until the apocalypse, but it would not save much money for organizations needing real, working decision support systems. Decision support, data warehousing, data marts, and business intelligence systems demand careful business planning (which means extensive business executive involvement), concentrated development and deployment efforts, and ongoing technical and business support. Those are all people-intensive efforts—expensive, highly skilled, experienced people.

Professional productivity applications are a broad class that can include anything from computer-aided design for commercial architects to laboratory tracking and inventory of bacteria cultures. These are more than merely enabling technologies in that they generally have built into them very specific tools and specialized information that only the professional working in a particular field would be interested in or would even know how to use.

Distributed applications can be of at least two types. One would be a back-office application that is spread across geographically remote locations. Take, for example, a spare parts inventory. If a company has six locations and each location maintains its own inventory of spare parts, it would be nice to be able to query all locations to locate a needed part.

In a very broad sense, client-server applications are distributed applications as well because, in theory, the application is divided between the client and the server. Client-server application architecture is discussed in more detail in Chapter 11.

Networked applications are the latest and most important of the application technologies. These are web-based applications and electronic commerce. What we are really engaged in when we order a book from Amazon.com, or point-click-and-ship a FedEx package, or even use an ATM (especially if it is not one of our bank's own ATMs) is networked applications. Networked applications soon will become so prevalent that the applications running on networks outside of an organization will be more important to the organization's success, or lack thereof, than the applications running inside the organization. And most, if not all, applications running inside most organizations will be running on intranets or extranets.

Networking is the area of technology growth that has the greatest impact on our current focus on IT in general. The Internet and the World Wide Web are directly responsible for the tidal wave of information capabilities we are experiencing. And networking technologies will continue to grow at a mind-boggling pace.

According to a Nielsen Media survey released August 1998, there are 79 million "Netcitizens" in the United States and Canada alone, which is a 36 percent increase over 1997's 58 million Internet users. And 20 million of these Netcitizens are buying goods and services over the Internet—that's not counting those who use the Internet to comparison shop before buying from traditional channels. Although Netcitizenship cuts across every demographic group, Nielsen found that over half of the total population between the ages of 16 and 34 are Net users.

Networks grow in direct response to user demands. And we are all demanding more and more from networked information and applications: as business users, as customers, as business partners, and as individual participants in this networked phenomenon—as private users and consumers.

Two years ago, not one in 1,000 people had bought anything over the Internet. Today probably nine out of ten of those who are reading this book have bought something over the Internet or found information on it about a purchase, whether in a business context or for personal use. For Internet users, comparison shopping can happen with a few mouse clicks and keystrokes while sipping coffee and wearing pajamas on Sunday morning. This is not a passing fad.

It is just too easy to buy books from Amazon.com, or a notebook PC from Dell—and that could be a $5,000 personal transaction. And the more we do it, the more we want to do it, from airline tickets to even automobiles. The Christmas shopping season in the United States revealed a new and somewhat stunning development. According to analyses of 1998 online holiday shopping, female online buyers for the first time surged significantly past male online buyers. According to International Data Corporation, this "feminization of the Internet is a very important shift, because women seek out different Web destinations than men, spend less time surfing online, and are the primary decision-makers in the majority of household purchases."

Everything we do demands more and more networking technologies and services. And we are turning more and more to the Internet and the World Wide Web as fundamental dimensions of all types of business. There has been a paradigm shift: The business applications running outside of a company will soon be, if they have not already become, more important to the success and well-being of the company than will the traditional business applications running inside the company. And the business applications running outside the company will be (and are) Internet and web based.

Chapter 11 covers application technologies in more detail, but there are some things that should be stressed here. First, applications need to be flexible and to evolve as rapidly as business conditions and social and economic climates around them. The time is past when we could take years to develop and deploy an internal application and expect that application to serve its purpose for 10 or 20 years. If applications are not built very rapidly, they stand a very good chance of being obsolete before they even come online. Above all that means that top-level executives must understand the strategic directions of their organizations in order to determine what types of applications should be invested in. Too many application decisions have been and are being made based on the immediate needs of baseline users and not the strategic directions of a business or public service organization. CEOs are approving multimillion-dollar expenditures every day based on the preferences of clerical workers while ignoring the longer-term needs of their businesses.

Second, the cost of applications is like an iceberg. The price of the software itself is just the tip, even when it is a packaged, "off-the-shelf" application. Deploying the application and training and adapting its users can double and triple the initial overall application costs. Supporting and maintaining the application can double and triple that. With applications developed in-house or custom applications developed by third parties, the cost can escalate by orders of magnitude. Read carefully Chapter 10 on enabling technologies before making decisions on custom-developed applications. These have a long history of coming in way over budget and months and years behind schedule—just the kind of things that undo the best business strategies.

All of which brings us back to the software infrastructure and an important new IT infrastructure component, application servers.

APPLICATION SERVERS

Application servers are a relatively recent development among software infrastructure technologies. Although the term is applied slightly differently by various software providers, in general application servers allow business application developers to create and deploy Internet and web-enabled applications. These Internet/web-enabled applications assume not only the existence of an Internet (and also intranets and extranets) but are ready to access the networked resources without requiring specific and extensive programming to do so.

In short, the application server links the client browser technology—what people are using—to business applications and information stored centrally somewhere (and we do not normally even care where) on the Net. Just as important, application servers can link business applications to the Internet, enabling users to interact with business applications from a browser outside the confines of a corporation.

Is that important? Emphatically, yes! Put another way, if an organization's applications are not Internet enabled, within just a couple of years those applications will be at best obsolete or at worst a competitive liability.

Why? Because we, as users, are becoming so accustomed to and comfortable with accessing applications and information through a browser that we simply will not use applications or information not accessible via a browser.

Application server technology is a rapidly evolving sector. Every key provider of software infrastructure technology has either developed application server capability (e.g., Oracle, Microsoft, IBM) or has bought up smaller companies that have these products (e.g., Netscape's acquisition of Kiva and Sun Microsystem's acquisition of NetDynamics). Application server technology is being hailed as one of the most important developments in recent years; according to some observers, it is perhaps as important to the enterprise IT infrastructure as was the introduction of relational database technologies two decades ago. Application servers are very likely to emerge as key component technologies, and much of their functionality will become embedded inside other software infrastructure technologies, particularly application integration technologies and even IMSs (e.g., Oracle8i).

Decisions made concerning application servers may or may not involve large capital outlays, but the ramifications of these decisions will remain with organizations for a long, long time. Those decisions could accelerate a company's competitive value or debilitate its overall capabilities. And it is very likely that someone, somewhere, inside the organization is trying to make decisions about application server technologies today, if they have not made those decisions already.

Should executives know about these decisions? Probably, since they are a key part of the big picture. Should executives get involved with these decisions? Possibly, but probably only to the extent that decisions about applications servers are consistent with other IT infrastructure strategies. Will decisions about application server technologies impact the business? That fact is assured. Remember, this is the technology that links business applications to the Internet and the World Wide Web. The better an organization does that, the better it will compete, the better it will serve customers and constituents in the future, and the happier shareholders and executives are likely to be.

Many of the components of the software infrastructure overlap and even blend into each other and, especially, into networking components. So the graphical depiction of these component technologies as discrete elements is a bit inaccurate.

The component boundaries should be fuzzy and wavy, and if each were a separate color, the colors would bleed into one another, in constantly flowing real-time animation. We have tried here to keep it more straightforward.

Obviously, technology is a rapidly evolving and constantly changing environment, as is contemporary business itself. I would like to provide a clear, clean, and crisp picture of information technology, frozen in time, as it were. Unfortunately, it is a moving target. Readers who keep the fundamental IT infrastructure model in mind should be able to make sense of components and their interrelationships as they evolve and develop over time.

Middleware plays a central role in many large organizations in maintaining and managing the blending and blurring of these software infrastructure technologies, especially among different applications and separate IMS. And since many commentators consider application servers to be middleware, it can get a bit confusing. (Just for the record, I do not consider applications servers to be middleware. Application servers are a new class of software infrastructure component.)

MIDDLEWARE

Middleware is an often-abused term among technology providers, and often middleware technologies themselves are bundled inside some other software infrastructure components. Middleware, in its strictest sense, consists of integration and monitoring technologies that facilitate the interoperability of two or more separate business applications, generally transactional applications. Additionally, some middleware technology provides extended systems management functions, especially between two or more disparate applications; these usually include, but are not confined to, load-balancing among systems resources and fault tolerance. Middleware is most commonly found among large transaction processing applications in very large commercial environments—banks, airlines, telecommunications, and the like.

What integration technologies do is rather simple to describe but not very easy to achieve, at least at enterprise and intraenterprise levels. These technologies connect disparate systems, applications, networks, and databases, and, it is hoped, make them operate together "seamlessly"—that is, transparently to the application and information user.

Do they actually achieve that? Yes, mostly. Are they viable solutions? That depends, mostly on the technologies needing integration and the degree of "transparency" required. Are they expensive? Yes, an important thing to keep in mind about middleware is that it is expensive, from the standpoint of both licensing costs and initial implementation and ongoing support costs (again, expensive people costs).

Because so many different systems, applications, and forms of information must be interacted with, if an organization is larger than the proverbial mom-and-pop shop, integration issues will arise from time to time. The IS staff will bring them to executives' attention. And although quick fixes will be tempting, business executives need to probe for longer-term solutions with the chief information officer and IS management.

A new segment of software infrastructure technologies is called enterprise application integration (EAI) technologies. The sole purpose of these technologies is to integrate fragmented applications and information resources within an enterprise organization. As good as many of these technologies are, they are only interim fixes. The need for integrating fragmented applications and information resources may indicate a deeper problem with an IT infrastructure—a lack of planning (both IS planning and business planning) and an absence of standards across an enterprise, which indicates a lack of strong leadership.

Some organizations find it more effective and efficient simply to dismantle fragmented legacy applications and databases and completely replace them with a standardized, open, and scaleable already integrated ERP environment. And some organizations were backed into doing just that in order to avoid Y2K problems. This is usually more feasible for smaller and medium-size organizations, generally organizations with fewer than 5,000 people. Massive replacement of fragmented software infrastructures always requires the leadership of a strong CEO and the support of an informed and dedicated board of directors. Larger organizations often find the quick fix offered by integration technologies too tempting to pass up. And many middleware providers are counting on the temptation of quick fixes for a large portion of their profits.

There can be, however, a number of valid reasons for implementing middleware technologies, especially in larger Fortune 500–type IS environments. For one, top-level business executives might devise new business requirements to meet emerging customer needs or market conditions; these new business requirements may involve a mix of existing applications, information, and systems. Take, for example, a large merger or acquisition. Two complementary business organizations with separate and different business applications, different databases containing different information, and separate and perhaps radically different IS environments now must function effectively and competitively as one organization—and accomplish this within a short time frame. The advantages and rewards of a large-scale merger or acquisition are usually found in the melding of resources, especially information resources, and the resulting competitive advantages. And middleware technologies stand ready to help bring all the disparate pieces together, from legacy mainframe applications and data, to existing client-server environments, to new and emerging Web- and Internet-based applications like electronic commerce. Although middleware integration can be accomplished within relatively short periods, keep in mind that these are not quick fixes and will be expensive to initiate, implement, and maintain.

If discussions concerning middleware appear on a meeting agenda or are raised by IS managers, ask questions immediately and understand what is being meant by the term. Is it integration or monitoring technologies that will tie together existing applications and databases, or is it new Internet- and web-enabling technologies, what is here called application server technologies? If the middleware is aimed at integrating existing applications and information, then the problems being addressed stem from preexisting conditions and possibly from previous mistakes or previous poor IS planning. If what is being discussed is actually what this book calls application server technologies, the discussion is forward-looking in nature, not focused on past situations that need correcting but on new opportunities. Finally, if executive management is calling for new business solutions that require integration of legacy applications and existing, disparate information systems, middleware technologies may be the only viable answer.

One of the primary sources of integration problems bubbles up from lines of business that may implement departmental or divisional technologies that, on the surface, appear inexpensive and easy to acquire but that sometimes quickly turn into isolated pockets of disparate information and applications. Integrating these applications and information resources can become more costly than the original departmental "solution."

An executive's rule of thumb concerning middleware might be this: If the application is new, if the technology under consideration is current, if Internet-harmonious networking is involved, *and if* someone mentions middleware, a red flag should pop up immediately. No modern networked application should be designed from the ground up with middleware in mind, unless that new application needs to be integrated with legacy applications and historical information. Ask lots of questions. And keep in mind that for other than large transactional applications (and almost all these are legacy applications), the functionality provided by most middleware should now be contained in the operating system, the information management systems, or the application server (as in regard to the Internet and World Wide Web), or it should be built into the application itself. Buying middleware for a new business application indicates that something probably is wrong somewhere.

SYSTEMS MANAGEMENT

Although the chief information officer and his or her staff are concerned with all of the components of the IT infrastructure, systems management is their special domain. All of these IT infrastructure components (software packages used in the enterprise ranging across operating systems, databases, productivity tools, and customized applications) need constant administration, tracking, tweaking, and management. System components need to be kept current, to be backed up (when you back up a PC file on a diskette, you are performing systems management), to be monitored, and to be *secure.*

All of these tasks—and a host of others—are deep "back-office" functions that IS specialists perform constantly and that require a variety of tools. In a sense, these systems management technologies are similar to the sophisticated shop tools that modern automobile mechanics use to tune and maintain luxury cars. Executives may not need to know too much detail about how the tools work or what they do, but since the company is paying for these tools, executives probably want to know that they are appropriate and necessary to the tasks at hand.

More detailed discussions appear in Chapter 7. For now, keep in mind that systems management is vital. The software is an expense in and of itself, but an even more critical investment is the one IS management makes in their people. The best tools in the hands of poor mechanics can do more harm than good. And along with network management and information management, the systems management function is among the most delicate in the IT infrastructure, not one on which to economize. The word "security" alone should be enough to underscore the critical nature of systems management.

INFORMATION TECHNOLOGY INFRASTRUCTURE REVISITED

Let us take one more look at the complete IT infrastructure model (see Exhibit 5.2).

There exists a vast software infrastructure supporting business applications, and decisions made about that software infrastructure will directly affect the capabilities and viability—and competitiveness—of applications and of an organization. And in our networked, knowledge-based global economy, the efficacy and soundness of this hidden software

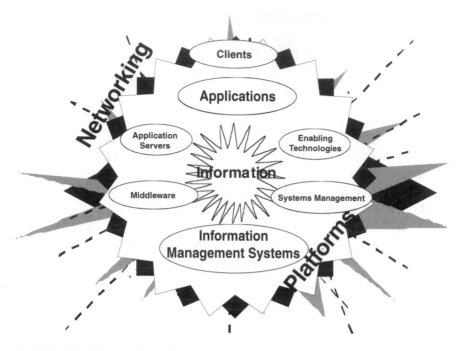

Exhibit 5.2   Networking Platforms

infrastructure translates directly into bottom-line profits or the lack thereof.

Even more significant, this software infrastructure can spell the difference between a firm's ability to perform, to carry out its mission, or abject failure, as illustrated by one of the U.S. Navy's new generation of "smart ships." Early in 1998, the battle cruiser USS *Yorktown* lay dead in the water for several hours and had to be towed back into port because of a "bug" in the Microsoft NT operating system of the computers that ran the ship's propulsion systems. In modern combat an immobile warship probably would not survive.

And so comes to mind the lines of the English poet George Herbert, "For want of a nail the shoe is lost, for want of a shoe the horse is lost, for want of a horse the rider is lost," and thus are lost the battle, the war, and the kingdom. With IT infrastructures, one line of faulty code can cripple an organization, and crippled organizations cannot compete in the information-based global economy. Like it or not, the global economy exists because of networked information and the information technologies that support it. And like it or not, top-level management is responsible for the continuous and effective operations of organizations that are now overwhelmingly dependent on viable IT infrastructures.

The best whiz-bang application may be running on a desktop or in a department, but if it is supported by a shabby, "un"secure, unreliable information infrastructure, it will be worthless.

Someone once said to me that when people buy a house, they are not interested in the plumbing. My answer was that they should be very interested in the plumbing, and in the electrical wiring, the gas lines, the phone connections, and the antenna, cable, and satellite hookups. If the gas, electricity, and water do not work, a picture-perfect Martha Stewart kitchen is not very useful.

The same holds true for the software infrastructure. Over time, the IT infrastructure must expand and adapt to meet the growing needs of an organization. New technologies will arrive. New application requirements will pop up, usually from competitive conditions and customers' demands.

The ability (or inability) of an organization's IT infrastructure to expand, adopt new technologies, and support new applications will determine whether a company can continue to provide value to customers and thereby continue to create wealth for shareholders today and into the future.

None of this is magic. None of it happens because someone repeated a chant, cast a spell, or waved a special wand. Nor does it happen because a technology vendor promises it to be so. It requires a tremendous, ongoing investment of capital resources, people, time, and, what this book is about, top-level executive involvement. At this point, readers should be much better prepared to become involved, to govern and manage more prudently and effectively the organization's information resources and the technology infrastructure that supports those resources. The chapters that follow will broaden and expand capabilities in these vital areas.

NOTE

1. For example, see William J. Drake, ed., *The New Information Infrastructure: Strategies for U.S. Policy* (Washington, DC: Brookings Institution Press, 1995).

CHAPTER 6

Networking Technologies

Heaven's net is indeed vast,
Though its meshes are wide, it misses nothing.

—LAO TZU

NEW FIRST PRINCIPLE OF
INFORMATION TECHNOLOGY

In *The Tao of Physics,* Fritjof Capra states that "the properties of the parts can only be fully understood through the dynamics of the whole. The whole is primary, and once a person understands the dynamics of the whole, he or she then can derive, at least in principle, the properties and patterns of the interactions of the parts."[1] As was said earlier, parts is parts. Now that we have a comprehension of the whole, we can look more closely at the parts.

In examining the IT infrastructure model and its primary components, the constantly informing dynamic of the whole must be kept in mind. No single information technology offers any value by itself, except perhaps as a curiosity. Information technologies and components must interconnect and work in concert to deliver any sort of value to an organization. Unfortunately, IT components usually are explained in isolation, by component technology providers themselves, who tend, naturally, to explain best that set of components on which their business is focused.

This and the next three chapters examine networking and platform technologies, information management systems, and the nature of information itself. Modern scientists no longer view nature as merely a

71

collection of individual building blocks, but rather, as Capra tells us, "as a network of relations." "Ultimately, there are no parts at all in this interconnected web."[2] The IT infrastructure ultimately is composed of various technology components, no single one of which either explains the whole or offers any organizational value in and of itself. Nobel laureate Ilya Prigogine states that bricks are not interesting in and of themselves. What is interesting are the purposeful and pleasing structures built with the bricks. In the same way, the organizational value of IT is derived only from the components working in concert, composing a networked IT infrastructure.

Information itself is at the core of Exhibit 6.1 simply because the fundamental activities are always gathering and sharing information and communicating knowledge that is in turn based largely on information and its relationships.

Platform technologies are vital because information transfer happens with electricity, and hardware and operating systems conduct and direct the flows of electrical current. The greater the raw processing power available to organizations, the more information-based capabilities organizations are likely both to have and to exercise.

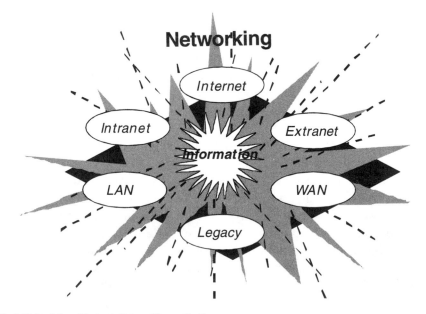

Exhibit 6.1   Networking Foundation

However, people have been accomplishing quite a bit for a relatively long time with comparatively crude and limited computer networking technologies. Technology has changed dramatically within the last decade, especially within the last five years. But think for a moment about how business and governments conducted their daily affairs 100 years ago or more. Commerce was conducted quite nicely during the nineteenth century around most of the world. And there were no telephones. Try for a moment to imagine what commerce would be like today without telephones. Now try to imagine what commerce will be like ten years from now when networking technologies have evolved and matured by a factor of 10 to 20 times what they are today, and when there are several billion global Netcitizens. It can be a bit mind-boggling.

Networked information has changed the ways people conduct commerce among organizations and between individuals. It is rapidly changing ways in which we relate with each other as human beings. Its effects are both immediate and widespread, from electing a populist governor (Jessie Ventura's campaign success resulted from an uncommon turnout among younger voters who, in large part, responded initially to the candidate's dynamic website), to central plots for movies *(You've Got Mail)*, to vital extensions of our intimate lives—from graphic and interactive pornography available on the Internet, to the infamous Starr report, also available on the Internet. To borrow the tag line from Cisco Systems' television commercial, "Are you ready?"

IMPORTANCE OF NETWORKING

Networking has become the central paradigm for modern science. Going back almost 3,000 years, Westerners thought of a building or a clock as the central paradigm of the material universe. With the development of an elaborate Newtonian model of the universe, that paradigm of parts composing the fundamental building blocks of a structure, our building paradigm became very elaborate, and the clocks became ever so more precise that they sometimes appear to wreak havoc with our sanity. But modern science in general and quantum physics in particular offered a new paradigm, that of a network of constantly interconnecting and interacting dynamic phenomena, of processes and subprocesses, of systems and subsystems rather than a set of mechanical building blocks, precisely ordered and behaving without variance to fix rules enforced through the universe.

The concept of the universe as a network, an intricate web of relations and interactions, has always been at the basis of Eastern thought. However, Western scientific thinking began rediscovering the fundamental networking principles of nature only with the inquiries into quantum mechanics. It is not that we threw out Newtonian mechanics. It is more that quantum physics helped us discover the limitations of deterministic science and prompted us to move beyond and to explore new frontiers of perception, information, and knowledge. And where science leads, business sometimes follows, right?

So much for the philosophical background. Let us talk about business issues. In an information- and knowledge-based economy, there are a couple of new and important dynamics at work. These dynamics have always existed, but they have been limited. Take, for example, the dynamics of value exchange in a simple commercial transaction. If I sell you a product and you give me money in exchange for that product, you have gained a new value (the possession of the product) and I have gained a new value (the possession of your money). The only thing is, I had to give up my product to get your money, and you had to give up your money to get my product.

A strange thing happens when we start dealing in information and knowledge. If I have some knowledge that would be valuable to you and that you would be willing to give me money for, I can exchange that knowledge for your money without really giving up the knowledge—I still will retain possession of the knowledge even after I have shared it with you. In fact, by sharing the knowledge I possess, I actually may increase that knowledge and its value by incorporating feedback and observations from people with whom I have shared the knowledge. In other words, information and knowledge resources are constantly increasing rather than depleting, in direct contrast to most traditional commercial resources, which are constantly depleting. With knowledge and information we can exchange value, while retaining the resources from which that value is derived, and at the same time increasing the knowledge resources themselves by the very act of sharing those resources. A future Nobel Prize awaits the economists who can bring meaningful order, lucidity, and precision to these concepts.

But what has that to do with the importance of networking? Spend just a couple of hours with a search engine like Yahoo! or Excite or with a business information service like Hoovers or the Wall Street Journal's Briefing Books. Look for anything of interest—information on competitor or partners, and not just about their products and services but about the individuals themselves who run the organization. Interested in investing in a particular stock but want to see the 10K information and a historical graph of five-year stock performance? A few mouse clicks and keystrokes and it is on the screen, ready to be read, printed, or stored. Not many individuals could even imagine having ready access to those kinds of information in 1993. Six years later, anyone can do it—that is, anyone who has a browser and Internet access.

Now imagine for a moment that these capabilities and the technologies that enable them evolve at the same pace they have during the past decade on through the next two decades. Imagine that the technologies keep getting faster, better, more reliable, more pervasive, smaller, and cheaper. That is what is happening. Projections are that during the year 2000, telephones in the United States will carry less voice transmission than data transmission. And three years after that, 98 percent of all telephony traffic of all kinds will be data and not voice. It is clear why many area codes are being changed. We need more phone lines for all that data to get to where it needs to go.

The good news, at least for the United States, is that much of these networking capabilities are in place and are being used. To move forward, top-level executives need to understand what new investments are required and what new ways of innovating and conducting commerce might be feasible or possible, decide how to finance these (the return-on-investment [ROI] models may be very different from traditional ROI constructs), and how to deploy new web-based commercial and public services over the Internet.

Here it is important to remember two things: First, networking technologies and network capabilities already have created a new business paradigm, just as the telephone in the twentieth century created a new business paradigm, just as air transport has, just as automobiles and trucks did before airplanes, just as railroads did before automobiles and trucks, just as sailing ships and navigation did before railroads. Every new plateau in the history of business and commerce has been marked by the introduction of a new way of connecting points of value interchange (new trade routes), whether Marco Polo by land or FedEx and UPS by air. In the past, mostly goods and some services were involved. Now connecting points-of-value interchange centers around information, very specifically, around networked information.

Second, the networking technologies considered here are Internet-based technologies, ones that conform and adapt to the standards of the Internet. What is more, these Internet-based technologies are in their relative infancy. A person would need to have grown up in a small town in the early 1950s to remember picking up a telephone and asking the local operator to connect you to a certain party. At that time rotary dialing was still a big-city phenomenon. And in the 1950s, futurists projected that if long-distance telephone usage kept increasing at its then-current pace, within 20 years every person in the United States would need to be a telephone operator.[3]

Relative to the Internet, that is about where we are today—where we were in the mid-1950s with telephone technologies. One important difference affecting the pace of networking technology advancements is something called "Internet time" or "web years," which are somewhat like "dog years"—a compression of time at a ratio of about eight or ten non-Internet years into just one Internet year. The U.S. government's report entitled *The Emerging Digital Economy* emphasizes that the Internet reached the 50-million-user mark within four years of its availability to the general (and business) public.[4] (Some credible estimates put the number of Internet users at 1 billion just a couple years after the turn of the twenty-first century.) It took the PC 16 years to reach 50 million users. It took TV 13 years to reach 50 million households. It took radio 38 years to gain 50 million listeners. So Internet time is very likely to help move networking technologies forward at a blinding pace, pushing all of us along with it.

Two business factors are also at work in advancing networking technologies, and we have little experience with either. First, the Internet and the technologies on which it is built are not owned by any single technology provider or even by a consortium of companies.

Nor are Internet technologies regulated or controlled by any government or specific international authority. Standards organizations influence the perimeters of technologies, but these often slow progress more than facilitate it. Internet technologies are "open" in the truest sense. And that means literally millions of technologists and developers around the world are working to advance Internet-based technologies and are working within a standardized model to which all efforts conform. They all work within standardized models not because someone is enforcing those standards, but because it is in everyone's mutual interest to conform to the standards. That, in and of itself, is amazing. Compelling business incentives motivate most Internet technology entrepreneurs, from ready venture capital, to stratospheric market capitalization.

A second business factor is that the compression of time is not restricted to technology development. "Web years" are a reality for everyone

Recall that the Internet is not actually an entity in itself. It is not a construct in space and time. The Internet is a concept, a defining and informing principle around which open networked information forms. When Robert Metcalf, one of the Internet's major contributing innovators, sometimes (and I hope with a sense of wry humor) predicts the collapse of the Internet, he refers to the growing pains that the Internet must constantly go through. Humankind will need someday to become accustomed to digital cash, to solve problems surrounding security and privacy, to expand bandwidths and increase reliability, to understand new investment dynamics, and to adjust political priorities and processes. There is still a lot of changes in store. But never for a moment think that the Internet is a flash in the pan or that it is a passing fad that will disappear like last season's fashions. The Internet has been over 40 years in the making, and much like the U.S. interstate highway system, which began around the same time and grew out of much the same concerns for U.S. national security and defense, the Internet is here to stay. It will be expanded, repaired, retrofitted, and constantly improved. In 50 years the technologies supporting the Internet will be vastly different and greatly enhanced, but the Internet will still be the information superhighway most of us first encountered in the decade before the turn of the twenty-first century.

connected to the Internet. Everything and everyone connected is immersed in real time—everything happens now. The only delays are the speed of the connections and the capacity of the bandwidths. Einstein and his colleagues were right: Time does not speed up. Time is relative to the observer, the participant. Time does not compress itself; more precisely, our perception of time is compressed.

Stan Davis and Christopher Meyer provide an engaging business discussion of these phenomena in their book *Blur: The Speed of Change in the Connected Economy*.[5] They offer three derivatives of time, space, and matter: speed, connectivity, and intangibles. Networking technology, specifically Internet-harmonious networking technologies, is in the center element of their equation: It provides the "connectivity." Speed is the compression of time. The intangibles are values we cannot quite quantify in traditional terms yet which are at the center of business and organizational pursuits—specifically, the intangible values of information and knowledge themselves. Without the connectivity of networked information, none of this has any substance. Because of connectivity, because of networked information, an entirely new world is rushing in upon us. Ray Kurzweil, in his book *The Age of the Spiritual Machine,* anticipates that there "will be far greater transformations in the first two decades of the twenty-first century than we saw in the entire twentieth century."[6]

NETWORK EVOLUTION

At the risk of disengaging a few of our readers at this point, I will take a brief step somewhat far afield to illustrate just how far back networking goes and where along the curve of progress present-day society lies. Australian aborigines are known for an ability to exchange information over distances of 10 and 20 miles or more simply by sending thoughts out to one another. This is not a magician's trick. Prehistoric humans exchanged a great deal of information in this way, particularly before languages evolved. We also are now beginning to understand concepts like spontaneous self-organizing, and not just in the context of, say, birds flying and swooping in precise formation without any apparent leader but with highly skilled athletes in a basketball or football game who react instantaneously and without thought to minute movements of other players. Bacteriologists are showing how bacteria can share information through networks. Physicists are discovering the spontaneous self-organizing capabilities of electrons streaming apparently randomly among electronic circuits.

As humankind evolved, as we developed languages and particularly as we began recording information, at first on cave walls and bones then later on parchment and paper, we began to rely less and less on naturally occurring networked information, to a point where we almost lost the natural networking ability altogether. The ability still lurks in the recesses of our consciousness and pops up from time to time, almost invariably connected with phone calls: "Strange that you should call, I was just thinking about you." But we have evolved out of using it. Possibly, the information we now share is too complex and too abstract for the natural networking capabilities of mental telepathy or synchronicity. Telepathic bandwidths also may be simply too narrow and lack real long-distance capabilities.

In an intriguing experiment performed in the 1960s, biophysicist Stuart Kauffman, a leading thinker in the field of complex self-organizing systems, built a network of 200 light bulbs wired together. Each bulb had an assigned relationship with two other bulbs in the network. Each bulb would turn on or off according to the state of either of the two bulbs it was connected with. This relatively simple network of light bulbs represented a possible number of on and off states of 10/30th. Kauffman anticipated the network would sooner or later settle into a repeated, self-organized pattern of on and off lights but thought that it would take some time before a repeated state would be reached. To Kauffman's surprise, the network of light bulbs very quickly explored only 13 states before it instantly settled into a repeated pattern of four flashing, on-off configurations.

As mentioned before, almost every major advancement affecting commerce and civilization seems accompanied by the introduction of a new means of *connecting*. From the wheel to ships, from roads to navigation, from the printing press to the telephone, each connects something human to something else human in a new way, over greater distances, and more quickly. And in the history of commerce, each advance expands the breadth of value interchange and shrinks the virtual distance between the points of value interchange, while concomitantly accelerating the pace of commercial cycles. The Internet not only ups the ante in connectivity but also concentrates on the mostly qualitative and largely intangible but very real values of information and knowledge, which have become the coin of a truly global realm. Just around the corner is a world where, as Frances Cairncross tells us in her book *The Death of Distance,* "transmitting information costs next to nothing, where distance is irrelevant, and where any amount of content is instantly accessible" to virtually anyone.[7]

Seen in this larger historical and commercial context, computer networking technologies represent the latest in a long line of efforts to exchange information and value and to shrink the distances between points of value interchange—getting closer to the customer, the supplier, and the resources of value creation. What seems different and even special about the evolution of computer networks into the Internet is that we may be getting back to where we started. But this time, instead of cave-man George sending his tribe a mental message that the buffalo hunting is good over the hills to the south, we are wiring the entire planet and making virtually every piece of information available and of potential value to just about anyone.

And do not think that the limited availability of PCs is the governor on this Internet information engine. Market demands soon will nullify the self-sustaining interests of some currently dominant technology providers. Almost anyone with a television set will soon have affordable Internet access. It is not that complicated; it is generally available; and it is reasonably affordable. A lot of people will be connected, and in the not-so-distant future.

SOME SIMPLE NETWORKING PRINCIPLES

Like most technologies, networks can start out fairly simple and straightforward, then quickly become complex and complicated. Let us start with something simple—a node. A node is a device attached to a network. We could call it a client, like a PC, or an appliance, perhaps like a smart pager, but a client implies some sort of interaction with a user. So while a client device can be a node on a network, a node is not necessarily a client device.

A node can be, for example, an expensive laser printer, or a central server containing Lotus Notes files that are shared by a workgroup. A node is anything that can be attached to a network, can be identified by the network, and can either send information out on the network or receive information from the network resources and other nodes.

A network server manages the network to which it is attached. The server is like a local traffic cop that not only directs information among nodes but also can store information for nodes that may not be connected at a given time. The network server also maintains information of its own, such as names, addresses, phone numbers, and passwords, as well as management tools that a network administrator uses. In a local area network (LAN) (see Exhibit 6.2), the server and nodes are usually wired together physically. Network wiring, like Ethernet, usually has physical limitations of a couple of hundred feet. So we connect these LANs together with more wire and special bridging technologies.

Exhibit 6.3 shows two local area networks connected to an Internet server, which, in turn, can connect to all the other servers on the Internet.

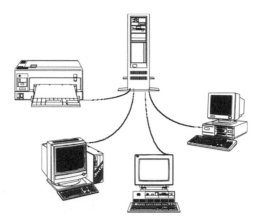

Exhibit 6.2   Local Area Network

Most of us know these servers as Internet service providers (ISPs), such as America Online, Mindspring/Netcom, and hundreds of others. Larger organizations maintaining their own Internet servers are themselves virtual ISPs for their internal users. If we are connecting to the Internet, we usually dial into an Internet server in some way. We are connected by flexible and movable connections, plugging into almost any phone, the T3 line, or the like, so we are not confined to limitations of fixed, physical wires. In this way, network servers provide network users with a gateway into the Internet, intranets, and extranets. Once we have a gateway like that, we can go anywhere we like and find any information we want—and

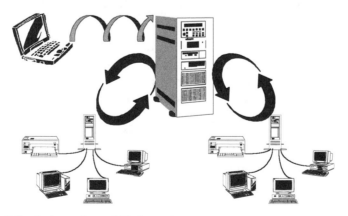

Exhibit 6.3   Intranets and Extranets

even be bombarded by information we do not necessarily want. It is the price we pay.

The physical network also consists of transport media—phone wires, cable, fiber optics, satellite transmission—and bridges, routers, and hubs. Bridges connect two or more LANs together, either in a local environment, one floor to another or one campus site to another, or among geographically remote LAN sites over longer-distance transmission. Routers connect similar networks into internetworks and usually have one input and several outputs. Hubs are generally more "intelligent" than either bridges or routers; in addition to providing connectivity among smaller networks and even individual devices, hubs manage a great deal of the information flow, optimizing internetworking efficiency.

Networked information exists because of a foundation of hardware and system software, and everything happens because electricity is moving in controlled patterns across wires and through the air and on increasingly intricate circuits called microprocessors. In other words, networked information is not smoke and mirrors. And the Internet and its related technologies are one of the all-time outstanding feats of science and engineering, modern or ancient. But more of that later.

The Internet, beyond the physical network, is comprised of protocols and sets of enabling technologies. *Protocols* manage the forms that data files go through as they move across a network from one computer to another. Unlike single-stream, analog voice transmissions over normal phone lines, data transmissions are usually broken up into packets of data, each packet neatly ordered and labeled with instructions—where to send it and how to reassemble it with its fellow packets into meaningful information. The protocol of the Internet is TCP/IP, for Transmission Control Protocol/Internet Protocol. TCP does the packetizing of the information, controls it during the transmission, and reassembles it at the destination point. IP is like an envelope in which we place the TCP packet; IP carries the packet across the network to the proper destination, determining the best and fastest routes.

Before the introduction of TCP/IP in 1974, and until it became widely distributed and stipulated (the U.S. Department of Defense made it mandatory in the early 1980s), protocols resembled a networking version of the Tower of Babel. There seemed to be a protocol for every different computer, for each different application, and for every occasion. One of the real benefits of the Internet was that it eliminated all that noise and settled on one highly efficient and flexible protocol for everything. Bob Kahn and Vint Cerf, who together invented TCP/IP, also gave us the term "Internet"; *Internet* Protocol was the first formal use of the word "Internet."

INTERNET ENABLING TECHNOLOGIES

The most common enabling Internet technologies are email and the World Wide Web. Some commentators also called these Internet "applications," but here "application" is reserved strictly for business applications that focus on business processes. "Enabling technology" refers to software that helps us perform more fundamental and less process-oriented tasks than normal business applications require. Enabling technologies are tools that help us either build applications or execute broader, less process-oriented tasks. For example, e-mail sends and receives text messages as well as data file attachments, like images, spreadsheets, and documents.

The World Wide Web is in some ways the Internet version of the Library of Congress catalog numbering system or the older Dewey Decimal system. With the World Wide Web we can assign a unique identifier to just about any individual piece of information stored in any system on the planet (or in outer space, for that matter) and, with a single mouse click, access that information over the Internet. And we can link from one piece of information to another by clicking on an embedded identifier, which usually appears highlighted in blue. In a few years, with 64-bit processors, voice commands are very likely to replace mouse clicks. We will simply tell a voice-enabled browser to go out on the Internet and bring us to a particular website or to a specific set of information contained in a particular website.

Other Internet enabling technologies include list servers (for broadcasting emails to list subscribers), File Transfer Protocol (FTP) (which sends copies of files between computers), newsgroups (which enable a user group to share email messages among themselves), and Wide-Area Information Services (which provide access to hundreds of topic-specific databases). This list will grow, most likely through a process approximating cell division.

While these quasi-applications are software, they are not part of the software infrastructure within the IT infrastructure but are part of the networking technologies. Much like the final major area of the networking technologies, the network operating systems, the Internet enabling technologies are embedded into the fabric of the Internet. We do not buy them or decide whether we want them or not. They are simply there. In contrast, the software infrastructure offers an endless number of choices and decisions, each of which enables business applications and all of which affect an organization's ability to fulfill its mission, and most of which are not by any means "free."

NETWORK OPERATING SYSTEMS

Organizations also can make some real choices about network operating systems. Some decisions are determined by legacy networks and systems and existing business applications, while others may evolve in response to market demands or to the availability of new technology. Network operating systems (NOSs) provide first-level management of network activities—mostly the traffic movements of requests for information itself. Two key roles of NOSs are access control (who can access the network and its services) and security (logons, authentication, virus/intruder detection, etc.). NOS services can become extensive. In fact, where NOSs were once distinct among themselves, with different protocols, different fundamental features and functions, they have now evolved into very similar offerings and are distinguishable by the state of their technologies rather than by the types of their technologies.

Almost all NOSs now use the TCP/IP protocol for internetworking, even though they may use a unique protocol for LANs or proprietary WANs. (For example, Novell uses SPX/IPX in its Netware NOS product.) And, quite naturally, all NOSs contain Internet support and Web server support. As a direct benefit of the Internet technologies now contained in all NOSs, users normally do not have trouble tying different legacy NOSs together. All NOS vendors offer upgrades of Internet technologies that facilitate internetworking. A vendor who does not offer Internet capability has an obsolete NOS. And if an obsolete NOS is part of an organization's IT infrastructure, it needs replacing.

Currently, Novell's Netware/Internet continues to offer the best technology among widely used NOSs and dominates 80 percent of the LAN markets. Banyan's Vines was Novell's keenest competitor but has diminished in market presence. A large U.S. corporation or a government organization may still use Vines, which in many ways is a superior networking technology.

Banyan's Vines and StreetTalk networking technologies were based on the concept of a logical network, which is more flexible and scaleable than a physical network, such as Novell Netware. But there are lots of pieces to any network, and most vendors providing the pieces saw more money in partnering with physical network providers. This scenario is common among technology providers—a superior technology gets shunted off into virtual oblivion by an inferior albeit workable technology that locks in distribution channels based on market clout, not on innovation or value. Microsoft, in early 1999, invested significantly in Banyan, which is now focused on network service and support. Microsoft plans to train Banyan support personnel on Windows 2000 and hopes to migrate Vines and StreetTalk users into Microsoft's Active Directory Services in Windows 2000 Server editions.

EMBEDDING NOS TECHNOLOGY IN OPERATING SYSTEMS AND HARDWARE

Two older trends made new again seem to dominate NOS technologies. The first is embedding NOS functionality into operating systems. Unix has always done this. Recall that Unix and its programming language C came out of Bell Labs (now Lucent Technology, Inc.) in the early 1970s, and the business of Bell Labs was to explore better and better ways of communicating, of telephony, of networking. Almost everything about Unix screams "connectivity, networking, internetworking!" And recall that the first law of Sun Microsystems, started in 1982, was, and still is, "The network is the computer." Sometimes life, even in high-tech companies, can be sweet and prophetic.

Then came IBM's OS/2 Warp Server, which offered combined application services and network services. IBM pulled the plug on OS/2 when it was apparent that Microsoft's NT Server was ruling the day. Microsoft had originally intended for its NT Server to compete against Novell in the NOS markets and to offer client-server application services. That way Microsoft could own the LAN and the clients all by itself. But the initial releases of NT Server, starting in 1994 and up to now, proved inadequate for most networking tasks. NT lacked several key functions, including Named Directory Services, so Microsoft was almost forced to market NT Server as a client-server application platform for departmental and line-of-business environments.

Once again and almost by accident, Microsoft stepped into a pile of gold. Chapter 7 discusses NT operating systems, now called Windows 2000, as well as Unix. They are mentioned here to show that general-purpose operating systems like Windows NT Server and Unix have most NOS functionality built in.

The second trend for NOS is to embed NOS features in the networking components themselves. There are lots of choices in networking technologies. And the good news is that all the choices conform to Internet technology standards. That contrasts with platform technologies, where vendors try to devise differentiated and proprietary technologies, saying "We have this great functionality but you can only get it from us"; network technology providers offer open technologies based on Internet standards, saying "We all do the same thing, but we do these particular things better and cheaper than anyone else."

FROM ARPAnet TO INTERNET

If you know this story, skip down to the next section on the World Wide Web. If you do not know the history of the Internet, if you have not seen the PBS video production or read the book *Nerds 2.0.1: A Brief History of the Internet* by Stephen Segaller,[8] you might want to take time to read these next few paragraphs. For one thing, the history of the Internet demonstrates the power of focused, publicly sponsored research divorced from any immediate commercial concerns. In an era where free enterprise and ultra-strength capitalism are twin gods, it can be humbling to realize that the next big leap in commerce and culture is occurring now because a young U.S. president in January 1961 dedicated his nation to putting a man on the moon before the end of that decade.

John Kennedy's promise, during the tense global climate of the Cold War, was not merely aimed at beating the Soviet Union to the moon. What sobered U.S. strategists in the late 1950s was that, if the Soviets could put a man in orbit, they were more capable than the United States of sending out nuclear payloads. The United States needed to develop heavy lifting technologies, and fast. In 1959, President Eisenhower requested funds from Congress to establish the Advanced Research

Projects Agency (ARPA), which was set up with $520 million buried inside a line item in an air force appropriations bill. So the machinery was in place and the money was there by the time Kennedy promised to send a man to the moon before 1970. Research funds began pouring from federal coffers into defense and aerospace research and development and into universities, which were in turn further funded to produce the next generation of engineers and scientists who would further the nation's technological progress. Several federal and state programs funded the university education of not just engineering and science students but language and literature students, history and psychology students, and business students throughout the 1960s and into the 1970s.

And did it work. Neil Armstrong walked on the moon on July 20, 1969, and on September 2 of that year, the ARPAnet came alive for a single-node test at the University of California, Los Angeles. A second IMP (interface message processor) was installed at Stanford University on October 1, and the first message was transmitted between two ARPAnet nodes, the characters "L" and "O"—or "hello," in computer shorthand. A month later a third node was installed at the University of California at Santa Barbara, and a month after that, a fourth was installed at the University of Utah.

The growing ARPAnet spurred curiosity and experimentation in universities around the United States. By the 1980s the ARPAnet had a couple of hundred nodes and growth was accelerating. Also at that time the National Science Foundation funded an effort among several universities in the Southeast, led by the University of Maryland, to establish new computer networks among universities that would be based on ARPAnet technologies but would not be part of the ARPAnet. The proposal grew into NSF NET, which began connecting supercomputing resources of universities, research organizations, and corporations.

At the time the PC was just beginning its roll into the future, and local area networks were more promise than function. Most of the networking being done on the ARPAnet, the MILNET (the military spinoff from the ARPAnet), the first-generation Internet networks (Whole Earth's 'Lectronic Link, or WELL), and the NSF Net was done primarily using Unix-based platforms. And as university computer science majors graduated and took jobs in the high-tech corridors of Silicon Valley and outer Boston, they brought with them an addiction for email and a thing called USENET—a techie form of a chat room. Exposed early to the virtues and benefits of the ARPAnet and various NSF NET technologies, especially the open network architectures and the TCP/IP protocol, these young computer engineers could see no reason for developing proprietary network technologies when the whole idea was to interconnect all computers. And the overriding compulsion was to gather information and share knowledge, at a time when that was not a very commercially viable notion.

In 1985 NSF NET's backbone was upgraded to T1 lines for higher-speed connections among the supercomputers that formed it. Later the backbone was upgraded to even more powerful T3 lines, again funded by the National Science Foundation. These high-speed connections provide the United States with its current Internet backbone; due to this technology funding, the United States is farther in front of other nations in availability of Internet bandwidth.

In 1992 the National Science Foundation Act was amended to allow commerce on the Net. A year earlier Tim Berners-Lee working at CERN (Conseil Europeen pour la Recherche Nucleaire) outside Geneva had published code for the World Wide Web on the Internet. In 1993 a group of graduate students, led by Marc Andreessen at the University of Illinois, Champaign-Urbana, developed the Mosaic browser; in that same year the Web grew by 341,000 percent. One year later, in 1994, Andreessen and Jim Clark formed Netscape, Architext Software (now Excite) was formed, and Jeff Bezos wrote his business plan for Amazon.com. Then things really began taking off.

Two things are interesting about this brief history. First, the Internet and all of its core technologies have in a real sense been given to us. If it had been left in the hands of technology companies, the Internet never would have happened, much less have produced the open, accessible, and virtually infinitely expandable interconnection of information and exchange of knowledge that it has. Technology companies would have tried to make every network proprietary. We would not have had the Internet had President Eisenhower not established ARPA in 1958.

The second interesting dimension of the Internet's history is that at every turn, something almost mystical seems to occur. Not that there have been any great leaps and bounds or radically new inventions, but each phase seems to build on the last, each concept is a refinement and an extension of the last, each technology improves and expands its predecessor. And they all seemed to coalesce during the early 1990s, making 1994 and 1995 watershed years for the next generation of commerce and culture, the real beginnings of a global knowledge-based economy and even a global information-based society. But then, in science's network paradigms, complex systems are characterized by steady, intertwining expansions of relations and variety. So all this is not really out of the ordinary.

The World Wide Web and browser technologies are fundamental to the Internet's commercially viable dimensions. The web and browser technologies allow us to point and click across the Internet, to locate and retrieve information, and to share both knowledge and value—to conduct commercial transactions, based both on information and on goods and services. Networked commerce is not just the wave of the future. It is the tsunami of the present.

Pundits have consistently and grossly underestimated almost everything about the Internet and web commerce. The volume of Internet business transactions, the value and impact of those transactions, the growth of Internet users, the valuations of Internet stocks, all boggle the minds of traditional business forecasters. Many want to dismiss it as an aberration, a temporary blip on their radar. Yet the Internet is not an overnight accident. It has been building for 40 years. Science, education, engineering, even politics has been caught up in the Internet's broad wake. Segaller ponders one of the salient ironies of the Internet:

> . . . the Net was responsible for facilitating social and political liberation in places as diverse as Myanmar, Russia, and China. . . . a Pentagon program prompted by Cold War rivalry has evolved into a communications medium that helps overthrow . . . tyrants. Today's tyrants are attempting to restrict or dominate computer networks, almost certainly in vain.[9]

And it is all just starting.

Think for a moment how a group of radical thinkers, brought up on a diet of new ideas and values that are broadly referred to as the "Age of Reason," extended the heritage of Descartes and Newton and the ideas of a deterministic universe, took these new values from science and philosophy, then shaped a new concept of government called democracy. What the rest of the world looked up as a "great experiment," what many doubted would last into the nineteenth century, is now the dominant form of world order. And the Internet and World Wide Web are not just outgrowths of those democratic concepts; they promise an even greater penetration of democratic principles and values as the twenty-first century begins.

WEB COMMERCE AND BEYOND

In web-based commerce, customers have infinitely more choices than ever before. The entire world is their shopping mall. And here we are not just talking about a giant yellow pages with expanded yellow-page ads. (Unfortunately, to many businesses websites are precisely that—overgrown yellow page adverts.) Customers are no longer captured when they walk into our store. They must be *engaged*. If they cannot immediately find the information they are looking for—even if they do not know precisely what that information is or if it is even here—or if they cannot perform a transaction easily and quickly, if pages or images download too slowly, if the information itself is not engaging, even almost entertaining—for any of these reasons and a host of others, all customers need to do is point and click, and they are almost instantly in a competitor's virtual store.

So when we think about web commerce we need to think beyond the commercial paradigms of the past and the present. We need to do more than just "webifying" the commercial transactions we have always done and delivering the same types of information-based services we have always delivered. To gain any real competitive advantage in Web commerce, business thinkers must be truly engaged and innovative all of the time. Much of the value an organization offers its customers and constituents will be the value of its innovation as these are expressed through websites and over the Internet.

Quality counts, yes. Availability counts, yes. Price counts, of course. But the web demands new kinds of innovations that will count as much as these and even more. Business, whether in goods or services, must engage customers and constituents and keep them engaged. That will not be easy. Think about TV commercials. They are very good at engaging viewers, but how long can most TV commercials keep us engaged even for the first time we see them? Think now about engaging customers and constituents repeatedly, and keeping them engaged, keeping them from pointing and clicking to a competitor's website.

The bottom line, so to speak, is that web commerce will become a vastly different set of activities for most businesses from anything they have done before. Just as many people prefer to engage in business with people they know and like, web customers will develop preferences for websites. Most of those reasons are within the direct control of a business's top-level executives, and most are directly related about the kind of IT infrastructure those executives have put in place, for infrastructures reflect the quality and capability of top-level executives.

A well-built IT infrastructure coupled with innovative top-level leadership can open entirely new frontiers for almost any organization. Take, for example, AMR Corporation, the parent company of American

Airlines. AMR's first chief information officer, Max Hooper, designed and built a forward-looking IT infrastructure before the days of the commercial Internet; it anticipated the web. That resulted in a spinoff of AMR's IT functions into its Sabre Technology subsidiary. By 1995 the Sabre Technology unit contributed 44 percent of AMR's pretax profits, while American Airlines contributed about 12 percent of pretax profits. Computers are not free, but AMR's capital and personnel expenses associated with the Sabre Technology unit are minuscule compared to the capital and personnel expense of the airline unit. So if you were chief executive officer of AMR, when would you start considering outsourcing your airline unit?

It is indeed a brave new world. There are new and wondrous things in it, and all of those wondrous things rely on networking. It is for a good reason that Internet stocks have been the darlings of Wall Street. No, not all of them are going to work out. Yes, many of them are overvalued, at least according to traditional valuation criteria. But there is little doubt that these Internet companies, and the ones to follow, will be at the epicenter of business and commerce in the first several decades of the twenty-first century.

KEY TECHNOLOGY PROVIDERS

Key players in networking technologies move fast, merge quickly, and transform and mutate often. It is the nature of networking to do that. The volatility and expanding valuations of Internet-related stocks testify to the dynamic nature of the players themselves. Among the current providers of network and Internet technologies, Cisco System, Lucent Technologies, Nortel Networks, and Fore seem strongest at providing enterprise-type organizations the physical components of the Internet, the network platforms technologies themselves. These companies seem to be in constant acquisition mode, which can make for constant transformation and turbulence. In late 1998 Northern Telecom and Bay Networks combined to form Nortel Networks; in January 1999 Lucent announced a merger worth $20 billion with Ascend Communications in order to compete more keenly with Cisco.

It is wise to choose one primary technology provider, establish ongoing relationships with top-level executives, especially the chief operating officer most directly responsible for meeting your organization's networking needs. One phone call, or email, from one chief operating or executive officer to another can mean more than all the requests for proposals (RFPs) and formal agreements generated lower down the ladder. In this age of electronically networked commerce, those personal executive relationships count even more than before. The personal communications among top executives from technology providers and the top-level business executives in customer organizations can alter for the better many of the large dynamics involved in building and maintaining robust, flexible, and viable IT infrastructures. The more informed top-level business executives are, the more productive and profitable that intercommunication with technology industry executives will be.

HIGH COST OF NETWORKS

M. Bensaou and Michael Earl, in their article on "The Right Mind-set for Managing Information Technology," underscore an important and unfortunate tendency among top-level U.S. executives: ". . . the cumulative and pervasive value-for-money mind-set can be destructive. It can bias investment decisions toward cost-saving automation projects; it can deter ideas for revenue-generating IT applications; and it can lead to the dangerously late adoption of IT infrastructure improvements."[10]

Although they are talking broadly about IT infrastructures, it applies to the networking infrastructure that is our new first principle of IT. The ROI for networking technology investment is much more visionary than it is number crunching. Top-level executives who lack vision, who cannot or do not shape innovative strategies and lead their organizations in new ways toward emerging opportunities, will fail to make proper investments, especially in the crucial underlying network infrastructure components, simply because they are wholly guided by crunching short-term "value-for-money" formulas. They are too preoccupied in counting the branches of a particular tree and know nothing about finding new paths through the changing forest. Some seem to prefer burying their heads in the sands of quarterly measurements while ignoring the shape not just of the future but of the present.

Quite frankly, I believe that large corporations are mostly incapable of leadership, either in business or society. I am not talking here about passionate, inspired entrepreneurs who break new ground and sail uncharted seas but about the class of professional managers who, rather than innovate and lead, simply enforce the measurements in place. Fortunately, over the next few years those executives who insist on counting the branches of a particular tree will find themselves in a special part of the forest labeled Jurassic Park.

While investment in networking technologies is not a good place to skimp, Internet technologies are generally very similar and relatively low cost, if not free. Of course, nothing is really free except bad advice. The people costs are high and will get higher. For the most part, it comes down to a competition between Netscape/AOL and Microsoft for the browser and related technologies. Consult with key technology providers, hardware and software, and determine whose advice is in the best interests of the organization. What kinds of things are current technology providers saying—the same things, or are they pointing in different directions? What is the mix of self-interest and customer interest and involvement among them? Be skeptical about vendors who mask self-interest as customers' interest.

As mentioned earlier and as will be reiterated later, networking technologies and information management system technologies are the two crucial components of any IT infrastructure. Get these two right, and an IT infrastructure will adapt, grow, and deliver value required by organizations, customers and constituents, and shareholders. Get either one of them wrong and we and our staffs will be fighting a rearguard action for a very long time.

EXECUTIVE DECISION FACTORS

Two items probably will dominate any executive discussion of networking technologies and infrastructure. One is bandwidth. Bandwidth is the single overriding factor in networking infrastructures, and there never seems to be enough of it. Whatever someone proposes or projects as network bandwidth requirements, double it, even triple it. Remember, if a web commerce site is too sluggish, customers will point and click to a competitor's site. Sluggish websites can be blamed on software infrastructure components, such as underpowered information management systems or poorly designed applications, but bandwidth is almost always the larger part of the equation. There may now be a question about never being too rich or too thin, but no one can ever have too much network bandwidth.

The second executive decision factor is cost. In the 1980s movie *Moonstruck,* Vince, the father of the main character, Loretta, owns a plumbing contracting company. He sells a young urban couple on using a better grade of pipe for their bathroom renovation: "There are three

In the 1980s and into the early 1990s, the U.S. National Science Foundation funded the construction of a high-speed, broad bandwidth Internet backbone in the United States with T1 and T3 technologies. That investment, built on continually by public and corporate organizations, now serves the entire world. Many Internet service providers (ISPs) outside the United States route their Internet traffic through the U.S. Internet backbone. Much in the way FedEx routes most of its U.S. packages through its hub in Memphis, then back out to each package's destination, most ISPs route Internet traffic through the United States, then back to the Internet address, even if that Internet traffic is destined for a site within the same country but on a different Internet network. The Internet in the United States is, in accordance with Internet design principles, a ganglion of interconnected networks. Outside the United States, the Internet is more like an airline's hub and spoke system, with non-U.S. Internet traffic flowing first through the U.S. backbone before traveling on to its ultimate destination. This phenomenon can have global economic and political ramifications in the first part of the twenty-first century. Think for a moment about what happens to metropolitan areas that have a key airline hub. Dallas, Atlanta, Cincinnati, and Salt Lake City are today's "port" cities, just as Boston, New York, Baltimore, and Charleston were 200 years earlier. Now think what may happen when electronic commerce participants can get faster and better access to information by clicking on U.S. sites than they can by pointing and clicking to sites within their own (or neighboring) national borders. We have not yet even experienced what those of us who live in earthquake country call the "foreshocks" of this coming phenomena.[a]

[a] For a deeper look into the ramifications of U.S. telecom dominance of the Internet, see "Global Telecom Rout" by Kenneth Neil Cukier in *Red Herring* (February 1999).

kinds of pipe. The kind you have, which is garbage. Then there is bronze, which is fine, until something goes wrong, and something always goes wrong. Then there's copper, which is the only kind I use. It costs money, but it costs money because it saves money." He likes the story so much that during lunch he tells it with great pride to his mistress. Networking technologies, like no other IT component, are the plumbing of an IT infrastructure. Invest in that plumbing, or later it will have to be torn out and replaced again. With network technologies, it is both wise and prudent to invest in quality components and services.

From networking and bandwidth, we move on to processing power. Keep in mind that in the wide world of networked information, no computer is an island.

NOTES

1. Fritjof Capra, *The Tao of Physics: An Exploration of the Parallels Between Modern Physics and Eastern Mysticism,* 3rd ed. (Boston: Shambhala 1991), p. 328.

2. Ibid., p. 329.

3. Stephen Segaller, *Nerds 2.0.1: A Brief History of the Internet* (TV Books, 1998), p. 15.

4. *The Emerging Digital Economy* (Washington, DC: U.S. Department of Commerce, April 1998), p. 7.

5. Stan Davis and Christopher Meyer, *Blur: The Speed of Change in the Connected Economy* (Reading, MA: Addison-Wesley, 1998), see pp. 5–8.

6. Ray Kurzweil, *The Age of the Spiritual Machines: When Computers Exceed Human Intelligence* (New York: Viking, 1999), p. 2.

7. Frances Cairncross, *The Death of Distance: How the Communications Revolution Will Change Our Lives* (Boston: Harvard Business School Press, 1997), p. 89.

8. Segaller, *Nerds 2.0.1.*

9. Ibid., pp. 21–22.

10. M. Bensaou and Michael Earl, "The Right Mind-set for Managing Information Technology," *Harvard Business Review* (September–October 1998), pp. 122–123.

CHAPTER 7

Platform Technologies

And now I see with eye serene
The very pulse of the machine.
—WILLIAM WORDSWORTH, *She Was a Phantom of Delight*

PHYSICAL COMPONENTS OF THE
IT INFRASTRUCTURE

If the physical components of the IT infrastructure were reduced to their essential elements, we come down to sand and electricity. Next comes binary mathematics, 1s and 0s, which literally tells electricity either to flow or not to flow in precise and intricate patterns etched onto silicon. From 1s and 0s, we build higher-level code, compilers and programming languages, data formats—information and enabling technologies—that in turn create the applications that allow us as users to interact with new and enriched forms of information, finally allowing us to pursue new kinds of knowledge and value. All of this is a result of humankind's ability to control the behavior of electricity on increasingly intricate patterns etched on processed sand. Humans have come a long way since the first wheel, but in a fundamental sense, we are doing much the same thing, establishing new and farther-reaching points of value interchange.

If we look at our IT infrastructure as a three-legged stool, one leg would be networking technologies, another would be platform technologies, and the third would be information management systems, all supporting information itself, the seat. The rest of the IT infrastructure sits atop the stool, a variable and flexible if not completely self-organizing complex system.

In this context, platform technologies include all hardware—everything that needs either a plug or a battery in order to operate at all—as well as operating systems, which are the layers of code just above the binary commands that tell the electricity when to flow and when not to flow. Hardware may light up without an operating system, but the first thing a computer looks for when it is turned on is an operating system to tell it what to do. That is why we see a blinking set of "000" on VCRs and microwave ovens after power has been turned off and then back on again. An operating system needs a couple of vital pieces of information; it is saying "Tell me what time it is so I know what to do."

That is what happens when we "boot" (or with Windows, when we frequently "reboot") our PC. We power up the electricity, and the instant the electricity turns on the hardware components, the processor looks for an operating system, either on the internal hard disk or on diskette or CD-ROM attached to the PC. The operating system loads itself into various parts of the hardware, brings up the desktop, and we are ready to open files, go out on the Internet to retrieve and send files (like e-mail), look for information and use applications at websites, use tools to build applications such as spreadsheets, and use prepackaged applications, such as Quicken or Mortal Combat.

Exhibit 7.1 illustrates the division between client platforms and server platforms, both of which consist of hardware and operating systems. Hardware is useless without an operating system of some sort. And operating systems are useful only with hardware. We can buy one without the other, but we can use neither without using both. In our context of an IT infrastructure, we refer to them together as platform technologies. First, we look at them separately, to distinguish among various types of hardware and operating systems, and then we look at them in combination, client platforms and server platforms. Those discussions will allow us to look at two-tiered and *n*-tiered client-server architectures, the area in which most executives will encounter strategic decisions about their organization's IT infrastructure. Platform technologies must be understood before we can grasp the ways in which we might invest in them, how they can affect the rest of IT infrastructure, and how they might impact organizations. Readers with a good grasp of platform technologies, clients, and servers might want to skip ahead to the section entitled "Client-Server Architectures."

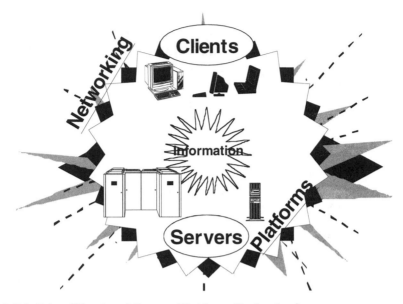

Exhibit 7.1   Client and Server Platform Technologies

CRITICAL COMMODITIES

More than any other single item, platform technologies, especially the hardware components, have become commodities. There are a multitude of reasons for commoditization of computer hardware—economies of scale, improvements and innovations in research and development, increased manufacturing capabilities and efficiencies, fierce global competition, and on and on. But hardware commoditization has had one overriding benefit: The parts are incredibly inexpensive. And hardware should follow Moore's Law for some years to come: About every 18 to 24 months the number and speed of integrated circuits on a microprocessor doubles while the cost of producing that microprocessor remains constant. This effectively triples and even quadruples the value of microprocessors. We pay the same but get three to four times more capability and performance.

Ray Kurzweil observes that this "Exponential Law of Computing" began over 100 years ago with the introduction of mechanical electrical card-based computing devices used in the 1890 census and accelerated up until Gordon Moore's observation first in 1968, later revised in 1975.[1] Kurzweil and others have drawn a comparison between the rapid advance of computing capabilities and the automobile industry, both of which started at about the same time. If the automobile industry had advanced at the same rate as the computer industry, a car today would cost less than one penny and go faster than the speed of light.

Other key factors in bringing us constantly higher performance at consistently lower prices are the high-volume manufacturing of computers, particularly PCs, which is a direct result of demand, which since 1995 or so has been spurred even further by the Internet and the fierce competition especially among manufacturers of Intel-based PCs and servers. This trend should continue for another couple of decades, until we reach the physical limitations of microprocessor manufacturing, when the circuitry is merely a few atoms thick and there is insufficient insulation between paths of electrical current. Ironically, at that point, the technology probably will get larger, although users will not notice it so much. Today's integrated circuits are built on silicon wafers, a two-dimensional process. We could easily go to three dimensions, not just stacking the circuits one on top of another but integrating them in three dimensions. With hardware, lots of things are possible.

Beyond the constantly lower prices for better-performing computer hardware, commoditization has driven additional benefits for business. More people using better computers results in more information being used to fulfill more purposes more efficiently and more quickly. To some that spells increased levels of public service at lower costs; to others that spells e-commerce; to still others that spells totally new lifestyles and occupational choices, such as a morning commute measured in steps from the bedroom to the home office rather than in hours spent in traffic. The ability to untie ourselves from the traditional, centralized office creates entirely new dimensions of economy, commerce, society, and culture. We can reestablish core family units without being isolated from either commercial or social processes. We can increase productivity simply by eliminating commuting dead time. We can raise the quality of our environment by polluting the air less and conserve natural resources by lowering our consumption of fossil fuels in internal combustion engines. Lower-cost commodity hardware makes most of that possible. The Internet makes most of the rest of that possible. New commercial and organizational models can make this a reality.

However, operating systems have not gotten cheaper. In fact, they have gotten more expensive. To be sure, we are getting a good deal more functionality, particularly in Microsoft's operating systems, than we got five or ten years ago, but we are paying more for that increased functionality. And in many instances we are paying for functionality we might not need or use, due to a practice called bundling, which is not restricted to operating systems. Almost any software provider does it. And it is not necessarily a bad practice. By designing software functionality into a package, the functions are integrated better and are likely to perform more reliably and more efficiently.

Why do software providers bundle their products? Producing good software takes a large investment in expensive human resources. One way for software providers to realize a decent return on investment (ROI) is to package the functionality in ways that justify certain pricing levels. Most of us do not need a large portion of what Microsoft's Windows desktop operating systems are capable of. Those who tinker inside Windows use that functionality. But we all pay one price, so that Microsoft can realize an acceptable ROI. It is just business, right? This gives us a hint about where we might be able to leverage software costs overall. There is wiggle room in licensing practices and pricing policies. Naturally, bargaining and bartering are more effective when we have real alternative choices. And it is up to an organization's top-level executives to establish and reinforce a management culture that continually maintains an open and flexible IT infrastructure so that choice itself remains a valid option.

The people expense will hit organizations in the form of support and services, whether internal with our own employees who support and administer our IT infrastructure or externally from vendor or third-party support. We can get the Linux operating system for free, but maintaining it requires Unix expertise. The software industry has promised to reduce the support and administration requirements of their products by embedding more and more of what systems administrators do inside the software itself, so that, for example, Microsoft Windows automatically configures itself to use new devices attached to a PC. But for the foreseeable future, the responsibilities of systems administrators and system managers will continue to grow in both complexity and criticality.

Thus, although we can characterize platform technologies as commodities, the hardware is really what is delivering lower costs to us. The operating systems are expensive to build and to maintain, and it is the systems administrator and managers who, over time, will cost us the most in this equation.

HARDWARE FUTURES

Once again we need to pay homage to the Cold War and the Space Race and the government funding that fueled research and development engines, both public and commercial, during the 1960s and 1970s and into the 1980s. The communications industry first developed the transistor, which was needed to build better telephone switches, which in turn replaced local telephone operators and then replaced the bulky, unreliable, expensive, and not easily expanded mechanical phone switches.

But once we started building packages called "capsules" to sit atop rockets that would carry them into space, we ran into another kind of space problem—the lack of physical space and the abundance of technologies that needed to fit inside. Things could be made smaller by using transistors

It is curious how many technological advances are propelled by war. Electromechanical computers were first developed in the late 1930s, when Alan Turing and his colleagues at Bletchley Park in England began cracking Nazi Germany's Enigma code. The Bletchley Park code breakers also developed in 1943 Colossus, the first electronic computer using vacuum tubes. Among other things, the Allies' ability to decipher Germany's "unbreakable" Enigma code allowed the United States and Britain to follow the movement of Nazi U-boats in the North Atlantic. This enabled the Allies to move massive amounts of war materiel and supplies from the United States to Europe and Russia during most of the war. In the Pacific, the U.S. Navy broke Japan's JN-25 naval code, which gave the United States a decided edge in the Battle of Midway and throughout the island-hopping campaign in the Pacific. In fact, a JN-25 message intercepted and deciphered by the Allies alerted them to the travel itinerary of Japan's top naval officer, Admiral Yamamoto. In April 1943 U.S. Admiral Nimitz ordered fighter aircraft to intercept and shoot down Yamamoto's plane as it approached Bougainville in the Solomon Islands. Some historians argue quite convincingly that one of the fundamental reasons the Allies were victorious in World War II was *information*, principally information derived from early computing devices which penetrated Germany's Enigma and Japan's JN-25 codes.

instead of vacuum tubes and mechanical switches, but more refinement and sophistication was required. People created integrated circuits, the immediate progeny of transistors, and once the microprocessor was developed, we got really good at making all sorts of hardware smaller and more powerful, delivering ever more bang for the buck. And people are still getting better at that. Not only does Gordon Moore's Law still pertain after almost 35 years, it shows no immediate sign of moderating in the future. Kurzweil thinks Moore's Law will be eclipsed by a new paradigm around 2020, but now we have little indication what that new processing paradigm might be.

It was mentioned earlier that there was the probability of creating microprocessors containing three-dimensional integrated circuits. Also just around the corner is a technology for manufacturing microprocessors called extreme ultraviolet lithography (EUL). The process has been proven in theory and demonstrated in the lab, and now there exists a consortium of microprocessor manufacturers, sponsored and coordinated by the U.S. Department of Commerce. Its task is to turn theory and lab demonstrations into manufacturing reality. When successful, EUL capabilities should shrink integrated circuits and microprocessor technologies by a factor of 5 or 10 initially and eventually by factors of 20 to 25 or even more. What that means is that the functionality of a late-1990s Notebook PC will fit into a device about the size of a digital wristwatch. Wristcomputers might be quite the rage as holiday gifts for the person who has everything around, say, Christmas 2003. Within a year or so after that, wristcomputers should probably be mass-market commodities.

Hardware will not only keep getting smaller, faster, better, and cheaper, it will also gain functionality. And that speaks directly to the proliferation of 64-bit microprocessors. Today most computers, especially PCs and Intel-based servers, use 32-bit computers. That means there are 32 bits of information within every byte (a single character or numeral) of data. Sixty-four–bit processors contain 64 pieces of information in every byte, but that does not merely double the content of a byte. It raises exponentially the amounts of information a processor can manipulate. Today's 32-bit computers can manipulate information which on paper would fill filing cabinets around the equator of the earth. Tomorrow's 64-bit computers will be able to manipulate information which on paper would fill filing cabinets from the earth to the moon.

But what does that mean for business and an organization's IT infrastructure? For one thing, it means real voice recognition and voice response. The process has been worked on for 20 years, and what is currently available is pretty impressive. At least we_____ are past _____ having _____ to _____ talk _____ like _____ this. With 64-bit technology, we will be able not only to talk normally to our EUL wristcomputer, but its vocabulary will be three or four times that of an average Ph.D.'s, and it will respond verbally, probably in any voice we select. Pointing and clicking on windows and icons will be things of the past sometime around 2005.

What may impact IT infrastructures even more is a shift from technological determinism—that is, technologists telling us how to access the IT infrastructure—to user determinism, or each person telling IT infrastructure caretakers how he or she wants to access the information and applications. Peter Keen tells about one chief information officer (CIO) who hates laptops, because they put his infrastructure at risk.[2] But, as Keen goes on to say, people like to talk. When the technology is available for true conversation interaction with applications, people will demand it. And when top-level executives assume greater control of their IT infrastructures, fewer CIOs will think of the infrastructure as their exclusive possession. That shift will occur in organizations when business executives become more comfortable with and in control of IT issues, when they shrink the gap between them and their organization's IS executives.

Even more important, 64-bits provides the kind of information compacting and content capabilities needed to deliver true, real-time, instantaneous spoken language translation. By around 2005 it will be normal for a person to be on the phone in, say, Chicago, speaking English and holding a long-distance conversation with someone in Beijing who is speaking in Mandarin Chinese, or someone in Atlanta speaking another kind of English with someone in Paris speaking Parisian French. And those long-distance conversations will travel over IP connections (remember the Internet protocol TCP/IP?). As mentioned, 98 percent of telephony traffic in just a few years will be data traffic. This sort of instantaneous voice translation traffic will be data, not voice, in the same way that music from a CD ROM is digital, not analog, as it was with tape or vinyl.

Finally, dozens of other hardware technologies are being worked on. Remember that EUL wristcomputer? How will they ever make hard disks that small? Well, the wristcomputer probably will not have a hard disk. More than likely it will use some sort of browser technology to connect to servers, where we users will store most of our occasional information and applications. But then, ten years ago, no one would have believed that people would be carrying 5 or 6 gigabyte hard drives inside four pound Notebook PCs. Which brings us to the last real hardware frontier, batteries. How are we going to power that wristwatch computer?

Battery technology could well be one of the first benefits of the International Space Station. The world probably does not need another version of Tang, but better battery technology is something everyone can benefit from.

OPERATING SYSTEMS WARS

The area of operating systems is fairly cut and dried. There is Microsoft, and there is everything else. So let us start with Microsoft. Microsoft's first operating system, DOS, was an accident that did not wait to happen. In 1980 IBM was looking for an operating system for its first personal computer. The hobbyist computers prevailing at the time mostly all used 8-bit processors, and the operating system they used was CP/M (Control Program/Monitor) from Digital Research. But for some unknown reason, the briefing book given to the IBM team responsible for buying an operating system for the first IBM PC said that CP/M came from Microsoft. So IBM called the small Seattle company that specialized in writing Basic compilers. (Compilers take code written in high-level languages, such as Basic or COBOL, and translate it into assembler language, a more arcane level of code that then takes in machine [binary] language to the hardware. This is discussed in depth in Chapter 10.)

In what Robert X. Cringley calls "probably his last gracious gesture toward a competitor, Bill Gates told the caller from IBM that a mistake had been made and gave them [Gary] Kildrall's number in Pacific Grove" near Monterey.[3] IBM followed through, made an appointment with Kildrall, and trekked out to California. But Kildrall was a no-show for the appointment, and other Digital Research people did not know what Kildrall wanted to do, and they certainly did not want to sign IBM's nondisclosure agreement (this meeting never took place, we were never here, etc., etc.) without Kildrall there. The IBM guys closed their briefcases and left for Seattle, where they had an appointment to discuss a Basic language compiler for the new IBM PC with a 50-person company called Microsoft.

When IBM asked Microsoft to sign their strict nondisclosure agreement, Gates and Paul Allen did so without hesitation and without legal consultation. Gates also convinced IBM that it would better to use a

16-bit processor than the 8-bit processor IBM had in mind, and that Microsoft could help with the operating system as well as with the language compilers. What IBM did not know was that Gary Kildrall's Digital Research had already developed a 16-bit operating system, CP/M-86, for the Intel 8086 and 8088 processors. Microsoft knew that because, as the leading supplier of Basic, COBOL, and FORTRAN compilers for CP/M and a leading reseller of CP/M, Microsoft was developing compilers for CP/M-86 before Digital released it.

Gates also knew that another small Seattle company, Seattle Computer Products, was writing a 16-bit clone of the 8-bit CP/M operating system called QDOS (Quick and Dirty Operating System). QDOS was almost a line-for-line clone of CP/M, altered for 16-bit Intel processors. Bill Gates bought the rights to QDOS for $50,000, a large investment for the then small company but one that was to pay off handsomely in the long run. QDOS became PC-DOS, which did not change much over the next 15 years; it still is the core of Microsoft's 32-bit desktop operating systems, Windows95 and Windows98. Only with Windows 2000, the renamed Windows NT, will Microsoft begin moving truly beyond the old 16-bit QDOS. Windows 2000 is a genuine 32-bit operating system built from the ground up, with versions for personal and professional desktops, departmental servers, and enterprise servers.

All of which brings us to Windows 2000, the next new operating system from Microsoft. Originally Microsoft and IBM teamed up to develop OS/2, the next generation of PC and LAN server operating systems. But Microsoft had an alternative. Digital Equipment Corporation had earlier set up a research and development project aimed at developing a 32-bit client-server operating system to supersede its proprietary VAX/VMS operating system. When top Digital managers saw a demonstration of the new operating system, they realized that it probably would break the business model Digital had built around its proprietary systems. Digital canceled the operating system project, and the project manager, Dave Cutler, took his work and his project team and pitched it to Microsoft. Microsoft saw an opportunity to build a client and server operating system without IBM's technology or business constraints, and it began focusing resources on Windows NT (the new name for the former Digital R&D project) while dragging their feet on OS/2.

But giving birth to a new operating system is not easy. When the first commercially viable version of Windows NT Server arrived in 1974, it barely held together and was neither reliable nor robust enough for most businesses to deploy. But NT had great marketing promise. Originally it was aimed at Novell's Netware markets. Estimates of more than 80 percent of enterprise networks still use Netware, so Microsoft was going after a large market. But the first several NT releases lacked enterprise-level directory services, a vital feature of enterprise networking and one that Netware Named Directory Services performed very well. NT's lack of key networking features forced Microsoft into marketing it as a departmental and line-of-business client-server application platform.

The gods of fortune once again smiled on Mr. Gates and company. Serendipitously, Intel processors capable of handling fairly robust business applications were evolving according to Moore's Law, better, faster, cheaper. Compaq, Dell, and other PC makers began building application servers that ran the NT Server operating system, at first NT 3.5, then NT 4.0, and NT 4.5, which were the only true customer-usable releases. Microsoft initiated a broad frontal assault to usurp the domain of Unix-based systems and mainframes throughout the enterprise. Intel, Compaq, Dell, and others were, of course, delighted. But Microsoft's server operating system still lacked the networking capabilities that its original target markets demanded, so customers tended to stay with Novell and Netware. Moreover, NT lacked the scaleability, reliability, and overall robustness of Unix. Meanwhile, Intel's processor technologies kept advancing, while Microsoft's operating system technology kept lagging farther and farther behind hardware advancements of all kinds.

But by now there was too much industry and customer commitment to turn away from Microsoft and NT and seek other alternatives—or was there? Everyone seemed completely mesmerized by Bill Gates's Pied Piper routine and blithely followed him down the road, except for a few miscreants, including Sun Microsystem's Scott McNealy and Oracle's Larry Ellison.

Now Windows 2000 is poised to enter at the dawn of the new millennium. The big question on everyone's mind is: "Will it work?" The big answer is, not likely, at least not for several years to come. Remember how long it took Microsoft to finally develop a workable clone of the Macintosh operating system and graphical user interface? Windows 95 arrived ten years after Macintosh; three years later, a revised (bug-fix) Windows 98 arrived. And that's just a PC operating system. Windows 2000 has PC versions, which should work well, and server versions, which probably will cause headaches and nightmares, depending on how deeply a user depends on them, for at least four or five years. Why? For one thing, it is a complex operating system.

Microsoft wants Windows 2000 Server to be all things to all people and to come in one package. The base code for Windows 2000 Server is approaching 40 million lines. Put into perspective, that is almost twice the size of mainframe operating systems and as much as three times the size of very powerful Unix operating systems. And every line of code represents a potential glitch, a potential bug. The more lines of code, the more potential hazards. Unix and mainframe operating systems have been used for decades, giving developers time to uncover and fix bugs and to build in added efficiencies and functionality. One IS manager, who oversees all three types of operating systems, said his mainframe is taken down once every year for maintenance; his Unix system goes down only when he takes it down for maintenance; his Windows NT servers need to be rebooted several times a day. One Fortune 50 company that has a limited business application running on Windows NT servers intentionally brings all of their Windows NT servers down every morning at 2:00 A.M. and reboots them to reduce the need for rebooting during the business day.

The real costs of these systems are in people-intensive efforts, not in the acquisition price. I will not be surprised to watch the dollars corporations everywhere had expected to save with Windows 2000 platforms be eaten up quickly by expensive support and service overhead during the first several years of server deployments.

An organization struggling with a crippled and limited IT infrastructure suffers less tangible hidden costs while it waits for emerging technologies to mature. Even a partially crippled IT infrastructure could have dire long-term consequences on an organization's capability to complete and fulfil its mission. And that does not include the soft dollars that disappear when highly skilled and costly knowledge workers are idled or rendered ineffective due to the frailties of a weak IT infrastructure. Smaller and medium-size businesses are at greater risk since their eggs tend to be collected into fewer baskets, but large organizations are exposed as well.

The alternatives to Windows 2000 are mostly all Unix operating systems. Unfortunately, the nagging compulsion of technology providers to devise proprietary and differentiated products has resulted in a fragmented Unix industry, where every version is just different enough to not work seamlessly and transparently with other versions, even if they conform to a purported standard. The leading Unix variants come from Sun Microsystems (Solaris), IBM (AIX), Hewlett-Packard (HPUX), Santa Cruz Operations (SCO Unix), Data General (DGUX), and

Compaq/Digital (Open VMS). And then there's Linux, which holds the best promise of driving the unification of the Unix variants.

Linux is an open Unix variant, which means anyone can download it for free from websites. Everyone who works with Linux agrees to post on the Linux websites any new development or additions they might make to the operating system. Most development and project managers might consider this uncontrolled chaos, but what is developing is something like a complex self-organizing system. The base Linux code was written by Linus Torvalds in Finland during the early 1990s. It works well on a wide range of processors, small and large. It is more robust and reliable then any Windows operating system released so far. Linux has an estimated 6 million users, making it the third most widely used operating system behind Windows and Macintosh.

And that frightens Microsoft more than any other challenge, even more than the U.S. federal antitrust action. An internal Microsoft memo from October 1998, known as the "Halloween Memo," demonstrates both Microsoft's concern about Linux usurping its enterprise markets and how the software giant's internal development processes are weakening the firm's ability to develop new technologies within acceptable time frames. However, Linux does not have much marketing muscle at all; Microsoft has more marketing muscle than Coke, Pepsi, McDonald's, and Michael Jordan combined. Linux has no real sales force behind it; Microsoft has multiple layers of distribution channels, each with multiple sales capabilities. As yet Linux has only nascent support, Red Hat Software and Caldera being most prominent. So what has got Microsoft so spooked? Remember those estimated 6 million Linux users? They are almost all Unix techies, and most are computer science students who will be coming into the worldwide IS labor pool in the very near future. Six million potential developers and managers for Unix-based systems, who openly denigrate Windows for its frailties and unreliability, portend a different future for platform technologies, and that future is not Microsoft's.

Intel now supports Linux as an advanced server operating system. All of the major IMS vendors—Oracle, IBM, Informix, Sybase—offer Linux versions of their core database products and offer support for these products. Remember the three-legged stool? For platform technologies we have Intel and Linux; for networking we have the Internet, which does not discriminate; and for IMS we have, well, everyone except Microsoft SQL Server, which runs exclusively on Windows NT/2000. So with Linux, we have everything required by our IT infrastructure, and it is all open, portable, scaleable, and reliable. On top of that, we have a growing and synergistic community of technical innovators and support specialists, those 6 million and growing Linux users and they are not confined to MIT or Silicon Valley or Redmond, Washington. They are in every computer science department in every college and university around the planet.

If the commercial release of Windows 2000 Server operating system slips any more than it already has (it is currently three years behind its original release dates) and if Windows 2000 Server editions do not live up to their advanced billing, Microsoft may find itself up a proverbial river with a broken paddle. Intel is fearful of just that scenario, which is why Linux looms so significantly in its thoughts. Intel continues to follow Moore's Law and cranks out better and bigger and cheaper processing power. Microsoft just got to 32 bits in 1995, when Intel was clustering its advanced 32-bit processors to enter the enterprise computing space. Now Intel is readying its 64-bit processors, while Microsoft is still promising the Windows 2000 Data Server that will support the clusters of symmetric multiple processors (SMP) that Unix has supported for over ten years.

All major IMSs support 32-bit SMP clusters, and most of the rest of the system hardware and software industries are gearing up for commodity 64-bit processors from Intel. Digital first released its 64-bit Alpha processors in the early 1990s. Oracle quickly adopted its IMS products to support 64-bit information environments. Sun Microsystems brought out 64-bit technologies, both hardware and operating systems, shortly thereafter. Again, Oracle provided the IMS. Almost all of the rest of the high-tech industry followed, except Microsoft, which claims Windows 2000 servers will run on 64-bit Intel processors. And it will, but since Windows 2000 is fundamentally a 32-bit environment, it will look at 64 bits as two 32-bit instructions rather than as one 64-bit instruction. Comparing software to automobiles again, what Microsoft is doing is a bit like going from a four-cylinder automobile engine to an eight-cylinder engine, but instead of using all eight cylinders to power the crankshaft, first four cylinders are used, then the other four, back and forth. Windows 2000 will not run in full 64-bit mode for some time.

So Intel needs to look elsewhere to find ways of delivering 64-bit capabilities to its customers and to what it hopes will be new and expanded markets. It needs a robust, reliable operating system that can exploit 64-bit processing, that has a global community of developers and support specialists, and that can exploit the Internet and World Wide Web. Linux fills the bill, and it is free! It is no wonder that the infamous

"Halloween Memo" showed us, for the first time clearly, the soft under-belly of the world's largest software company and, arguably, one of the world's most powerful business organizations.

Thus, even though we may think of platform technologies as commodities, decisions about them and the roles they might play in IT infrastructure strategies are not *no-brainers*. Only one thing is clear. Multiple types of hardware and operating systems will continue. Windows 2000 will need to coexist and interconnect with Unix and other open systems platforms. Microsoft realizes this, and although not many inside the technology industry are naïve enough to forget about Trojan horse business tactics, most observers believe Microsoft is sincere about integrating with open systems rather than simply obliterating Unix. That is wise on Microsoft's part. If the specter of a Linux-Intel platform combination was not enough to put Microsoft on the ropes, that in combination with the U.S. Department of Justice's antitrust actions have backed it into an uncomfortable corner. Now comes Steve Jobs and Apple with a wildly popular iMac desktop. As Tom Peters says, "It's not a question of whether you are paranoid or not. It's whether you are paranoid enough."

For the most part, I have been talking about platform technologies in terms of servers because that is where the operating systems wars are taking place, and that is where most executives are looking to find a new round of cost savings in their IT infrastructure, specifically from Intel-based servers running Microsoft operating systems. I hope I have communicated not only where savings are likely to come from (the hardware itself) but also where savings are *not* likely to come from. Even if an operating system is totally free and open, like Linux, it must be supported and maintained by educated, skilled, and expensive professionals. And although software providers keep building in more functionality that lightens the load on system managers and administrators, the rapidly accelerating complexity of IT infrastructures and of the market demands will only increase the need for highly competent system managers and administrators well into the foreseeable future. Be very skeptical of anyone who says differently.

VARIEGATED CLIENTS

Client platform technologies may seem a bit more straightforward than server platform technologies. For one thing, Microsoft currently owns the lion's share of desktop and mobile (notebook) clients, and it is doing fairly well in the still-emerging palm client arena with its Windows CE products. Apple maintains a fiercely loyal customer base, one that seems to be expanding rather than retreating, especially among college students and discontented former Windows users. But Microsoft would need to misstep very, very badly to lose its stranglehold on the business desktop in the very near future.

But there are other types of clients as well as a relatively new category of clients called "network appliances." Earlier I mentioned the EUL wristcomputer, NCR's Internet-ready microwave oven, and the capabilities of Web TV. The Net Computers, TV and cable set-top boxes, screen phones that deliver email and Internet access, new generations of cellular phones and pagers, smart cards, smart cars, and smart keys are not futuristic fantasies. They are all here today, and they will become more and more pervasive as each day passes. The important point to keep in mind is that, with the advances of technology already in the works, do not assume that Microsoft desktops will be the only client organizations will ever need. Today's clients could easily become tomorrow's eight-track cassette players.

What top-level executives need to keep most in mind is flexibility. The IT infrastructure must be flexible and adaptable to technologies that have yet to be invented but that, when introduced, could well change the competitive dynamics of businesses and the abilities of public service organizations. Thus an IT infrastructure must be designed with a built-in open systems strategy. In the days when proprietary and vertically integrated systems were the rule, many organizations were tied too completely to their proprietary technologies. The past is littered with the corpses of businesses that remained tied to closed legacy systems while their competitors sped by them by rapidly adopting new technologies.

Clients can be categorized by two characteristics. One is the type of user interface they provide: character based or graphical. Character-based clients, like a "dumb" terminal, provide limited user interface capabilities through a keyboard. Graphical user interfaces, such as Windows and Macintosh, provide extended capabilities through a point-and-click mouse as well as a keyboard, and offer enhanced information display through dynamic and animated graphical displays. Although people will continue to view information through future client technologies (vision is one of humankind's primary information-gathering capabilities), voice commands directed at clients which interact with information and applications on servers will become more prevalent. Business applications will become voice responsive as well as graphically responsive. Although a number of business application and enabling technology providers offer limited speech recognition before 2000, the real integration of voice responsiveness will most likely follow the evolution of 64-bit software during the first decade of the twenty-first century.

The second characteristic of client technologies is the amount of intelligence contained in client devices. At the high end are Unix workstations and PCs, both of which are powerful stand-alone computer systems, with processor power, memory, and storage. At the opposite end are "dumb" terminals, which have only enough intelligence to recognize electricity when it is turned on and feed information from a connection onto a screen in alpha-numeric characters. In between is a range of client technologies that will get broader as we move into the twenty-first century. The most important of these are web browser clients, which have intelligence enough to support the activities of a browser but little or no storage. In the late 1990s, these were known as Net Computers (NCs) and were offered as replacements for more expensive and less easily managed PCs. In fact, using a PC to access the Internet and work with websites and their applications employs only a small part of the PC's capabilities: the screen (output display), the keyboard and mouse (input), some memory and intelligence, and the modem connection to the Internet. A Net Computer can be considered a slice of a PC intended strictly for Internet and web use. Web TV is the same thing, except that the regular TV, rather than a separate monitor, functions as the output display device. And most of the Internet and web appliances to come are variations on that same idea.

Guess who loses when it comes to intelligent clients that are not PCs? Mostly Microsoft. These devices have much simpler operating systems burned into their electronics. There is no need for a Windows client operating system like Windows 98 or Windows 2000. PC hardware manufacturers also saw the onslaught of Net Computers as a potential loss—not as much hardware, not as much profits, right? So in the best traditions of prudent capitalistic thinking, what did PC manufacturers do? They drove down the prices of their fully intelligent PCs even further, first to under $1,000, then even lower. If a NC would cost $500, and a low-end, fully configured PC could sell for just a couple of hundred dollars more, customers would buy the new low-cost PCs. Of course, that makes Microsoft happy, because the Windows PC operating system costs the same, regardless of the hardware cost. PC manufacturers would need to find manufacturer and distribution efficiencies to maintain margins, but Microsoft could continue shipping the same licenses at the same price levels.

CLIENT-SERVER ARCHITECTURES

The low-cost PC is only a temporary measure fostered by PC manufacturers and Microsoft to extend the life of "fat" clients (software programs that run on end users' computers that compute business logic to execute on a server. Typically fat clients require installation on end users' computers as opposed to being automatically downloaded, such as a web page.). Another measure is the fundamental two-tier client-server architecture of the Windows 2000 operating systems. This architecture consists of a fully configured PC client, with the complete capabilities of a Windows 2000 client operating system, plus a LAN that connects the fat clients to a server. As illustrated in Exhibit 7.2, the server provides the information (the databases) and part of the business logic (the application), while the client provides the user interface (presentation logic) and also part of the business logic.

The idea is that users work mainly by themselves on a client PC, creating documents, devising spreadsheets, working with an application on their desktops. Sometimes they need to send information to or retrieve information from a server, and perhaps less frequently they need to interact with an application that is wholly resident on the server. The server is a repository of shared resources, principally shared databases. The client is the versatile platform for applications, enabling tools, communications, information manipulation, and everything else. This paradigm emerged in

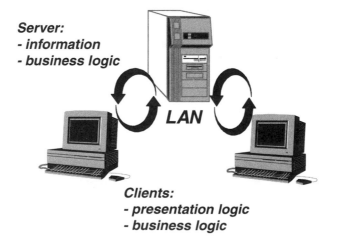

Server:
- *information*
- *business logic*

LAN

Clients:
- *presentation logic*
- *business logic*

Exhibit 7.2   Two-Tiered Client-Server Architecture

the mid to late 1980s before the Internet became commercially accessible, therefore before Internet connectivity principles and options were widely understood by IS professionals. As mentioned earlier, many technologists now believe that if networking specialists and IS specialists had communicated better in the 1980s, two-tiered client-server architectures would never have emerged; *n*-tiered architectures instead would have been the way to go (see Exhibit 7.3).

With *n*-tiered architectures, clients come in a variety of shapes and sizes (variegated clients). All they need is some intelligence, a connection to the Internet, and a web browser. For those who labor at spreadsheets or computer-aided design, PC and heavy-duty "fat" clients are also part of the *n*-tiered client mix. Fundamentally, *n*-tiered servers provide both applications (business logic) and information and are not locally restricted to a certain set of clients. In other words, users can access several application servers and several database servers on an intranet or extranet and not be concerned in the least where those servers are physically located.

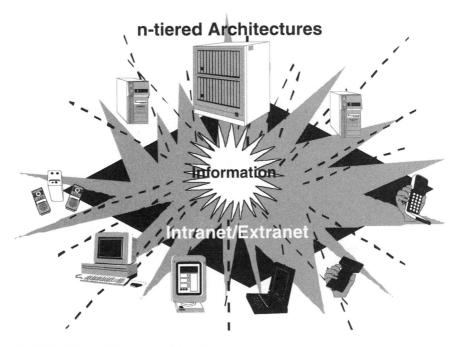

Exhibit 7.3 n-Tiered Architectures

So why should top-level executives care about the difference between two-tier and *n*-tiered architectures? It has everything to do with costs and capabilities of IT infrastructures. Variegated clients, Internet appliances, and NCs are not only specialized according to tasks but invariably are less costly to deploy (since they are simpler by design to operate) and to maintain (since they do not require constant operating system administration and upgrades).

More important, since business logic and information are housed on powerful servers, applications and databases can be maintained and administered by fewer competent IS professionals in more concentrated central locations. Estimates are that it takes roughly two to four IS professionals to manage and maintain the elements in a two-tiered client-server environment compared to one IS professional in an *n*-tiered architecture. A lot of that has to do with the reduction in time spent administering software on individual clients. "Fat" client advocates argue that they offer centralized administration of software, so that each PC does not need to be individually administered and that fewer administrators are needed, just like *n*-tiered architectures. It sounds good in theory, but it does not work well in practice. Every individual's desktop is different. Every individual's preferences have been set into his or her desktop operating systems somewhat differently. And many individuals have different devices attached to their PCs. Centralized administration of PCs rarely works to reduce the number of administrators and managers required to maintain a population of PC clients, regardless of whether each client costs $5,000 or $500 to purchase. The ongoing cost of administering and upgrading the PC operating systems cranks up the costs.

Another hidden cost is the cost of two-tier applications themselves, especially enterprise applications like ERP. In order to take advantage of the client-server architecture, an application's business logic is divided between the client and a server. User logic, that is, tasks and information processing required to solve a problem for a specific user, is executed on the client. Shared logic, that is, tasks and information processing required across multiple users to keep an organization fulfilling its mission, is executed on the server. This makes sense until the time comes to upgrade the application software to a new release. Usually there is little problem upgrading the server side of the application, but problems and sharply higher costs arise when upgrading clients. Again, unless the "fat" client desktops have been very tightly controlled by IS, all desktops are different, and every attempt to upgrade that desktop's application logic may require costly individual attention from an IS specialist, the same as when upgrading the "fat" client's operating system.

Potentially worse is the fact that two-client server architectures are generally rigid, allowing for very little flexibility in the face of changing organizational demands or in the adoption of new technologies. If a two-tiered application architecture is in place, and something impacts business practices and models (such as a merger or deregulation or increased regulation or even global economic conditions), the business logic on the servers and all of the clients would have to be adjusted, since the business logic is divided among servers and clients. With n-tiered architectures, only the logic on the application servers must be adjusted. Obviously, an organization using n-tiered architectures can adjust its business logic faster and at lower cost than can an organization using two-tiered client-server architectures. Lower costs, greater flexibility—that is what n-tiered architectures are about.

But what about the platform technologies supporting these architectures? Aren't they different? Yes, but only in one regard. Windows 2000 is designed from the ground up to be a client-server operating system for two-tiered architectures. That makes sense for Microsoft, which is mainly in the business of selling operating systems licenses. Companies in that business want to sell an operating system on every desktop and want to sell an upgrade to that operating system every 18 to 36 months. They also want to sell operating systems for every server. By selling server operating systems that tightly integrate with desktop operating systems, they will sell more and more desktop operating systems. For every server operating system sold, 10 to 20 desktop operating systems (and the upgrades) will be sold. In fact, companies could give away the server operating system just to sell the desktop operating systems. But that would not be fair. A company may decide just to charge a whole lot less than the competition for its loss-leader server operating system. That way maybe the antitrust investigators will not notice.

But what about the hardware platforms? Aren't two-tiered servers lower cost than n-tiered servers? Not at all. The same Intel-based servers found in Windows two-tiered architectures work just as well in n-tiered environments. The Windows 2000 Server operating systems do not work as well as do the Unix operating systems simply because the Windows servers look for "fat" Windows clients. Unix servers look for all types of clients, and in intranet/extranet environments, all types of clients—fat, thin, or in between—that have a browser can access server resources.

What makes *n*-tier servers appear more expensive is that they can support very large Unix servers and even mainframes (the kinds of servers which Windows 2000 cannot support very well, if at all), the smallest Intel-based servers, and the largest Intel clusters and 64-bit configurations. In short, *n*-tiered environments offer a lot of choice and flexibility. Some choices can lead to higher per-unit acquisition costs, in which case users need to decide whether the cost savings of reduced IS administration in consolidated large servers outweighs the lower initial acquisition costs of a number of smaller Intel-based servers. Unix-driven and Internet-based *n*-tiered architectures offer choice and flexibility.

Two-tiered client-server architecture aids technology vendors who provide client-server components, not organizations needing cost-efficient and flexible IT infrastructures. The *n*-tiered architectures, emerging as they do from the open networked information concepts of the Internet and World Wide Web, offer greater flexibility and better cost efficiencies. Two-tiered client-server application architectures should die a natural death, but top-level executives must understand to what extent their IT infrastructures incorporate two-tier architectures, then make it clear to all managers that, regardless of perceived immediate value, the organizational standard is *n*-tiered architectures. Anyone proposing two-tiered should be prepared to defend its rigidity and costs with his or her career.

KEY TECHNOLOGY PROVIDERS

Through the first half of the first decade of the twenty-first century, in most larger organizations Unix and Windows 2000 will coexist with legacy systems (mainframes and minicomputers). Small and some medium-size organizations may be able to swap out entire platform technologies for Intel-based hardware and Windows 2000 operating systems, depending on the flexibility and scaleability required by their business models and organizational needs. In larger organizations, and the divisions and departments composing them, several operating systems (usually Windows and Unix) and several hardware technologies will have to coexist. The demands for flexibility and scaleability will increase rather than lessen in coming years.

The good news is that almost all providers of platform technologies recognize and accept this fact of coexistence. The largest providers of Unix systems, Sun Microsystems, Hewlett-Packard, and IBM, have extensive coexistence capabilities both available and in development. The same is true for Compaq and its Digital platforms as well as Intel and its server support of Unix, especially Linux. Even Microsoft understands and has committed to coexistence with Unix in particular as well as mainframe platform technology.

Intel will continue to push the envelope of Moore's Law, and more powerful and lower-cost hardware can be expected well into the twenty-first century. Microsoft faces its biggest challenge ever—getting Windows 2000 Server operating systems functional, stable, and scaleable by 2001. Too many large organizations have bet part of their farms on NT, now Windows 2000. If it does not deliver, Microsoft's ambitions for the enterprise markets may be squashed. Microsoft's future rests on events that will occur between 2000 and 2002.

EXECUTIVE DECISION FACTORS

Two decision factors loom large among platform technologies: flexibility and cost. Flexibility really speaks to the architectural choices made. It is important chiefly because it enables users to adapt IT infrastructure and its capabilities to changes in business, economic, and social climates, as well as allowing users to take advantage of emerging new technologies.

The second EDF is cost. The largest cost efficiencies in IT infrastructures are likely to be found among platform technologies, especially among hardware technologies. But costs related to platform technologies are not just acquisition costs. Beyond the cost of initial acquisition is the total cost of ownership, which is heavily burdened with very expensive costs of competent professionals who implement, manage, and maintain the various parts of the IT infrastructure.

Finally, there is the cost of missteps. To paraphrase John Ruskin, if low purchase price is the chief buying criterion, built in should be a budget for adding to it when what was purchased does not meet expectations. When that cost is added in, normally users find that they would be better off spending the bit extra up front and buying something that would meet expectations. Be judicious but skeptical about costs when platform technologies deals seem too good to be true.

Networking technologies provide connectivity and bandwidth. Platform technologies provide processing power as well as storage, input, and output. The next chapter examines information itself and the information management systems that codify, manipulate, and manage it.

NOTES

1. The Age of the Spiritual Machine, pp. 20–30.
2. *Computerworld,* January 11, 1999, p. 49.
3. For the best version of the complete story, see Cringley's *Accidental Empires: How the Boys of Silicon Valley Make Their Million, Battle Foreign Competition, and Still Can't Get a Date* (New York: HarperBusiness 1993), especially Chapter 7, "All the IBM Stories Are True."

CHAPTER 8

Software Infrastructure Overview

Any sufficiently advanced technology is
indistinguishable from magic.
—Arthur C. Clark, *The Lost Worlds of 2001* (1972)

DATA, INFORMATION, AND KNOWLEDGE

As Exhibit 8.1 illustrates, information remains at the very core of the IT infrastructure model, and information is the fundamental feature of the software infrastructure itself. Conceivably, networks and platform technologies could exist that deal exclusively with electrical impulses that have nothing to do with information as it is thought of. But in business systems, in the types of IT infrastructures discussed here, the software infrastructure has no raison d'etre without information.

However, the term "information" usually is used rather loosely. It is rarely differentiated from data or from knowledge. There has been a great deal of focus on the interrelations among data, information, and knowledge in business since the early 1990s. In a larger sense, much of humankind's preoccupation and many of our endeavors have centered around information and knowledge ever since we first began understanding where to find food and shelter in different seasons of the year. It is best to lay out some concepts and ground rules about information itself before we go further.

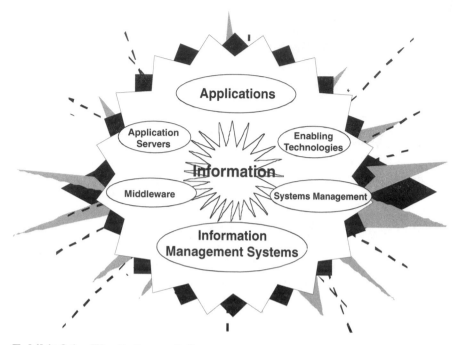

Exhibit 8.1   The Software Infrastructure

A simple analogy has been floating around high-tech circles for some years. Take, for example, the outside temperature, expressed in Fahrenheit or Celsius. Let us say it is 92°F outside. That is a data point. It has no meaning in and of itself. We do not even know where *outside* is, except that it is probably in the United States since the temperature is expressed in Fahrenheit, not Celsius. So data in and of themselves are just that, data.

Data in context becomes information. "Ninety-eight degrees F is warm this time of year for San Francisco" puts the data into the context of location and time of year and renders a comparative evaluation. People only began putting data into context and rendering some meaning from the context and the data with computers in the late 1970s. Prior to that, human observation was required to make the connections between contexts and data and to render useful information and meaning. Relational databases began allowing us to query data in ways that would generate useful information independent of human oversight and intervention. Somewhat crude at first, the query-and-response capabilities of relational database systems (RDBMSs) and their SQL query tools accelerated rapidly during the 1980s and into the 1990s.

Now that we have information of the temperature, we can take it a step further to knowledge. In its simplest form, knowledge is what we do with information. One pioneer of modern knowledge management theory, Karl Erik Sveiby, following the leads of earlier twentieth century philosophers such as Ludwig Wittgenstein and Michael Polanyi, calls knowledge *"a capacity to act."*[1] In our analogy, we might say, "It's 92°F outside [data point], which is warm for San Francisco this time of year [information context], so we should go to the beach rather than snowboarding at Lake Tahoe." We go from data, to information, to knowledge, from information, to knowledge, to decision, to action.

Obviously, there is a lot more to epistemology than simple analogies suggest. Peter Drucker coined the term "knowledge management" and for decades has shown us how knowledge and information are the real bases of commercial value. In the end, as Drucker tell us, what we sell, one way or another, is ultimately some kind of knowledge, or *"know-*how." Unfortunately, in the rush to make new fortunes, hardware and software providers jumped on a self-perpetuating knowledge-management bandwagon, resulting chiefly in devaluing the concepts of knowledge as they relate to modern business. One way to tell that a trend has gotten out of hand is by the number of conferences and trade shows that it generates seemingly overnight. Using the measurement of the number of trade shows and conferences popping up about it, knowledge management seems a bit overrated. The quick-buck artists generally fade away after the first blush of interest in a hot new field. Knowledge management and its co-conspirator, intellectual capital, are not dead, nor are they overnight wonders. Both will evolve and mature and will impact business and public service organizations much more than is generally thought in the late 1990s. And, yes, networked information is at their heart.

As serious students of knowledge and information always emphasize, information and the knowledge workers who use it as their raw material are the core assets of almost any business today. We live and work in a global information and knowledge-based economy. A larger problem for business is that we do not know how to measure the asset value of information or knowledge except by selling them, packaged in books or in software, or sold as processes and services, as law firms and consultants do. These examples do not measure the asset value of information and knowledge themselves but rather track their residual effects. Ultimately, *know-how* coupled with information produces just about every commercial value that exists. But because both know-how and information are more tacit than explicit, more intangible rather than tangible, they are more difficult to quantify as assets and list on a balance sheet.

The fault lies not with information and knowledge but with the limitations of accounting systems. Business accounting fundamentals go back to the fifteenth century and have not really changed much since then, although they have gotten a lot more complex and complicated. Since Luca Pacioli invented double-entry bookkeeping in 1494, the printing press, the Protestant Reformation, the rise of Newtonian science, the Age of Reason, the American, French, Russian, and Chinese revolutions, the Industrial Age, two world wars, a cold war, and now the information-based economy and the Internet age have occurred, yet people are still trying to track it all with a limited two-dimensional quantitative balance sheet.

At the risk of being overly simplistic, the first two things we want to keep in mind about information and knowledge is that (1) they are largely unaccounted for by traditional business measures, and (2) information and knowledge provide the foundation for the creation of value and wealth in every sector of every economy. Intangible assets are at the core of business and organizational pursuits but are difficult if not impossible to quantify. Now comes the manager's lament: "How can I manage what I cannot measure?"

Chapter 2 discussed how top-level executives' responsibilities are expanding to include the governance of information and the information technologies that support both information and knowledge workers. Here we need to peer more deeply into the nature of information itself, particularly as it figures in the management and measurement schemes of modern business and public sector organizations.

No data have any value until they are put into action and achieve some intended result, through a process we call knowledge. And as investigations into epistemology for over 2,000 years in the West and as Eastern mysticism for nearly twice that long have consistently revealed, knowledge is ultimately individual in character. Knowledge requires the unique perception of "objective" phenomena and the formulation of a subjective valuation derived from those uniquely perceived phenomena in order to come to a conclusion or set thereof that prompt a specific course of action.

People gather data and information, convert it to knowledge, make decisions based on knowledge, execute those decisions, and, it is hoped, achieve a desired result. No step of this process can be skipped. Management traditionally has assumed responsibility for making and executing decisions. Yet today management must assume responsibility for the entire cycle by paying attention to the data-gathering and information creation steps. Let us go back to the weather analogy and, for sake of illustration, assume that the temperature reading was in error. Rather than 92°F it was really 29°F, in which case it would be a very bad decision to go to the beach instead of snowboarding.

People do their best to agree on perceptions of phenomena and to come to some conclusion and action, but in the end, the agreements and consensus usually involve argument and compromise. Take, for example, a jury trial or even the impeachment trial of President Bill Clinton. If the ordeal of the Clinton impeachment proceedings and subsequent Senate impeachment trial made anything clear, it was that intelligent, experienced, and informed individuals shaped absolute and conflicting perceptions of a set of ordinary phenomena and clashed on subsequent courses of action, all of which threaten the health of a global economy and the stability of world politics. And this was mostly because two varying yet not altogether different sets of values, Republicans' and Democrats', rendered opposing perceptions of the same set of phenomena. Both sides looked at the same set of phenomena, came to different conclusions, and fought over those conclusions for different reasons.

It gets even stranger than that when we bring modern science into the picture. Newtonian science tells us that we know something by observing it. But as Gary Zukav tells us in *The Dancing Wu Li Masters,* "According to quantum physics, it *isn't there* until we do observe it!"[2] Particles and waves do not exist as entities but come into being only as we observe them, or, more properly, as we observe their effects. Quantum mechanics shows how waves can be particles and particles are also waves, extending wave-particle duality to something called "self-actualization." Phenomena exist because people are there to observe them, and people exist because we observe phenomena. Without people, the phenomena do not exist; they only have a tendency to exist. Without phenomena, people do not exist; people have a tendency to exist.

This is the focus of a field of modern science called "complementarity." Classical science thought of the universe as a set of objects. Modern science sees the world as interactions and potentialities or tendencies. Properties do not belong to objects, entities, or independent phenomena, and without properties, objects, entities, and independent phenomena can be said not to exist. Properties belong to interactions between objects, between entities, and between phenomenon and observer. So the universe is self-actualizing, just as each person is self-actualizing. That does not mean that if a tree falls in a forest and no one is there to see or hear it fall, it does not fall. Lots of other objects and entities were there to see or hear or interact with the falling tree.

So what has all this to do with asset value of information and knowledge? Information and knowledge derived from it have business or organizational value only if some human interaction manifests a value through economic, commercial, or organizational participation. Put another way, commerce, broadly defined, is an interaction among individuals, and sometimes objects, that results in an exchange of value and the creation of wealth of some kind. Commerce is one of several ways that human beings connect with each other and with the world outside of each individual. It is in those interconnections we become *"self-actualized."*

What makes the asset value of information so intangible is that information value has no real objective existence in and of itself, but, like particles and waves in quantum physics, it has a tendency to exist. The value of information reaches an extant state only through transitory interconnections among constantly changing entities and consistently shifting observations. Just as modern physics has discovered that, at the subatomic level, the universe is more qualitative than quantitative, we are discovering that the real fundamental assets of business and commerce, information and knowledge, are more qualitative than quantitative, more dependent on perception and interconnection and less amenable to quantitative measurement.

Bottom line: We are working in new dimensions. That does not mean that the traditional measurements of business have to be discarded. Just as quantum physics did not throw out Newtonian science but rather needed to expand beyond the limitations of classical physics, we do not arbitrarily dismiss double-entry accounting as irrelevant in a modern information-based economy. Accounts payable will always be accounts payable. But mountains of investigation have shown that traditional business measurements do not yield satisfactory or even workable pictures of business and organizational realities.

There are no quick answers or easy formulas to the problem of the asset value of information. Perhaps there may never be. The information revolution of the last quarter of the twentieth century probably will extend well into the first quarter of the twenty-first century. A third dimension of commerce and organizations that was there all along but which two-dimensional measurements prevented us from fully engaging is being discovered.

INFORMATION: THE CORE OF THE SOFTWARE INFRASTRUCTURE

Information is at the core of the IT infrastructure model because everything coalesces around the intangible asset of information. Without information, there is no reason for an IT infrastructure to exist. The IT infrastructure is about information; it is built with technologies, but it is about information.

The software infrastructure is an infrastructure within an infrastructure where, instead of just moving information around microprocessor circuits and networks, users begin to manipulate and process information to create value that can be transformed into goods, services, and wealth. We look closely at information management systems, enabling technologies, applications, application servers, middleware and systems management, but along the way keep in mind that each of these components of the software infrastructure has only one purpose; the manipulation, processing, and transformation of information.

EVOLUTION OF THE SOFTWARE INFRASTRUCTURE

The software infrastructure evolved over the past half-century, from the earliest computers, ENIAC and Univac, which were programmed with mechanical switches and wires and fed information on punch cards, to the emergence of Fortran and COBOL and BASIC, which allowed programmers to write higher-level instructions that would in turn be compiled into assembler language that could give binary instructions to hardware. Writing early business applications in the 1960s, programmers needed to define input and output formats, create data formats and data stores specific to a particular business application, and then write instruction sequences that told the processors what to do with the information they would receive via punch cards.

What started with manually coding practically every aspect of an application and its data evolved into discrete tools and components that can be integrated to produce more sophisticated applications using more intricate information while delivering results faster and at lower cost. The software infrastructure is largely invisible because, once again, we seem always to focus on each of the parts, sometimes paying attention to how one part interconnects with another but almost never seeing them as a dynamic whole supporting information-based business activities and organizational functions.

Of all the discussion surrounding the Y2K problem, not one commentator has nailed the real reason this trillion-dollar problem came about. Everyone mentions limited memory and limited storage in first-generation business computers, but these had little influence on why the date format was shortened by two digits, creating the last great headache of the twentieth century. Nor were programmers unaware of what they were doing back then. During the very first week of the first programming course I ever took, in August 1967, the instructor mentioned the Y2K problem. He said there would be hell to pay when everyone finally realized what would happen when the century date turned. He probably never thought that this particular hell would cost over $1 trillion.

The problem arose not particularly due to limited memory. Although memory was not nearly as abundant as it is today, it was used primarily only to hold the programs while they were being executed. Programs contained date fields, but it was of little consequence so far as programs or memory were concerned whether the year in the date field was two digits or four digits. In the 1960s and 1970s, good programmers were able to code a business process, say accounts payable, in 3 to 5 kilobytes of program code; there is plenty of room for a four-digit year. (By way of comparison, today even the simplest programs normally exceed several megabytes of code, at least 200 times the size of most early business application programs.) Nor was storage a particular problem. Most storage devices were magnetic tapes, and they held a lot of data even then. Spindle disk platters were more convenient for data search and retrieval than were tapes, but most platters held plenty of data. No, it was not memory, and it was not storage; nor was it processing power. Processing power just dictates how fast data is processed, not how much data can be processed.

The real culprit behind the Y2K problem was *input!* There were no screens. There were very few keyboards attached to computers, and those were so crude as to be almost useless for genuine input purposes. The only real input medium was punch cards. And every punch card had 80 columns, so that only 80 alpha-numeric characters of data could be contained on each card. Those 80 columns were expensive real estate. And since a large portion of the data had to do with transactions—daily, weekly, monthly business transactions—a date accompanied almost every transaction. The data for each transaction had to fit onto one 80-column punch card. Programmers who created input formats that spilled over onto two punch cards were ridiculed.

So why, when we evolved from punch cards to cathode ray tubes (CRTs) and direct keyboard input, didn't someone say something to correct the impending doom of the Y2K bug? No one from data processing wanted to upset executive managers with the news that they would need to redo a lot of old data and programs in order to avoid a potential business and organizational disaster at the turn of the century. For one thing, executive managers cared only about results: output; they didn't want to be disturbed about input, which was the real source of the problem. And for another thing, unlike today's executives whose vision and leadership reaches well into the future, executive managers from the 1960s through the 1980s could care less about what might happen on January 1, 2000; they cared only what happened immediately and how it affected this quarter's measurements.

Thus the real culprits behind the Y2K bug were the executive managers who reneged on their fiduciary responsibilities by not paying attention to their (crude) IT infrastructures and their ramifications for the future.

In the next chapter, we want to keep in mind the whole of the software infrastructure as we examine each of its components. And we begin with the most fundamental of its components, information management systems, the technologies that house, manipulate, and maintain information. And as we will see, IMSs have an extensive history indeed.

NOTES

1. Karl Erik Sveiby, *The New Organizational Wealth: Managing & Measuring Knowledge-based Assets* (San Francisco: Berrett-Koehler, 1997), p. 37.
2. Gary Zukav, *The Dancing Wu Li Masters* (New York: Bantam, 1984), p. 86.

CHAPTER 9

Information
Management Systems

I am the very model of a modern Major-General.
I've information vegetable, animal, and mineral,
I know the Kings of England, and I quote the fights historical,
From Marathon to Waterloo, in order categorical.

—SIR WILLIAM S. GILBERT, *Pirates of Penzance*

FROM ETCHED BONES TO INFORMATION
MANAGEMENT SYSTEMS

Around 20,000 years ago there began appearing in southern Europe humankind's first "database." James Burke and Robert Ornstein in their book, *The Axemaker's Gift,* tell us about "magic wands," which are really carved bone or antler horn and are referred to by archeologists as "batons," that "seem to represent the first deliberate and detailed use of a device which would serve to extend the memory, because with it knowledge could be held in recorded form outside the mind or the sequence of ritual. . . . In all likelihood the carvings represent the first form of information notation."[1]

One example, the French La Marche bone, dating from about 13,000 years ago, bears a series of marks in sets and subsets that reveals an "exact sixty-mark notation of the lunar calendar"; the bone's "entire calendar covers a period of 7.5 months with remarkable accuracy."[2] It would be another two or three thousand years after the La Marche bone until humankind began domesticating animals, and another couple of millennia after that before people began cultivating crops. So it turns out that gathering and recording vital information and passing it on as knowledge are some of humankind's earliest endeavors, if not its oldest profession.

Most writing evolves from forms of recording commercial and government data, food and livestock inventories, taxes and tokens, and the like. Numbers and pictographs came first; words—strings of pictographs, symbols, and numbers—came later. But all of it was aimed at recording information, and by recording information, it was further aimed at ordering, making sense of and controlling, the physical environment and the commercial and social environments.

That puts information at the core not just of our IT infrastructure, as illustrated in Exhibit 9.1, but also at the center of humankind's progress since the end of the Pleistocene epoch. In a very real sense, people have been building databases of one type or another since the end of the last Ice Age. Gathering, ordering, storing, maintaining, manipulating, and retrieving information are at the core of practically every human endeavor. And these form the very heart and soul of commerce and of organizations engaged in business and public service.

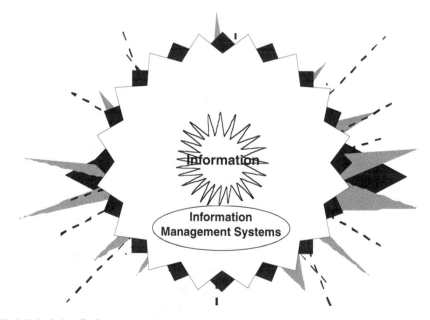

Exhibit 9.1   Information Management Systems

Therefore, if there is one component in the IT infrastructure that we absolutely, positively need to get right, that component is information management systems. If information is correct, current, secure, and broadly and easily accessible by users who need it when they need it, applications are likely to yield desired results. If an application does not yield results, the application can be changed. If an organization has made the right IMS decisions, data move effortlessly to the new application. If additional applications are needed, they can be developed and implemented. The information will be there, ready for its new uses.

If a flexible and scaleable network infrastructure can be built and a robust and open IMS be established at the heart of the software infrastructure, the other components of the IT infrastructure will fall into place and evolve and adapt to expanding business demands and shifting organizational requirements. Applications will evolve and change constantly, as will platform technologies, middleware, system management, and user interfaces. For that matter, networking and IMS technologies will continue to evolve and improve. But a good IMS will build and build, adding and delivering new kinds of information to meet evolving user demands. One constant in the relentlessly changing worlds of business and public organizations is a need for consistent and accurate information—the raw material of a knowledge-based economy and the cornerstone of humankind's modern evolution.

IMSs are more than just databases. They are a combination of databases and information management and manipulation capabilities that define and store information as well as ensuring its integrity, security, accessibility, and connectivity. As mentioned earlier, Oracle's current IMS offering, Oracle8i, is only roughly half RDBMS; the rest is information management functionality that occurs outside the rows and columns of the Oracle RDBMS.

Although all relational databases essentially do the same thing—store and maintain data—IMSs are not all created equal. And although all IMS providers can tell good stories, what they actually deliver can differ significantly. Those differences can have lasting effects—positive or negative—on an organization's ability to deliver value to its customers and constituents. Once again, business decisions about IMS technologies are not default, commodity decisions.

Information management systems are not just databases. We are talking about information at the heart of our organizations, about our organizations' abilities to fulfill their missions. The decision on which database to use should not be made strictly on a cost basis. There are real technological differences among the choices. IMSs are not commodities and are continuing to evolve as rapidly as any other software infrastructure technology, and even as rapidly as the Internet itself. Wall Street sometimes seems to think that the market for databases has been saturated. (Remember that databases are a core part of IMSs.) As usual, Wall Street's vision is myopic. Only a first beachhead has been established on this new information-based economy; industrial era cultures are just barely beginning to shift. Think of all the information in all the libraries in the world; think of all the information in the file cabinets in every business on the planet. We have only scratched the surface in making all that information accessible by computers over the Internet. Every piece of information will someday be stored in a database. And Wall Street thinks that the demand for databases has passed. It is reminiscent of watching "Wall Street Week" in 1979 and listening to the panelists debate whether the Dow will ever exceed the 1,000 mark.

INFORMATION MANAGEMENT SYSTEMS EVOLUTION

IMSs not only maintain the storage of data, without which no application can exist, but they make certain that the data are correct, current, consistent, and secure. Early IMSs were rigid and hierarchical. Frequently referred to as "flat file systems," these early data stores were built to resemble the contents of manila file folders, usually along the lines of a business form (e.g., a personnel file or a vendor file).

Most often associated with business applications built on COBOL, flat files were built into the application itself and generally did not share data with other applications. For example, if information about an employee's insurance benefits were contained in a human resources application, those data were not automatically accessible by a payroll application. A custom program could link a specific field of information to a mirrored field in another program—called "networked" files—but these were unique to an application and time-consuming (read "expensive") to build. During the 1970s, hierarchical and network data stores called "networked databases" provided early databases that could, with planning and programming, make a single data store available to multiple applications. The hierarchical networked databases could store both information and specific (more or less rigid) relationships. Some of these are still in use today.

The Year 2000 problem provides a good example of just how critical a mistake in IMS planning can become. Ultimately it will cost businesses and governments worldwide over $1 trillion to fix the problem. Some organizations will mutate, and others may die because of this problem. The root cause of the problem was the input limitations of the 80-column punch card. But the ongoing persistence and expansion of the Y2K problem can be assigned to poorly thought out managerial expediencies and poor IMS planning—a simple yet $1 trillion mistake.

The perpetuation of hierarchical and networked (flat-file) databases in organizations is more of a liability than anything else. The Y2K bug has made many organizations upgrade their flat files to relational databases while upgrading core legacy business applications to current-generation ERP applications. If any organization continues to maintain any types of flat-file data stores, top-level executives need to know why. Data caretakers must propose projects to migrate into modern IMSs that have been selected to anchor the organization's new IT infrastructure.

Relational database systems first began appearing in the late 1970s. E. F. Codd, working at IBM's research labs in San Jose, conceived the theory of RDBMSs. But it was a small start-up company, then called Software Development Laboratories, headed by a programmer named Larry Ellison and his former boss from Ampex, Bob Miner, that delivered the first commercially viable RDBMS in 1975. Ellison's first customer was the U.S. Central Intelligence Agency; the CIA's project was code-named "Oracle." Ellison soon changed his company's name to that code name. IBM wanted to discourage (if not squash) the use of RDBMS technologies, preferring instead to perpetuate the IMS flat-file model that ran on its mainframes. Once again that ugly tendency of technology vendors to stifle advances and protect their "locked-in" customer base raised its head.

Although it took awhile for RDBMs to catch on commercially, by the late 1980s virtually all next-generation business applications were being built on RDBMS foundations. Oracle, Informix, and IBM DB2 were the early RDBMS leaders, followed in the mid-1980s by Ingress (later acquired by ASK, which was in turn acquired by Computer Associates), Sybase, and Interbase (acquired by Borland, now Inprise, then later set free).

Microsoft SQL Server is a late entrant in RDBMSs and was originally a code base acquired from Sybase (Sybase's SQL Server Version 4.2 release). Microsoft's SQL Server 7.0, released in late 1998, is a new product, reportedly written from the ground up by Microsoft, although it has plenty of aging Sybase code at its heart. Microsoft SQL Server 7.0 and its progeny will replace its predecessors (SQL Server 6.0 and 6.5) as Microsoft's RDBMS for the Windows 2000 operating systems.

It should be clear by now that, left to their own devices, most technology companies with an appreciable market share tend to protect, perpetuate, and exploit that market share and not seek to advance technology. If it could have done it, Microsoft would have killed the Internet. It may even still want to do just that. And Microsoft is not alone. Kevin Werbach keenly observes that many of the companies building the next generation of the Internet "want to tie those pipelines to the content and services they are selling, and control interconnection to the world at large. Their intractability may damage the network's openness *and* slow down its development."[a]

In other words, if we subscribe to XYZ company's fiber optic Internet service, we may not be able to access content of or exchange email with subscribers to ABC company's satellite-based Internet service. This is not good old-fashioned free enterprise. It is more like exploitation of public resources, if not outright theft of what belongs already to all of us. Werbach goes on to observe that "the tragedy of the cyber-commons is that competitive access benefits all providers collectively but few individually."[b] Proprietary networking technologies and the business models that attend them have no real place in the twenty-first century. Proprietary networking technologies would be a giant leap backward. They benefit neither customers nor users and serve mostly to limit humankind's progress while holding us hostage to inferior—and overpriced—products and services, replacing an information superhighway with a ganglia of private toll roads.

---

[a] Kevin Werbach, "The Architecture of Internet 2.0," *Release 1.0: Esther Dyson's Monthly Report,* February 19, 1999, p. 1.
[b] *Ibid.*

Although all RDBMSs are more or less alike in that they conform to E. F. Codd's original criteria for relational databases,[3] each vendor's product is slightly different. More important, RDBMS can and do differ considerably in their capabilities and the functionality they integrate. So while RDBMSs may conform to Codd's 12 rules, vendors implement basic functionality differently and integrate different sets of information management capabilities into their IMS packages. What we buy from an IMS provider depends a great deal on what that particular IMS provider defines as an IMS. There is some serious caveat emptor going on here.

KEY INFORMATION MANAGEMENT SYSTEMS PLAYERS

Oracle

Oracle has always held the dominant market share in RDBMSs and has always taken the lead in integrating information management functionality with its RDBMSs to offer increasingly more capable IMS products. Its products (Oracle8i is the current release) are generally recognized as the most flexible and open, scaleable, reliable, secure, and best-performing RDBMSs on the market. And Oracle itself is generally acknowledged as the technology leader in IMS, the standard to which all others compare themselves. Oracle also runs on the widest assortment of platform technologies and is supported worldwide by legions of engineers and consultants.

One former Oracle development manager, who now uses different IMSs in his current job, says that when he worked at Oracle, he thought that, aside from all the marketing sales hype, all RDBMSs did pretty much the same things in pretty much the same ways. He says now he did not understand the differences until his current company actually started using the different RDBMSs. He believes that Oracle is superior "by a wide margin." Another user of various brands of RDBMSs, in the financial services industry, put it more simply: "Oracle just doesn't break. The others can and do." These kinds of statements by RDMBS users are consistent, almost even universal. So it is not surprising that Oracle continues to dominate market share for relational databases in particular and information management systems in general.

Some critics might protest: "Isn't Oracle also the most expensive RDBMS?" No, and yes, maybe. Oracle's basic RDBMS, which runs on Windows NT/2000, Unix, and most other operating systems, from desktops to mainframes, is priced competitively with anything on the market at any given time. It is when we start adding what Oracle calls "enterprise" features and functions that the price begins to rise. To make matters a bit more confusing, what Oracle calls its basic system is more closely similar to what Microsoft calls its "enterprise" RDBMS, SQL Server 7.0. Microsoft does not yet have what Oracle calls its "enterprise edition." A vendor's sleight-of-hand marketing and nomenclature does not deliver enterprise-level capabilities.

Once again, the real expense of IMS will not be in the initial cost of the license; it will be in the people-intensive dimensions of implementing, deploying, maintaining, and administering the IMSs. Most Oracle people will say upfront that Oracle database administrators (DBAs) are high-priced professionals, commanding annual salaries in the United States of $90,000 and more. And Oracle DBAs are difficult to find and recruit and perhaps even more difficult to retain. But that is not because Oracle's IMS is necessarily more difficult to manage than others. Oracle's IMS generally can do more than other IMSs, so there is a degree of difficulty. But it is more a case of Oracle's cultural arrogance resulting in fortuitous honesty. Like proud owners of a professional sports team that consistently wins championships, they frequently take pride that their players are the highest paid in their league. There's a bit of that behind the openness of Oracle people when they cite the value of Oracle DBAs: "We got the best, and they're the best paid!"

However, sometimes Oracle competitors try to leverage to their own favor the high cost of Oracle DBAs. One competitor trains its sales cadre to tell customers that if they can run a word processing program, they can administer its RDBMS. Be very skeptical of those kinds of claims. If it seems too good to be true, even in the realms of fast-moving technologies, it probably is too good to be true. And if vendors making those claims have a short history in building the particular technology and in supporting customers using that technology, be even more skeptical. They may not know what the real problems are.

As mentioned many times before, it is not the technologies themselves that represent the highest cost factors in an IT infrastructure, it is the professionals who implement, deploy, and maintain those technologies. There are no exceptions. There are alternatives, such as outsourcing, but there are no exceptions. The people costs of building and maintaining IT infrastructures will always represent the largest cost, at least in our lifetimes.

Oracle and IMS providers in general must be commended for the meaningful strides they are making in reducing administrative tasks through technology. Oracle's latest IMS offering allows fewer DBAs to manage a greater number of distributed RDBMSs than before, so one DBA might be able to perform the management functions it took three or four DBAs to perform just a few years ago. Good news, yes. However, the number and size of RDBMSs are rapidly increasing, as are the number of applications and the overall extent of and demands on our IT infrastructures. So, at best, users can hope to perhaps break even on administrative costs, whatever brand IMS was chosen. Highly competent database administrators will still be needed. They are an organization's first and best line of defense against criminal hackers and info terrorists.

IBM

IBM's DB2 runs a close second to Oracle in robustness and enterprise capabilities. As with Oracle, support and consulting are world class and worldwide. Performance, scaleability, security, reliability, and future viability are on par with Oracle. The difference? IBM software traditionally runs best on its own operating systems and hardware. And although IBM recently has made DB2 available on Windows NT and other Unix platforms, IBM's sincerity of commitment to other-than-IBM platform technologies has yet to be proven. As with Microsoft's commitment to coexistence with Unix, we must remain skeptical of possible Trojan horse tactics. Oracle has proven its commitment to the broadest possible range of platform technologies for over two decades.

Informix and Sybase

Informix and *Sybase* are very similar to each other in size, market share, and technical capabilities, and their products can compare favorably with Oracle8 and IBM's DB2. Both Sybase and Informix have endured some rough waters recently, and both are surviving and have loyal customer bases. But neither company has seen revenue expansion over the past few years. Some industry observers attribute that to a slowdown in RDBMS markets, but numbers from Oracle, IBM, and Microsoft would belie those analyses. It would seem more a case of industry consolidation around the big three.

Moreover, neither Informix nor Sybase has come out strongly on Microsoft's Windows NT/2000 operating system, although both have products available. Oracle RDBMS and Microsoft's SQL Server far outdistance all others on NT, including IBM. This may underscore a potential shortcoming for Sybase and Informix. Windows NT/2000 will no doubt be a major factor in business IT infrastructures as we move into the twenty-first century. Therefore, not commanding a meaningful market share here can become a longer-term weakness for both Informix and Sybase.

Even more important, their slow starts in the Windows NT/2000 platform markets highlight a potential weakness in the research and development (R&D) capabilities. Microsoft, Oracle, and IBM have bountiful resources to fund and manage R&D. That "deep-pockets" R&D capability may become one of several deciding factors in longer-term market viability among IMS providers, as it is in any area of the software infrastructure.

This leads to another red flag, at least for organizations with international locations—the availability of worldwide and world-class support and consulting. Deploying and maintaining direct and indirect resources globally requires a great ongoing commitment. These life-lines can weaken quickly if not well funded and committed to. Employee cutbacks in technology companies usually affect the quality of service and support delivered in its smaller markets. And we might just have a critical business using that vendor's technology in a "smaller" market. This makes it incumbent on both IT staff and business managers to know where these technologies will be deployed and that adequate support, service, and consulting are available for all sites, for the foreseeable future.

If either Sybase or Informix is already a part of an organization's IT infrastructure, there is no immediate reason to abandon either of them. Additional or new investment in Sybase or Informix IMS technology would need to be based on added value provided by the vendors themselves, and many of these companies' customers are quick to point out what forms that added value can take—responsive service and support, specialized solutions, close account management, good channel partners, among other things.

Computer Associates

Computer Associates' (CA) Ingres/Jasmin object-relational database product may prove to be viable and attractive to some organizations. Yet while CA can generally offer support, service, and consulting worldwide, its business is not significantly concentrated on database. CA could buy Informix or Sybase or Interbase and substantially replace the Ingres code at any time. CA has a history of shuffling technologies.

Interbase

Interbase illustrates the point that superior technology does not always win out. Five or so years ago, Interbase offered very probably the best RDBMS technology available. But before it could gain any appreciable market penetration, Interbase was acquired by Borland (now Inprise), which wanted to sell it as a shrink-wrapped product. Now Interbase has been spun off on its own again, but lack of R&D resources will keep it from keeping pace with Oracle, IBM, and Microsoft. Interbase lacks support and consulting services. However, a company like CA could snap it up and revive Interbase's fortunes.

Microsoft

Microsoft should continue to dominate the Windows NT/2000 platform. As of this writing, Oracle holds a slim market share lead over SQL Server on NT, but that may change when SQL Server 7.0 begins shipping because SQL Server 7.0 is integrated with Microsoft BackOffice on NT. Not that product integration brings notable advantages to the customer in scaleability, reliability, security, or performance; it does not. BackOffice integration is more product packaging than anything else.

What integration does mean is that users get SQL Server 7.0 virtually for free when they buy BackOffice. So it becomes a no-brainer decision for small businesses and for many mid-tier organizations. The apparently attractive "cost of acquisition" that comes with Microsoft's bundling tempts many departmental or divisional heads to implement Microsoft's SQL Server 7.0 without regard to integration issues at the enterprise or intraenterprise levels, which should be a red flag for top-level executives.

Finally, SQL Server 7.0 can run only on Microsoft operating systems, which have been consistently unreliable and which continue to lack the scaleability and flexibility required by enterprise organizations of any size. Even more important, with SQL Server Microsoft is inviting (some observers would use the word "locking") its customers into a proprietary architecture. While this is very beneficial for Microsoft's business, a proprietary software infrastructure holds few benefits for organizations larger than mom-and-pop enterprises.

So even though Microsoft may claim large unit shipments of SQL Server 7.0, most will be used by smaller organizations with limited needs or will go unused. Many organizations purchase BackOffice licenses for their NT Servers, but use Oracle or IBM or Informix or Sybase for their information management component. And these organizations are not doing that because they like spending the additional money.

If an organization is concerned about scaleability, reliability, security, and performance, executives need to ensure that their people avoid default decisions in favor of SQL Server 7.0 and make Microsoft compete on merits other than the price of an initial software license. Although all components in an IT infrastructure are critical, the information management systems are "the gray matter."

The IMS is one place not to make a selection based on cost of initial acquisition. A company's data will stay with the organization for a long time and must be absolutely correct, current, secure, and uncorrupted. All the other components of the IT infrastructure will evolve and adapt. The IMS will evolve as well with new releases, revisions, and added capabilities and improved performance. But what is stored inside the IMS is the collective information that the organization uses to perform its various missions, to deliver value to customers and constituency, and to create wealth for shareholders.

Not many chief executive officers would contest the notion that information is, at the end of the twentieth century, an organization's most valuable asset. Top-level executives must always keep in mind that IMS is the vital component in their company's IT infrastructure, containing and protecting the organization's information assets. It is where the firm's "family jewels" are kept.

OBJECT-ORIENTED DATABASES

Object-oriented databases and object-relational databases represent the next evolution of IMS. Here are some key points to keep in mind.

First, objects contain both information and behaviors for that information (i.e., what can or cannot be done with that information). RDBMSs (and previous DBMSs) contain only data; behavior is imposed on that data from other sources (software). For example, we could have information on a vendor from whom we buy services. In an object-oriented environment, we could assign that information an attribute which says that the information is "read only" and can be altered only by users with specific security identification (e.g., purchasing agents).

A line-of-business manager could, for example, access that information and read about a vendor's status or about the status of an order placed with that vendor, but he or she could not alter the information. Only a purchasing agent authorized to alter that information could do so. That kind of behavior could be programmed into our purchasing application, but it is more efficient and far more flexible to attach the behavior to the information itself, so that the behavior is there even if the information is used in another program (e.g., with an inventory control application).

Second, objects can be reused in any number of applications and will retain both the information itself and the associated or permitted behaviors. For example, the Y2K problem would not need a line-by-line fix in every application that has a date field; we would simply adjust the "date" object, and every time any application accessed that "date" object, it would access the correct annual progression.

Finally, objects and object-relational databases are efficient at handling types of information beyond data (characters and numbers). As we begin using more images and more video and audio types of information, there will be a greater need for object-relational and object-oriented database. Not coincidentally, Oracle, IBM, and Informix are all prepared to deliver some of those capabilities today. Early in 1999, Oracle delivered an Internet-ready version of Oracle8i that handles a wide variety of information types on websites, over the Internet, and on intranets and extranets.

Widespread use of pure object-oriented IMS is quite a long way off, although the technologies are mature enough to use today, and there are several mature object-oriented databases available. But massive stores of relational and flat-file data exist, and neither business nor government can afford simply to throw them away. Our knowledge-based economy craves the integration of all types of information, not the exclusion of one type in favor of another. Probably the remaining flat-file information should be moved into RDBMSs so that it can become a part of our modern IT infrastructures, but most likely object-oriented capabilities will evolve almost seamlessly alongside RDBMSs.

We can expect the current leading providers of RDBMSs to continue to integrate object-oriented functionality with relational capabilities. Oracle, Informix, and IBM are doing just that. Only Microsoft seems to be choosing a different tact. It tends to integrate object capabilities into its operating systems rather than in SQL Server. This creates a proprietary environment where applications developed to run on Windows NT/2000 and Microsoft's SQL Server 7.0 will most likely need to be largely rewritten to run with any other database. Proprietary environments offer absolutely no benefits to customers.

INFORMATION MANAGEMENT SYSTEM STANDARDIZATION

The most effective single action any organization can take to make its applications interact more transparently and securely, while performing more reliably and operating more efficiently at lower cost levels, is to standardize on a single IMS, one that meets all of an organization's requirements, both in the near term and for the foreseeable future. And guess what? It is neither difficult nor prohibitively expensive to do precisely that.

Standardization requires leadership and commitment, especially from top-level management. If that leadership and commitment are present, standardization of IMS will happen in relatively short order. Leading IMS providers, particularly IBM and Oracle, offer ancillary technologies and tools as well as services to help smooth this process. And IMS providers usually will compete fiercely for a bid to standardize a large organization's IMS.

Remember the high cost of those database administrators? This is one more incentive for IMS standardization, and cautionary tales abound here. A well-known manufacturing organization had gotten its ERP applications from SAP up and running, using an Oracle database as the supporting IMS. When executive management began asking for some business intelligence capabilities, IS management selected a data warehousing product that used a Sybase IMS rather than selecting Oracle's own data warehouse. They also implemented a third-party information integration product that would take Oracle-based information from the SAP applications and transform it into Sybase information to be used in the data warehouse to generate the business intelligence capabilities executive management wanted.

This did not happen during the dark ages. It happened in the spring of 1998. And what were executive managers thinking about all this? They just wanted their business intelligence from the applications. Had they had the benefit of reading this book, they would have known better. And not only would they have saved two-thirds of the money spent to get to that business intelligence (it was over $10 million), but they also would have maintained a better integrated and more flexible software

infrastructure that offered better support and lower ongoing maintenance costs.

Unfortunately, this cautionary tale is not an isolated incident. It happens in almost every organization, large and small, and it is happening
today and every day. It happens because top executives are mostly ignorant about the IT infrastructure that is so very vital to their organizations
and have not assumed responsibility for their company's information assets and the technologies that support them.

The IMS standardization process is clearly worth top-level executive consideration and involvement. The information is the most vital
part of the organization. That is why this is called an *information*
infrastructure—the core component is the *information.*

NOTES

1. James Burke and Robert Ornstein, *The Axemaker's Gift: A Double-Edged
   History of Human Culture* (New York: Grosset/Putnam, 1995), pp. 29–30.
2. *Ibid.,* p. 31.
3. E. F. Codd, "A Relational Model of Data for Large Shared Data Banks,"
   Communications for the ACM 13, 6 (June 1970), pp. 109–117.

CHAPTER 10

Enabling Technologies

> *Man is a tool-using animal. . . .*
> *Without tools he is nothing,*
> *with tools he is all.*
>
> —THOMAS CARLYLE, *Sartor Resartus* (1834)

CASE FOR TOOLS

Everything anthropologists tell us about what separates humans from other primates points to our use of tools, beginning with the first striking instrument (a randomly selected bone, if we are to believe the opening scene of *2001: A Space Odyssey*), and reaching past our current enabling technologies into a high-tech tomorrow we cannot even begin to imagine. Human beings are somehow naturally drawn to tools, everything from hammers and screwdrivers, from knitting needles and power drills to chef's knives, kitchen gadgets, and gardening implements. And so it comes as no surprise that tools are core components of the IT infrastructure. Here the category has been broadened somewhat by calling it "enabling technologies," because some of the technologies to be discussed may not at first seem to be tools in traditional software parlance.

As illustrated in Exhibit 10.1, enabling technologies are tied closely to information itself; they are used to build business applications that will use information resources. Enabling technologies encompass the fundamental tools of the computer science trade, computer languages and development tools, as well as technologies focused on person or group productivity (spreadsheets, groupware, workflow, project management,

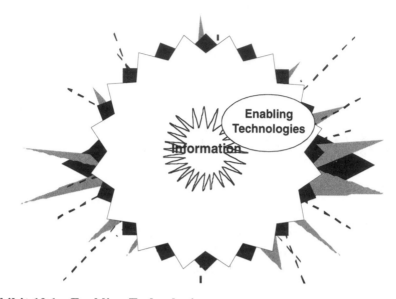

Exhibit 10.1   Enabling Technologies

document management, etc.). An enabling technology is any piece of
software that specifically helps people to build business applications,
which in turn help people use information as raw material in the creation
of value for the organization and for its customers and constituents.

Readers who know what computer languages and enabling technologies do and who have some idea of how these work might want to skip
the first section of this chapter. While we may never need to select an
enabling technology, we use them every time we touch a computer in almost any way. Understanding how these work will help us gain that desired comfort level with IT.

FROM BINARY MATHEMATICS ALL
THINGS SHALL COME

Let us go back for a moment to the two basic elements of the IT infrastructure, sand and electricity. Everything that happens in the IT infrastructure happens because electricity is flowing in intricate patterns
called integrated circuits etched on silicon—at least, that is how we are
doing it at the end of the twentieth century. Electricity either flows or
does not flow in those patterns according to the software commands it is

given. Those software commands reach the electricity in forms of 1s and 0s, binary mathematics or first-generation language, also called "machine language."

Assembler language (2GL) lies a layer above the binary commands. Assembler programmers are generally concerned with writing hardware commands that direct different hardware functions, like going to the disk drive, searching for a specific file, retrieving a copy of that file, placing it in memory, then displaying it on the screen. So when we select, for example, a Microsoft Word document and double click on the file name, a host of precise electrical operations are executed through assembler language (2GL) into machine language (binary, 1GL), and the result is displayed on the screen. But assembler is an arduous language with which to program, and it is closely tied to the hardware itself. Different processors have different assembler languages, a fact that must be kept in mind. Not all assembler languages are created equal. And assembler languages along with compilers (which are discussed next) are very likely to have an impact on 64-bit capabilities in the very near future.

During the mid-1960s FORTRAN, the first widely used third-generation language (3GL), was quickly adopted by programmers for scientific, mathematics, and engineering applications as well as some larger business applications, such as aerospace manufacturing materiel control. In the late 1960s, COBOL gained broader acceptance as the 3GL for business applications. COBOL was followed by a number of versions of BASIC, which most commentators at the time thought was a misnomer. (Most BASIC languages were not much less difficult than other 3GLs.) BASIC 3GLs were used mainly for smaller departmental applications; COBOL was used most often for what we now would call enterprise-level applications; and FORTRAN was the 3GL of choice for engineers and scientists. These languages, especially COBOL and BASIC, were much closer to declarative commands containing verbs and objects and, as a consequence, were easier to learn and easier to use.

Between the 3GL and the 2GL sits another piece of enabling technology called a "compiler." Compilers take the more easily programmed 3GL code and translate it into assembler language (2GL); assembler language then turns the code into binary 1s and 0s that in turn give the computer hardware on-and-off commands that electricity can understand. Compilers, which turn higher-level (3GL) programming languages like FORTRAN, COBOL, and C into assembler languages (2GL), can have a direct impact on how well program commands are executed at the hardware level. (In the late 1970s, Bill Gates and Paul Allen started a new

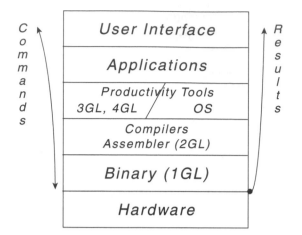

Exhibit 10.2   The Computer Languages Stack

company by providing BASIC, FORTRAN, and COBOL compilers for 8-bit hobbyist computers; Microsoft was born from such humble compiler beginnings.) The computer languages stack is illustrated in Exhibit 10.2.

ECONOMICS OF PROGRAMMER COSTS

Early in the history of business computer systems, processor and memory resources were the most expensive components. A mainframe computer in the mid-1960s had a mere fraction of the capacity and power of an average notebook computer that practically every businessperson carries on airplanes today. And the price for a single 1960s mainframe is equal, even in 1990s dollars, to the price of several dozen mainframes today, each of which has orders of magnitude of more computing power than the 1960s predecessors. Programmers, however, were comparatively inexpensive in the 1960s, at least relative to the cost of the computing power available. In the 1960s and well into the 1970s, there were few college courses for computer programming. Out of necessity, large companies took it upon themselves to train programmers for specific projects; they looked for job applicants with aptitude in logic and languages, which turned up as many English and language college majors as it did mathematics and engineering students. Programmers were paid upper-level clerical salaries (this writer was paid $450 per month in 1967 by a large aerospace manufacturer), but because their work weeks were usually extended by 10 to 15 hours of overtime, programmers' take-home pay began reaching into the moderate ranges of middle-management pay scales. In the early and mid-1960s these relatively inexpensive programmers slaved away with assembler languages, which, being close to the machine language of 1s and 0s, made more efficient use of processor resources.

In the late 1960s, computing resources were becoming a bit more abundant because business demands for automated data processing were gaining momentum and urgency. Since a COBOL, FORTRAN, or BASIC programmer could develop and deploy a business application much faster than could an assembler programmer, business organizations bit the bullet and started buying more processing power, and the great shift from writing applications in 2GLs to writing them in 3GLs got under way—and a new corporate bureaucracy had emerged, the data processing department, later to become the IS (information systems) or MIS (management information systems) department.

The cost of processor power became more affordable with the introduction of minicomputers from Digital Equipment Corporation, Data General, and others. Colleges began establishing computer science curricula, training computer specialists in software as well as hardware, which in turn raised the price of programmers. Microprocessor technologies in the 1970s would lower the cost of processing even further (Moore's Law again), and juxtaposed to the decreasing cost of memory and processing power, the cost of programmers continues to increase.

FOURTH-GENERATION LANGUAGES AND PRODUCTIVITY TOOLS

As mentioned earlier, around 1969 Dennis Ritchie developed the C programming language, a new 3GL, at Bell Labs. C has some core features that made it useful only as a 3GL in writing both systems and applications software, but other features made it more amenable to networking environments where packets of information prevailed. C is a modular language built to create programs in component chunks that could be easily broken up into packets, transmitted electronically to another computer, and reassembled back into the program's original form.

C is a more streamlined and a more efficient language than COBOL and BASIC. That compactness and modularity gave rise, in part, to C's progeny C++, which in turn helped to introduce objects into programming languages. C++ made it relatively easy to take a program routine that a programmer might use over and over, define that routine as an object, and call the object to execute the routine rather than rewriting the routine every time. Programmers had been using shortcuts like this for a long time, but this new generation of computer languages would come complete with a wide range of commonly used objects so that programmers would not need to create their own.

Languages like C++ and SmartTalk were more or less 3.5GLs, not yet real 4GLs. But C++ gave rise to Visual C++, one of the true fourth-generation languages, which made programming even less arduous by allowing programmers to select almost Lego-like building blocks (object components) and to build their programs with less line-by-line coding. Visual Basic, Microsoft's flagship 4GL, followed much the same path, coming out of QBasic, an earlier 3GL. Fourth-generation languages enabled programmers to perform more designing and testing and less coding, thereby increasing programmer productivity while decreasing application development time.

One key difference between 3GLs and 4GLs is that 3GLs are characteristically process based. In other words, they are usually best used to automate manual, transaction-driven processes, such as customer billing. Fourth-generation languages, being object based and more conducive to design experimentation, can better address the needs of information-driven applications, that is, applications that perform a great deal of information manipulation and are not simply automating previously manual transactions.

This distinction between information-driven applications and transaction-driven processes is important because it underscores another shift in business computing, from automating previously manual business processes to using information in new ways to create value. If, for example, we automate customer billing, we have not created new value except that we are billing customers faster and, it is hoped, more accurately than we did before, and at a lower clerical cost. This is a new value for the chief financial officer (CFO), but it is not necessarily a new business value that reaches our customers and constituents. As Tom Peters jokingly tells us, the nirvana for most CFOs is cutting all costs to zero, which is easily done by just shutting the doors and going out of business altogether.

If we are to stay in business and if we are to progress, we need to look for new uses of information. We need to use information as raw material in building new value for customers and constituents. Using information in this way calls for much more than automating previously manual processes. If, for example, we develop a program that plots the prices and behaviors of individual stocks over five years and compare these plots with similar histories of other investment alternatives, we are doing something with information that was not previously being done manually. That creates new value in the form of better decision-making capability, which in turn can result in better returns on investment. If we can deliver to customers better products and services customized to their preferences as revealed in their buying habits, and deliver these faster and at better prices, we are increasing value to customers through the application of information. We are not just automating manual transactions as we did during the first several decades of commercial computing.

This capability to apply information and information technologies in new ways, to create new customer value with the raw material of networked information, is crucial to a business's success in an Internet-harmonious and Web-centric global economy. Today most companies' websites are little more than elaborate yellow-page advertisements. Old products in new packages do not represent new value, not in Internet time. 4GLs and productivity tools arrived at just the right time to help us extend once more the reach of commerce and human interaction.

Fourth-generation languages and productivity tools allow us to work with information as a raw material to shape new uses for it, new products,

Take a tour of the websites of your company and those of your competitors. Also take a tour of the websites of a category of companies you patronize, such as airlines, hotels, or bookstores, and ask: "If my decision on which company to do business with was based largely on the experience of that company's website, which company would I select to get my business?" That's not an unrealistic exercise. What is more, a number of very realistic estimates tell us that, within as little as five years, fully 50 percent of all economic decisions will be either made or heavily influenced in just that way. Add to that the projections that within a couple of years after the turn of the century, over 1 billion people are likely to be regular users of the Internet and the World Wide Web. We have always had a tendency to do business with people we like and with companies whose cultures we feel most comfortable with. The Web extends those tendencies, allowing us to select among even farther-flung points of value interchange.

and new services. Rather than simply automating manual transactions—although 4GLs and productivity tools do that too—these technologies allow us to enable new organizational value, for the customer and constituents as well as for shareholders and institutions. That may be one reason "Internet stocks" are so highly valued. It certainly is not because of the book value of the companies, or most of their price:earning ratios. And it fuels our desire to jump into Internet stocks when we hear friends who got tenfold returns or more on investment in less than a year. Enabling technologies have been largely overlooked. Tools for Internet and web applications are not overly abundant right now, and the area is not only ripe for innovation but also requires smaller start-up investment. One visionary and a handful of software engineers could build the next knock-'em-dead web application development tool in a garage, only the garage is just as likely to be in New Bedford, Massachusetts, or New Delhi, India, as it is likely to be Silicon Valley.

Productivity tools range from individual productivity technologies such as spreadsheets, word processing, and presentation tools to group productivity environments such as Lotus Notes, Microsoft Exchange, project management and workflow and document management. Professional productivity tools include specialized computer-aided design or financial analysis workstations. Virtually all of these tasks are not so much an automation of previously manual processes but newly enabled productivity that extends the use of information in creating new organizational value. In short, users are not simply getting customer bills out faster with fewer clerks; they are creating new business value with information.

All enabling technologies are in one way or another accessing the processing power, memory, and storage of the hardware. They talk in languages to the electricity coursing around those intricate patterns etched in silicon. Enabling technologies are what users employ to express themselves to the technologies that in turn make things happen.

DO SOFTWARE ENGINEERS DRIVE FUZZY TRAINS?

There is some debate over the term "software engineer." Software engineers do not need to be publicly certified, as civil engineers do. They do not have any real professional oversight body, as electrical engineers have. They do not belong to unions, as railroad engineers do. Software engineers are all programmers, but all programmers are not software engineers, although most think they are.

Software engineers build software products from the ground up: enabling technology products, platform technology software, networking software, IMS software, or application software. They design the functionality and features. They may do some of the coding as well, but mostly programmers do coding. Software engineers are responsible for designing and overseeing the actual building of software products, much as architects design and oversee the construction of buildings. And yes, they sometimes call themselves software architects.

Why is this distinction important to top-level business executives? Software engineers build information capabilities into software products, capabilities that businesses not only need but need to determine as well. Heretofore, organizations have been pretty much at the mercy of the people who built the software. Users could do only what the software allowed. Users could not even think of doing something new unless offered software that could do it.

But then, in the mid-1980s, several things began happening, independently but simultaneously. First, IS departments began experimenting with a couple of new technologies. One was relational databases, which allowed complete separation of the data stores from applications, in turn allowing more and different business applications to use the same centrally stored and maintained information. Although Larry Ellison and Bob Miner installed their first RDBMS at the Central Intelligence Agency in the late 1970s, IS departments in large businesses experimented with RDBMSs for several years before adopting the technology in mainstream applications. Executives in some companies were reluctant to share their information internally across organizational chart lines, a reluctance that persists today. Today's top priority in knowledge management is to develop a knowledge-sharing culture inside even small organizations. In all networked organizations, influence not authority is power, and information and knowledge are shared freely, not hoarded. Only through the leadership and example of top-level executives can organizational cultures change from information-hoarding to knowledge-sharing.

In the mid-1980s, larger IS departments also began experimenting with CASE technologies. CASE offered a great deal of promise. With it, business managers could build business models and scenarios, which would be fed into the CASE engine, which in turn would automatically generate, integrate, and test application programs. Development time would be dramatically reduced, programming costs would drop, and business managers could request changes on the fly as well as design new business processes at will. But there was a problem, one that did not lie so much in the technologies as it did in the methodologies. The starting point for CASE is a business model or a business process scenario, which needed to come directly from business management. Business management, it turns out, is not very adept at building models or scenarios. Moment-to-moment business issues pressing in on management leaves them precious little time to engage in lengthy and abstract cogitation about the nature of their business. They could delegate the task to MBA business planners, and many did just that. But then the managers had to delve deeply into the reams of MBA output, editing, emending, and expanding, which also sucked up valuable managerial time. So the great promise of CASE has yet to be realized.

Also in the mid-1980s, the PC was moving beyond personal productivity tools such as spreadsheets and word processing and into the realm of departmental applications. Novell and Banyan began delivering LAN technologies that actually worked most of the time, which in turn allowed departmental users to share not only devices but information and applications in an emerging two-tiered client-server environment. By the late 1980s, more powerful PCs and LAN servers made client-server departmental applications a viable alternative to some centralized IS functions. By 1990 the PC and LAN price points had dropped to within the signatory authority of most corporate operational vice presidents, and a large and growing community of Visual Basic (and other 4GL) programmers were willing to develop applications reasonably cheaply on contract.

No longer did users need to go through the litany of the IS department saying how what was wanted could not be done, not in the time frame we needed or within the resources budgeted. Users could just get themselves a LAN server and a Visual Basic guru and build it on their own. And that's just what many line-of-business and operational managers started doing.

There were (and are) two serious consequences of this phenomenon. First, most of the business applications followed a simplistic and mostly "*un*informed" development cycle. Business managers would outline the process they wanted to improve or a new information application they thought would improve competitive capabilities. Developers would lash together a prototype application, populate a database with some sample data, then demonstrate the prototype. After a couple of adjustments, when the business managers felt they had seen what they wanted, the developers went off to build the real application.

The managers got quick if not instant gratification from the prototype demonstrations and expected the application to be deployed in short order and at low cost. But before they could barely finish patting themselves on their backs, the project usually fell behind schedule and crept increasingly over budget. Too often, the deployed application either did not live up to expectations or business or organizational conditions had changed, making it inappropriate or even irrelevant. Operational managers began learning that building and demonstrating a prototype was one thing, and building and deploying a business application—on time and on budget—is quite another.

The second problem with independently developed departmental applications, even if they come in on time and on budget and do what they are intended to do, is that they are almost never a part of the organization's larger IT infrastructure. Departmental applications tend to be isolated from everything else, creating separate islands of information and disparate business processes. Unfortunately, at the end of the 1990s probably every major organization has at least a few of the pesky isolated departmental applications.

Web-based technologies will take us a long way toward remedying these fragmented applications and integrating them into the IT infrastructure. Chapter 12 looks at a new software infrastructure technology, application servers, that will play a key role in achieving that integration. A whole new class of enabling technologies is emerging specifically to improve and extend the development of web applications, applications that assume the existence of an Internet harmonious network, of World Wide Web capabilities, and of enterprise-level components like storage area networks.

Building a web application with Java or similar enabling technologies is one thing. Testing its scaleability to proportions required by the World Wide Web is another. Tools to do this, such as SilkControl from Eventus/Segue, are inching over the horizon. It is probably too early to call this new generation of enabling technologies that do not simply generate code and programs but ensure flexibility and robustness for Web applications 5GLs, but someone is bound to do so soon.

THE JAVA WARS, OR WILL TECHNOLOGY COMPANIES EVER GROW UP?

Sun Microsystems shipped the first version of Java in January 1996, and the world of application development has never been the same. Java, like most breakthrough ideas, is a rather simple concept. Write a software program once and let it run on any microprocessor, regardless of processor type or operating system. Programmers could produce and maintain programs that really did not care what kinds of clients or servers they ran on. And Java was Internet and web ready. Java programs could run on small clients (network computers and even cellular phones) as well as on large servers, including mainframes. Java was the *ne plus ultra* in openness, scaleability, and flexibility. And guess who was upset by that? Microsoft was so upset it licensed Java from Sun Microsystems, then gave it some major proprietary tweaks so its version would run only on Microsoft Windows clients and servers.

But Java held too much promise for developers and businesses to be stifled by internal industry rivalries. U.S. federal courts made Microsoft adhere to Sun's Java specifications, at least for the time being. Microsoft undoubtedly will come up with a reverse-engineered Java clone that will come bundled with its other development tools, so that any developer using Visual Basic or Visual C++ will already have a Microsoft clone of Java (which runs only on Windows clients and servers).

So here we have an enabling technology that can be all things to all users and deliver rapidly developed, sophisticated Web-enabled business applications over the Internet to the smallest microprocessor-based appliance and the largest mainframe computers. Java's programming language is very similar to C++, so programmers can learn it easily. (Today Java is the most widely taught programming language.) Java, in fact, represents the next generation of programming languages. But Sun left out one thing: Java does not need a Microsoft operating system to deliver applications and information to users. It only needs a browser. The Java wars are actually a larger and more important issue than the browser embedding issues that are at the heart of the U.S. Department of Justice's case against Microsoft.

Unfortunately, the computer industry's ingrained propensity for proprietary technologies which serve to lock customers in has fragmented the Java effort even further. There is a clone called Kaffe from Transvirtual Technologies in Berkeley, California. There is one called Chai from Hewlett-Packard. Thirteen smaller software companies have developed "real-time" versions of Java and their own consortium. So we have what some high-tech watchers are calling "Unix redux."[1] Unix was implemented slightly differently by each Unix platform provider, which gave Microsoft NT Server the window of opportunity it needed to achieve rapid broad-market penetration. While Sun, H-P, IBM, Novell, and the dozen or so other smaller software companies fragment Java, Microsoft can sit back and proffer its own Java clone with little or no real competition. Yet Sun, IBM, and Oracle seem committed to Sun's version of Java. If those three, aided by AOL/Netscape, can row the Java boat in the same direction, the Microsofties in Redmond may be in for a tough fight.

Bottom line is that the Java wars are not in the interest of customers, the business executives who are reading this book. But, ironically, they illustrate the benefits of publicly funded research and development divorced from the interests of technology companies.

GREAT RAPID DEVELOPMENT RACE

One last area of enabling technologies deserves a brief discussion, if only because it may turn up one day on a top-level executive's desk for budget approval. And that is something called Enterprise Rapid Application Development (ERAD). Like integrated CASE in the late 1980s, ERAD offers a lot of promise but is largely untested in enterprise combat conditions. Moreover, it can be confused with earlier rapid application development (RAD) tools that essentially allowed developers to piece together program components according to user-defined requirements for business applications, or with component-based development that developers could use in conjunction with line coding to build client-server applications. All 4GLs are really RAD tools.

ERAD promises to reduce server-side programming chores further and to manage the distributed development of large applications. This last capability will prove useful to companies with distributed development environments, that is, programmers working on the same development project in geographically remote sites. As a hypothetical example, consider a new commercial banking application, the cornerstone of a firm's competitive global strategy, that is being developed by a team of programmers located at the firm's headquarters in New York, at the communications center in Kansas City, and at a technology subsidiary in New Delhi, India. ERAD promises to make management of far-flung development efforts more efficient, delivering robust business applications faster and at lower cost.

The kicker is that ERAD will be expensive to license in personnel and services. And it may not pay off. If not, the businesses depending on new ERAD business solutions will be hurt the most. Top-level executives who have not considered carefully the business risk involved with massive new enabling technologies like ERAD leave themselves highly exposed.

EXECUTIVE DECISION FACTORS

For the present, top-level business executives should bear in mind three things. First, enabling technologies are tools that build applications and should be standardized throughout an organization. Tools are not like ball-point pens; developers should not select the 4GL they will use according to their own personal preferences. Not only does that perpetuate fragmented IT infrastructures, but it increases overall IT costs by expanding the redundancy of skill sets needed to develop and support applications. Central IS needs the authority to standardize enabling technologies and to enforce those standards, even if enforcement means putting rogue operational managers on the hot seat. Operational managers need always to innovate their processes and their uses of information as raw material, but they need to do that using corporate standards, unless they can prove that corporate standards are not workable. And the burden of proof must be on the business manager who wants to leap outside the standards. Only top-level management can establish that type of managerial culture. IS executives are mostly powerless unless board-level officers participate.

Second, top-level executives should understand the broad scope of application development and support cycles. They need to know that software development is a rigorous process that requires detailed planning and design, performance and scaleability testing, information and network integration, and close management of all processes.

Finally, top-level executives should encourage central IS to search constantly for new enabling technologies and to scrutinize their own established standards, being always on the lookout for emerging technologies that can enable next generations of business applications faster and at lower cost. The hidden cost of enabling technologies is not so much the cost of the tools themselves but of the skill sets required to use the technologies effectively and efficiently. Programmer costs, in real dollars, actually have not gone up since the 1960s. Compared to the quantity of computer code generated and the business capabilities enabled by applications of all kinds, programmer costs probably have declined in real dollars. Users are getting a good deal more for about the same money. But, as with any other area of the software infrastructure, while fewer software professionals who use more efficient software tools may be needed, the best, most competent people should be hired, and they should be very well led and managed.

Again, the larger costs of the IT infrastructure are people costs. Top-level executives must be directly involved if not directly responsible for the quality and capability of the people in their IS functions, beginning with the chief information officer (CIO) and chief technology officer (CTO). If the CIO or CTO is not reporting directly to the CEO, why not? There are a number of valid reasons why this might occur, but for every legitimate reason there are a half-dozen bogus, outdated, and bureaucratic reasons offered up. IT infrastructures are so vital to the success and health of any organization that CEOs need a close and comfortable working relationship with their CIOs and CTOs.

It is in the area of enabling technologies where the effects and efforts of a CIO and central IS are most keenly felt. It is relatively easy for a CEO and his or her executive committee to standardize information storage and manipulation. But the proliferation of enabling technologies and variety of tasks they perform makes this jungle more difficult to manage. Pick the right people, give them clear guidelines and authority to act, then monitor their performance. But above all, do not hesitate to get close to the action, ask questions, learn and adapt, and direct.

Networked information, the most powerful force business has ever known, is being unleashed globally for organizations both large and small. And if you doubt that, think back to October 1997 when the baht fluttered in Bangkok and the Hong Kong dollar fidgeted, then financial markets crashed in successive time zones moving westward to Wall Street. That was not money moving around the globe. That was networked information about money moving instantaneously around the globe. Enabling technologies quite literally determine the behavior of the bits and bytes of information that in turn determine the success, or lack thereof, of every modern organization.

Over the next half decade enabling technologies will evolve even further and faster. Right now leading edge companies are using advancing technologies like neural networks, evolutionary algorithms, and recursive information architectures to push the application envelope beyond where many theoreticians believed possible just five years ago. As we move from the age of the smart machine to the truly intelligent machine, enabling technologies will change rapidly. Only one thing is certain—they will always ultimately direct the flow of information and electricity, unless or until future machines use something other than electricity.

NOTE

1. *Forbes,* January 11, 1999, p. 111.

CHAPTER 11

Applications

The mechanics of running a business are not very
complicated when you get down to essentials. You have to make
some stuff and sell it to someone for more than it cost you. That's
about all there is to it, except for a few million details.
—JOHN L. McCAFFREY, former president, International Harvester

VISIBLE SURFACES OF THE INFORMATION
TECHNOLOGY INFRASTRUCTURE

Everything discussed to this point has laid the foundation for business applications. Business applications have been defined as software that is purposely built to accomplish any given set of business functions, from accounting to manufacturing, from customer care and sales force automation to on-line shopping and business intelligence. Commercial applications ultimately have something to do with the interchange of value between or among people. These applications extend and enhance that value interchange; they create new value while lowering the cost of value creation, raising profitability and increasing shareholder wealth. Tall orders, but that is exactly what they can do. Exhibit 11.1 illustrates the various categories of applications discussed in this chapter.

There is little question that information technologies are transforming the nature of business itself and our economy in general. One *Business-Week* survey estimates that the new networked information economy was directly responsible for 37 percent of all new jobs created during 1998. According to a U.S. Department of Commerce study, the continually

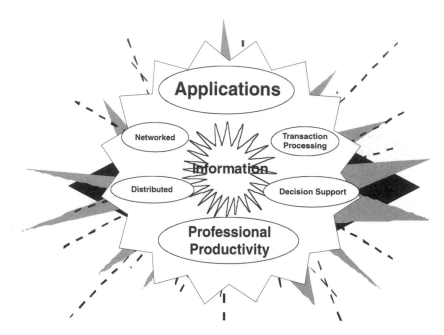

Exhibit 11.1   Business Application Technologies

decreasing prices of information technology lowered inflation by one full percentage point, counterbalancing the rise in prices in other industries: "Without the contribution of the IT sector, overall inflation, at 2.0 percent, would have been 3.1 percent in 1997."[1] Just as important, the investment community, particularly in the United States, is beginning to understand that deflation can be beneficial to an economy. The IT sector continues to demonstrate that significant and prolonged deflation can characterize a vital and healthy industry and the economy to which it contributes. Moreover, what Wall Street pundits generally see as a temporary and puzzling phenomenon in the wildly popular Internet stocks may perhaps be indicative of a larger and deeper shift among investors who seem to show more confidence in companies' long-term potential than in short-term quarterly performance.

Technology in general has always been an agent of transformation, from the first stone-edge ax to the Internet and World Wide Web. In recent years, entirely new businesses have emerged and rapidly evolved based on networked information technologies. Some have grown in less than half a decade from inspired business vision to billions of dollars in transactions and tens of billions of dollars in market capitalization. New relationships among businesses and customers and among government organizations and constituents are evolving, and, perhaps even more surprisingly, new, dynamic and more profitable relationships are occurring among business organizations themselves. All of this is directly attributable to networked information technologies and the new business applications they enable.

All the components that make up commercial IT infrastructures pull together to support the business applications, which in turn extend and enhance the efforts of business professionals, from file clerks to chief executive officers (CEOs).

FROM BATCH PROCESSING TO ON-LINE TRANSACTIONS TO TOMORROW

Recall those 80-column punch cards discussed in Chapter 9, the real culprits behind the Year 2000 bug. In many ways, those 80-column cards represent the epitome of batch processing—everything was done in batches. Clerks took transmittal forms and original paper transactions, *batched* them together, and hand carried them to be keypunched and verified in *batches.* Then transactions on 80-column cards were carried to the computer room, where the cards were then fed into card readers in *batches,* processed by the computer in *batches,* then finally results were printed out on "green bar" paper in *batches.* Many steps and many people were involved to move from actual transaction to processed result.

Things began to change in the 1970s with the introduction of character and block mode cathode ray tube (CRT) screens. Operators could enter information directly onto an electronic form displayed on the screen, verify and correct the information visually, then send it electronically to the computer to be processed in, guess what, *batch* mode. Even though the technology had introduced new capabilities that eliminated several of the steps and a few of the intervening people between transaction input and processed output, applications were still *batch* oriented. Why? Because that is the way they were always done. Although the technology for interactive business applications was available early in the 1970s, batch-mode applications persisted well into the 1980s, when on-line transaction processing (OLTP) applications began eclipsing batch processing.

All this illustrates a law of commercial computing: *Hardware technology capabilities will always streak ahead of software technology capabilities, which in turn will always evolve faster than the commercial use of these advancing technologies in business applications.* And this is one of the gaps this book is urging business leaders to shrink by being more aware of emerging and evolving information technologies. If OLTP technology was available ten years before businesses really started using it, imagine what would have happened if one company had had the foresight and courage to implement OLTP technologies just five years ahead of its competitors. The pace of IT evolution and of business change has stepped up dramatically with Internet time.

Scientists and engineers are usually the first to take advantage of hardware and software innovations, while commercial applications of evolving technologies usually lag behind by half a decade or more. This plodding tendency of commercial applications can be directly attributed to the shortcomings of business managers and top-level executives. Scientists and engineers approach their work with vastly more innovative mind-sets than do most business professionals; scientists and engineers are by nature more curious, more inventive than are most business professionals, and have a general desire to keep pushing the envelope, so to speak. Most business professionals are conservative by nature; maintaining the status quo and satisfying quarterly earnings expectations have traditionally required minimum innovation from them. Of course there are breakthrough pioneers among business leaders who are revered and imitated, but they come along infrequently, a Richard Branson here, a Ted Turner or a Larry Ellison there.

Even in the advertising trade, a supposedly more creative business pursuit, there is surprisingly little real innovation. Take, for example, the world's most watched televised event since the first Apollo moon landing, the Super Bowl. Several years ago many people began focusing on the commercials, since the games themselves were usually so boring. Now the commercials are getting to be as boring as most of the games. Exceptions to that rule for Super Bowl XXXIII, which aired January 31, 1999, were two commercials from two on-line companies, Monster.com and Hotjob.com. Innovation seems to be a fundamental part of only one business culture, the high-tech industry itself. Perhaps that is due in part to availability of venture capital, which encourages innovation. It is also probably partly due to the fact that most high-tech innovators are engineers of one type or another. But all of us are a part of the IT industry; in fact, the rest of us are the most important participants in the IT industry. We live and work in a dynamic era of change and progress, like none other before it. The artist Ben Shahn observed, "Ever since I could remember, I'd wished I'd been lucky enough to be alive at a great time— when something big was going on, like a crucifixion. And suddenly I realized I was."[2] Unfortunately Shahn died in 1969. Imagine what he would have thought were he alive today.

The historical dearth of innovation among business leaders is beginning to show signs of ending. A global information and knowledge-based economy seems to be creating something akin to what Ilya Prigogine calls a state of nonequilibrium.[3] Complex system thinkers and chaos theory tell us that states of nonequilibrium tend to evolve toward new states of equilibrium, and that these shifts occur not gradually but with sudden disruption. In short, the game is changing, and just as with any other sudden evolutionary shift, those game players who can innovate and adapt will survive and thrive. Those who cannot will become extinct.

The ability of business to transform technology into commercial value through the application and interchange of information should dwarf anything produced by the industrial era. And the key to it all is using the current application of technology by top-level business executives. This new breed of business executive does not merely use what technology providers sell but can determine and direct combinations of technologies that will expand organizational capabilities. These IT-savvy executives have a firm grasp of a broad range of IT issues and capabilities. They can communicate decisively with their own internal IS managers and also with technology and service providers in order to build better and increasingly innovative business processes with newer and more powerful technologies.

Ray Kurzweil, inventor and futurist, predicts that by 2009, a $1,000 PC will perform 1 trillion calculations per second, and 10 years after that, a $1,000 PC will equal the processing power of the human brain (about 20 million billion calculations per second). Ten years later, in 2029, a $1,000 PC will have the processing power of 1,000 human brains. That is hardware capability. Software may take a good deal longer. And it probably will not be until the last third of the twenty-first century before business applications harness this sort of power.

What if a very bright, very innovative business leader applied the technology Kurzweil is predicting and did it just a couple of years ahead of the curve? That would probably make Fred Smith's innovation of overnight delivery services and logistic management and Jeff Bezos's innovation of on-line retailing seem to be interesting but minor accomplishments.

When the first group of new 64-bit processors arrived in the early 1990s (Digital Alpha chips), some observers estimated that software would advance at the rate of about one bit per year, meaning that enabling technologies would not take full advantage of 64 bits of information processing until roughly 2020. And so far that prediction seems to be on track.

Technology is almost invariably capable of doing more at any given time than business thinkers are capable of directing it to do. So when computer technologies were first introduced to business processes, previously manual processes, like customer billing, were automated. Before every manual business process could be automated, along came relational databases, PCs, and local area networks, so financial managers and computer developers thought, "Gee, let's create a client-server architecture and build applications that run on desktops but share RDBMSs on servers. That way clerks could do input, verification, correction, processing, and output right there at their desktops, all the while sharing the common databases."

Then along comes the commercialization of the Internet and some really nifty capabilities like the World Wide Web and Web browsers, which germinate *n*-tiered architectures—and all of this, from RDBMSs, PCs, LANs and client-server to Internet, Web, and *n*-tiered architectures happens in less than ten years. Replacing LANs with intranets means, for one thing, that a work group no longer needs to be defined by physical proximity. LANs have physical restrictions; the wire tying everyone together is just so many meters in length. Intranet work groups can be defined by groups of interest and endeavor. With an intranet, members of a work group can be disbursed geographically around the globe. That is a major paradigm shift for most organizations. But then with Internet technologies, shift happens.[4]

But how much have business applications changed? Well, SAP, PeopleSoft, and others did introduce financial, human resource, and manufacturing applications in the early 1990s that were designed for client-server architectures. These moved forward during the mid-1990s to begin providing integrated ERP environments, which today more than two-thirds of businesses consider to be their most strategic computing investment. Yet even these contemporary ERP systems are lagging behind the technology curve. Most need to be retrofitted for the Internet and web.

Now that the Internet and web have entered into the mix, commercial application providers are beginning to display a bit of out-of-the-box thinking. They are racing to enable their products with web and intranet/extranet functionality, which in turn leads these applications into new possibilities that reach far beyond the automation of transactional processes. During the first half decade of the twenty-first century, most businesses will view the applications they are running on the web and Internet, outside their organizational firewalls, as more important to the success and ongoing vitality of their business than ERP applications currently running inside those corporate firewalls. For example, Delta Airlines invested $50 million in a contract with a small, $22 million-a-year company, iXL, to marry web interface design with high-volume transaction processing. Says Delta chief information officer (CIO) Charles Feld, "We're going to be an electronic airline—everything from a cultural point of view to customer service to the way we communicate inside."[5]

Many software vendors like to distinguish between two types of applications, as "front office" and "back office." Back-office applications are the traditional ERP applications, such as accounting and manufacturing, that customers never see, much less touch. Front-office applications, also broadly called customer relationship management (CRM) or enterprise relationship management (ERM) by application providers, get closer to the customer with applications like customer service, sales force automation, marketing resource management. There are several problems with this distinction between front office and back office. As we become more and more interconnected via the Internet and web, more and more boundaries begin to blur. For example, users can go to Amazon.com and look up their own account, check the status of any order (Amazon.com retains a six-month order history for every customer), and change their profile and preferences (users can alter information in their own customer files). Those are all traditionally back-office functions, but users are touching them as customers.

Let us broaden this a bit and look at supply chain management, which not only allows constituents of the supply chain to participate in informational activities that traditionally have been internal to an organization but demands it. The organization still controls the transactions, but the information surrounding those transactions must be accessible and even malleable by suppliers, the constituency of the supply chain. At the end of the twentieth century, users have not traveled very far at all down the road of electronic commerce or e-business yet. Some new vistas are beginning to open. In five years, people are likely to look back on twentieth-century e-commerce somewhat the way today's airline pilots look back on the planes of the late 1920s.

When it comes to what we think of as business applications, there are no solutions; there are only temporary fixes. Take, for example, the enormous rush among large companies to convert aging financial and manufacturing systems to ERP systems during the last two-thirds of the 1990s. Individual companies spent huge amounts to implement ERP using SAP, PeopleSoft, Baan, Oracle, and other platforms, despite the fact that ERP may already be an antiquated model.

While we do not need to throw out newly deployed SAP financial applications just yet, we can be virtually assured of one thing: By about 2005, users will look critically at those ERP applications, and what will stand out will be inadequacies and obstacles. These applications were built around 1980s' business practices and assumptions and were consistent with economic conditions of the industrial era. Yet economic conditions are rapidly changing.

So what are business executives to do about business applications? For one thing, we need to keep in mind that even the best business applications address problems that only business executives themselves can define. If problems can be defined based only on the way things have been done before, then applications implemented will solve only yesterday's problems. By anticipating tomorrow's realities, then we might be able to begin building application foundations that will help solve tomorrow's problems when they arrive and give us the flexibility to future changes.

That brings us full circle back to the IT infrastructure itself. Without a solid foundation, without a robust, flexible, and open IT infrastructure, an organization's future is limited. No business application by itself can provide a cure-all for the future. And if we do not build a solid, flexible and open IT infrastructure that can support whatever new business processes and directions we might devise, our organizations will be unable to evolve, survive, and thrive.

Business applications address real and well-defined problems and can provide known advantages, but we must ensure that those applications are an integrated part of the IT infrastructure that can evolve and adapt to meet new unimagined challenges. Standardizing information management systems and enabling technologies will go a long way in assuring the viability of an organization's IT infrastructure. The next chapter discusses application servers and middleware, which will play important roles as organizations move forward and adapt to new economic conditions and business demands. But for the moment, keep in mind that without that robust, flexible, and open IT infrastructure supporting the business applications, any business application is likely to be obsolete before the ink is dry on the vendor's order form. Now let us take a brief tour of the various categories of business applications, starting with on-line transaction processing.

ON-LINE TRANSACTION PROCESSING APPLICATIONS

The good news is that the fundamentals of conducting business are not likely to change very rapidly. Accounts payable is likely to be accounts payable for a long while. Accounts receivable is likely to be A/R for a while. What goes on in the back office will not change as rapidly as what goes on in the front office. So we are not likely to need to tinker much with internal workings of on-line analytical processing (OLTP). What is changing is how the information generated by on-line transactions will be used.

Airline frequent flyer programs are good examples of using transactions to extend and enhance customer loyalty. American Airlines introduced the American Advantage program in the early 1980s, and air travel experience has not been the same since. To institute a frequent flyer program, all an airline had to do was to add a member identification field (a frequent flyer number) in each transaction record and tie it to a rather straightforward application form. The accumulation of miles and points began very quickly to establish and perpetuate customer loyalty; then the frequent flyer information itself became a valuable commodity and a means of generating more wealth for the AMR Corporation. The transactional information was there all along, clicking away and accumulating; it just needed a small tweak to become accessible and valuable, to the customer, to the company, and to other businesses.

OLTP applications must be viewed not just as a means of getting customer bills out faster and at a lower cost, but also as a continually growing repository of potentially valuable information, valuable in new ways for our organization, for our customers, and for other businesses as well.

BUSINESS INTELLIGENCE APPLICATIONS

According to Peter Drucker, technology has not had the impact on business that many observers and managers had anticipated because IT mostly focused on operational tasks, such as asset preservation or cost control, which are not executive tasks and do not lead to business success, which is "based on something totally different, the creation of value and wealth." Executives have not used technology "because it has not provided the information they need for *their own tasks.*"[6] A major premise of this book is that executives need to actively engage in technology issues because information is at the heart of creating value and wealth today. And Drucker is right about technology not providing executives the information they need to perform their own tasks—at least until recently. That's what business intelligence systems (BISs) are aimed at doing.

In many ways business intelligence systems represent the new generation of what used to be called "decision support systems." However, they bring a whole lot more capability and power to the party than their forerunners did. For one thing, BIS can use information gleaned from OLTP applications in conjunction with OLAP tools as well all sorts of external and internal information residing on extranet and intranet nodes within and outside of organizations.

Data warehouses and data marts are a part of the broader functionality of BIS. These can be rather straightforward, such as a data warehouse containing all the ticketing transactions for a particular airline, a data mart containing just the travel information of the airline's frequent flyers, or just the information of the airline's elite levels of frequent flyers. Or they can be very elaborate, extracting and transforming data from a number of internal and external resources.

Currently available OLAP and BIS tools require a good deal of training and familiarity. Executives and managers need to think through what kinds of intelligence they would like to see on a more or less regular and repetitive basis from BIS. In a few years enabling technologies should have evolved to the point that business executives themselves can use them to slice and dice information on an ad hoc basis. Savvy business executives should be demanding this sort of capability now from their internal IS managers and from BIS vendors. The more relentlessly business executives push IS and technology providers, the more likely business executives are to get what they want and need.

BIS and data warehousing can appear deceptively simple. The business benefits—including keener customer knowledge, more responsive products and services, enhanced competitive advantages, increased sales, and better margins—can make top-level executives salivate. But the reality is often different. These projects involve major investments—the average data warehousing project costs roughly $2 million just to start, and frequently ends up costing tens of millions of dollars before it is productive. They present prodigious technical challenges even for experienced IS professionals, and they run into the hierarchical culture's resistance to sharing information and knowledge. The discouraging reality is that as many as half of all data warehousing projects fail in their first attempt, and some fail on their second attempt as well. And each attempt can take up to a year to work itself up to failure or partial success.

However, when they do succeed, data warehousing projects can deliver not just promised benefits but entirely new levels of business capabilities. Fleet Financial Group invested $28.1 million in a data warehouse project that ran eight months beyond its projected deadline but actually came in $10 million under budget. Management is now projecting a return of $100 million within three years of initial project completion. A senior vice president for Fleet says, "The warehouse itself doesn't make money. It's the decisions that the warehouse helps you make that make the money."[7]

It is not uncommon for long-term costs to run upward of $100 million for a data warehouse, nor is it uncommon for data warehousing projects to enable business decisions that directly generate $100 million in additional annual business revenues. It is a high-stakes game that relies more on the perspicacity, commitment, and involvement of top-level executives than anything else. It also helps a great deal to select the right partners, especially consulting organizations with a data warehousing track record in your industry.

Top-level executives need to understand their own roles in BIS and data warehousing. First, they need to envision the range of business capabilities that internal transactional information, when sorted and ordered, could deliver to the organization—better customer understanding, margin improvements, faster time-to-market with improved, more competitive products and services, customer retention and market expansion, and a multitude of other benefits limited only by the vision and imagination of the top executives themselves. In short, imagine the possible, draw what-if scenarios, engage the organization's IS professionals, and direct them to explore ways of getting from present point to future possibilities.

Top-level executives also must assume responsibility for building a knowledge- and information-sharing culture within their organizations. In this area in particular, there are no substitutes for leadership, not just by edict and example but through ongoing involvement. Business intelligence systems generally deliver less than satisfactory results in organizations whose culture is one of information hoarding rather than information sharing. It is our modern-day equivalent of the old garbage-in, garbage-out axiom.

In a networked information economy, hierarchical structures tend to disable organizations of all sizes. If there is a single evolutionary change executives should understand and support that change is from hierarchical structures where authority is power and where information and knowledge is hoarded, to networked organizational cultures where influence is power and knowledge and information are shared, and not strictly because of monetary incentives but as a result of being a contributing member of a networked organization. If flocks of birds in flight and colonies of bacteria can do it, surely business people can do it. In fact, information sharing through networks is part of our fundamental human nature. And it is the responsibility of top-level executives to lead their organizations toward networked structures. More responsive business intelligence systems and better data warehouses will be delivering new levels of competitive capabilities for information-sharing organizational cultures.

Throughout the high-tech industry itself, flatter, networked organizational structures are the norm rather than the exception, a phenomenon that is becoming more and more characteristic of knowledge-based companies in general. There tends to be fewer layers of hierarchical management and authority between knowledge workers—the individual professional contributors—and top-level management—the "suits." It is not a matter of eliminating a hierarchy of management completely. Rather it is a matter of power being derived from influence in a networked culture rather than from authority in a traditional hierarchical organization. The need for top-level executives and senior managers does not disappear, but their roles shift from one of power and authority to responsibility and accountability. Top executives continue to remain responsible, through their boards of directors, to the company's shareholders, who provide the capital, the means of production. And this becomes even more meaningful when we consider the fact that at the end of the twentieth century, shareholders are, by and large, the knowledge workers themselves, the individual contributors who create and deliver value for the company's customers.

And do not be tricked by vendors claiming that their lower-cost data marts are a viable solution to higher-cost data warehouses. While data marts initially may cost as much as 70 to 80 percent less, they create another problem. Unless carefully planned and controlled by central IS, data marts create and perpetuate isolated and incompatible pockets of business intelligence. This occurs especially when data marts initially costing less than $100,000 total start popping up in departments, with each department using different databases and different sets of analytical tools. As data marts multiply, they frequently lead to "a chaos of incompatible technologies, duplicate data and an overwhelming demand for systems maintenance."[8]

Eventually the information residing in these data marts will need to be gathered into at least a networked virtual data warehouse in order to serve the organization as a whole. Doing so may require dismantling the data marts and starting all over from scratch. Not only does that effort waste large amounts of money, it wastes something even more valuable: time. And in Internet time, organizations that squander time can die.

Finally, while a robust, flexible, scaleable, and open IT infrastructure provides the foundation for all business applications, no application depends so intimately for its success on a sound IT infrastructure as do business intelligence systems, decision support, and data warehousing. If an organization, through the concerned, informed, and prudent governance of its top-level executives, has standardized its information management systems and its enabling technologies, if it has invested well in its networking infrastructure and its platform technologies, and if it has managed well its criteria for openness and flexibility, the absolute cost of implementing BIS, including data warehouses, will be lower, and the probability of success of those projects will be higher—and projects will get done a lot faster.

STRATEGIC PLANNING APPLICATIONS

A new class of business intelligence applications, variously called strategic enterprise management or enterprise performance management, is beginning to emerge and hold substantial promise for top-level executives and their managers. These applications aim to give organizational strategists ways of peering into the future while arraying key business metrics that should monitor and help determine progress, or the lack thereof, toward fulfilling a given strategy. These off-the-shelf analytic applications are cutting edge (in 1999), and as they see broader use among business executives, they should evolve and mature.

Several mainstream ERP providers have announced analytic programs. PeopleSoft began shipping its Enterprise Performance Measurement package in 1999. SAP has announced its business warehouse analytic package. Oracle has announced four business analysis applications: Balanced Scorecard establishes performance metrics for strategic plans, and activity-based management uses cost information to help determine business decisions. Both should be available during 1999. Coming in 2000 from Oracle are Strategy Formulation, which helps devise global business strategies, and Value Based Management, which gives executives an investment community perspective of their organization.

Business intelligence tools from Gentia (U.K.), Omnivista Software, and Hyperion offer more business analysis and strategic planning. But this is a nascent area of software specialization and is not expected to pass the $500 million market mark until sometime after 2000. Like many new technologies and extensions of existing technologies, strategic planning and business analysis applications offer alluring capabilities if not executive nirvanas. These applications will need a good deal of real customer testing before their functionality and usability becomes broadly accepted.

These strategic planning applications may provide a viable alternative to large in-house staffs of dedicated MBAs crunching strategic data into executive strategy reports and white papers. And they could give smaller and medium-size organizations strategic planning and verification capabilities that they have never before had. This is one of the areas alluded to in the second shrinking-the-gap analogy. Top executives need to be constantly aware of these kinds of developments and be ready to adopt the technologies at the earliest appropriate moment. Early adopters will encounter the pitfalls and hurdles presented by most newly emerging technologies, but they also will have opportunities to influence the direction these products take as the technologies evolve. It may be worthwhile for some organizations to establish a pilot project team of business analysts, strategic planners, and an IS professional (particularly one experienced in data warehousing) and charge the team with road testing these new executive productivity tools and monitoring progress and experiences.

Two things need to be kept in mind here. First, these emerging "executive productivity" applications are of value only if they are sitting atop a well-built and maintained IT infrastructure. These applications suck up information from a variety of resources, chiefly from ERP and CRM applications, which in turn should be sitting atop robust and standardized IMSs. If ERP applications and other relevant organizational applications are not in place and functional, and if the IMSs are shabby and loosely linked, the best strategic planning application will give top-level executives a mish-mash of irrelevant information.

Second, an off-the-shelf strategic planning application may provide a baseline for top-level managers and may well eliminate some strategic staffing costs, but it is unlikely to deliver any silver bullets that magically accelerate an organization beyond its competition. In fact, the competition is very likely to be using the same or similar tools. These applications may make top-level strategic activities more efficient, but they probably will not render strategic decision making any less difficult than it is today. They may give executives some empirical indicators or verifiers, but they will not, at least in the very near future, supplant executive experience and insight, intuition, and plain old gut feel.

PROFESSIONAL PRODUCTIVITY APPLICATIONS

Professional productivity applications are usually extensions of professional productivity tools, such as computer-aided design or magnetic resonance imaging, but specifically customized and packaged for a targeted professional task. Some of the most innovative uses of emerging technology pop up first in these areas. For one thing, some of the brightest professionals in the most demanding fields are users of these technologies. They are typically out-of-box thinkers and may come up with some screwball ideas that often pay off well for entire organizations and sometimes even transform entire industries.

If an organization has pockets of professionals who could use professional productivity applications, executives should encourage active and ongoing evaluation of those applications. Typically these areas have been stand-alone or locally networked. Large strides in Internet and web capabilities probably will transform professional productivity applications coming from technology providers as well as from professional associations and support organizations. And advances in professional productivity applications and the networked information resources associated with them should be global as well as national.

DISTRIBUTED AND NETWORKED APPLICATIONS

Distributed and networked applications are discussed together because they resemble one another in many ways. Distributed applications generally refer to a class of business applications used by organizations with geographically remote sites. The applications may have centralized functions, such as central data stores containing all customer information or centralized billing or customer services, along with remote applications, such as order entry, local service parts inventories, or branch sales forecasting and tracking. Generally these distributed applications run on proprietary networks and are strictly for internal organizational use. Sun Microsystems was one of the first major companies to erect a globally distributed ERP environment, using Oracle financial and manufacturing applications and its own high-end Unix servers. Others have followed closely on Sun's heels, and still more will follow now that Internet technologies make distributed applications more affordable from a networking perspective and lower-cost, more powerful commodity hardware makes it more feasible from a platform perspective.

Networked applications are built not just with geographical remoteness in mind but with the notion that the network is the computer. This different mind-set involves several basic assumptions. First, information and applications could be anywhere on an intranet or an extranet or anywhere on the broad Internet itself. Where any particular application or piece of one may be located physically does not matter to the application user. The same is true of any information resource or, for that matter, any computing resource. It is all transparent to a user.

Typically, distributed applications have been built with a two-tiered client-server paradigm in mind. Networked applications usually are built with a n-tiered client server architecture in mind and assume the existence of and access to an Internet-harmonious network and to the World Wide Web. As a consequence, network applications tend to be more open and accessible to application participants outside of an organization—for example, e-commerce customers at Amazon.com or parts suppliers and product distributors and retailers who are part of a manufacturer's supply chain.

Most distributed applications based on earlier paradigms, specifically two-tiered client-server models, are migrating to networked application environments, which allow them to take advantage of lower-cost Internet-harmonious networking and open up their architectures to new and heterogeneous server capabilities and emerging Internet client technologies, such as the wristcomputer. Fortunately for users of distributed applications, software providers are now delivering a new class of middleware technologies called application servers that smooth this transition from older distributed applications to newer network application environments. The next chapter discusses both middleware and application servers.

EXECUTIVE DECISION FACTORS

First, be skeptical of any business application vendor who wants to demonstrate his or her "solution." What the vendor usually is saying is, "Here's what I have, here's how it is used, here's how you can shoehorn yourself into using it." Such vendors are trying to sell what they have without understanding a firm's problems. The vendors who will really help a firm will not just listen to specific problems/situations but will ask penetrating questions. And they will solve the problem in pieces, for no single vendor has all the pieces. In fact, take it as an encouraging sign if a vendor recommends partnering with additional technology and service providers to come up with a total solution. Only a handful of companies can cover most of the components that make up the software infrastructure, and even then there are holes.

Informed and involved top-level executives can determine the fate of their organizations by viewing the software infrastructure and its components as a breeding ground for innovation, then demanding that technology component and service providers help realize those innovations. In the past, users have done little more with information technologies than what technology providers allowed. Many organizations will continue to take what is offered to them then do the best that they can with it. The organizations that will thrive in an economy based on networked information will view information technologies as a master chef views his or her kitchen, a collection of interrelated components and tools with which to create and deliver value for customers and constituents, thereby creating wealth for themselves and their investors.

Avoid making decisions about business applications based on the preferences or dislikes of clerical or even managerial employees. These systems and the information they generate are the life-blood of a business. They will need to meet business information needs not yet thought about or anticipated. Whether a current A/P manager or a longtime inventory control manager likes one application over another is not the main criteria. How the application integrates with the IT infrastructure and the application's own flexibility and openness are the key criteria.

With applications as with all other parts of the software infrastructure, the largest costs are not the software and hardware, although these can be substantial. The largest costs are people costs, the programmers and the systems managers and the cost of training users, from clerks to vice-presidents. These people costs will shift over time, as software becomes more intelligent, easier to install, and more intuitive to use, but these people costs will not go away any time soon. Business is about people and value interchange among people. As Peter Drucker tells us, companies do not make money; companies make shoes. Money is only a certificate value that we exchange for another value, the shoes. The whole process will always be about people.

NOTES

1. *The Emerging Digital Economy* (Washington, DC: U.S. Department of Commerce, 1998), p. 5.
2. Quoted by Kurzweil, *The Age of the Spiritual Machine* (New York: Viking Press), p. 189.
3. Ilya Prigogine, *The End of Certainty: Time, Chaos, and the New Laws of Nature* (New York: The Free Press, 1997), passim.
4. Paraphrasing Tom Romero, as quoted by Ray Kurzweil, *The Age of the Spiritual Machine* (New York: Viking Press).
5. *InformationWeek,* January 25, 1999. http://www.techweb.com/se/directlink .cgi/IWK19990125S0023.
6. Peter F. Drucker, "The Next Information Revolution," *Forbes ASAP,* August 24, 1998, p. 48.
7. Chris Costanzo, "On Data Warehouses, Their Value is Clear," *American Banker,* March 4, 1999, http://www.americanbanker.com/a0304401.9mb.
8. *CIO Magazine,* January 15, 1999, p. 51.

CHAPTER 12

Middleware, Application Servers, and Systems Management Technologies

You can't always get what you want
But if you try sometimes
You just might find
You get what you need.

—MICK JAGGER, KEITH RICHARDS, *"You Can't Always*
Get What You Want," 1969

TOOLS OF THE TRADE

As Exhibit 12.1 illustrates, middleware, application servers, and systems management have been combined in one chapter, for two reasons. First, these are all very much computer "back-room" functions. While they have a direct and profound impact on information technology (IT) infrastructures and their capabilities, these technologies are the exclusive domain of IS professionals, who usually work in centralized information systems (IS) organizations. Second, there is a bit of overlap among the functionality delivered especially by middleware and application server technologies as well as by some systems management technologies. In fact, it is sometimes a challenge to get software vendors themselves to position their offerings among these various software infrastructure component categories.

181

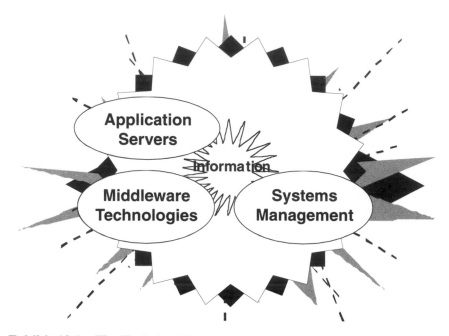

Exhibit 12.1   The Technical Components

As esoteric and obscure as these back-room technologies may be, top-level executives need to be familiar with them. These components not only round out the capabilities of an IT infrastructure but are crucial to the ongoing operational health of the entire infrastructure. Dozens of small yet critical software components ensure that the IT infrastructure remains up and running and delivers its networked information services.

PART 1: MIDDLEWARE TECHNOLOGIES

Let us suppose that, in our current business, we want to do something to-tally new with IT. Unless we are a Jeff Bezos and can build a new enter-prise from scratch and a new IT infrastructure from the ground up, we probably will need to take into account existing applications, databases, and systems. We also will be interconnecting with applications, data, and systems of other organizations, suppliers, and customers.

Broadly speaking, this is where middleware technologies enter the picture. Middleware helps integrate disparate platform technologies, information, and applications. Most especially it helps integrate transactions among different applications. When we do something as simple as swipe a credit card through a magnetic strip reader to get an automated authorization from a credit card company, middleware is making that transaction work.

Middleware, in a fundamental sense, is the virtual hub that directs traffic flow among all sorts of data and applications on disparate systems around the world. Middleware is not snap-in technology. It is purposefully built for a specific set of transactions, and it can get complicated very quickly. It also can deliver a wide range of possibilities and benefits to business processes, especially transaction processes and related information applications. For example, Delta Airlines installed IBM MQSeries messaging middleware that allows a variety of Delta's applications running on different platforms to exchange critical information, such as automatically updating passenger information on a gate agent's screen so that the agent knows when a connecting flight has arrived and does not give away a needed seat to a stand-by passenger.

Middleware is buried deep in the bowels of the software infrastructure, but because of the kinds of things it can do to integrate applications, data, and systems, it can have a very immediate and noticeable effect on customer service. In fact, middleware technologies can provide some of the quickest ways to improve customer service while cutting costs and increasing profits. And what is more, a rather mature and growing middleware industry can provide a plethora of middleware choices and plenty of assistance and support.

That is the good news. The other news is that middleware is not off-the-shelf technology. Middleware technologies are expensive, and the expense is not for software licenses. The introduction of middleware to a software infrastructure requires careful planning and design by an organization's IS staff, which can easily run into hundreds of people-hours. (And these are some of any organization's more expensive people.) The implementation cycle for middleware technologies is some of the trickiest and most expensive around. As most business executives have learned with ERP software, implementation costs quickly surpass licensing costs. That same lesson applies to middleware technologies. And the ongoing care and feeding of middleware integration must be factored in to the costs.

The problem with middleware integration is, just when users get everything integrated and working the way they want it to work, something changes, and they have to go back, check everything, and make sure everything is working properly. Say we have an IBM mainframe running MVS operating system with transactional applications using DB2 data that is integrated with a Sun UltraSpark Unix server supporting an SAP accounting application using Oracle data, which is in turn integrated with a Compaq Win2K server running a Visual Basic application using SQL Server 7.0 data. And these applications are all glued together with middleware technologies. Say Microsoft provides a new, updated release of the Win2K server operating system that fixes a rather pesky bug and has some new performance enhancements that could improve the efficiency and speed of the Visual Basic applications by 50 percent or more. When the new Win2K operating system release is installed, what happens to the middleware integration among all three applications? And can the user afford to take all these systems down for a couple of weeks while everything is tested?

There are some obvious ways around all this. Microsoft will tell users to scrap the mainframe and the Unix applications, redevelop all the applications in Visual Studio, and run everything on Win2K-powered Intel servers. Sun would like for users to do the same thing, but on Solaris-powered Spark servers with Sun Java. And IBM—well, it probably would say that it had told users decades ago never to buy anything but IBM systems. But in most large and midsize organizations, *heterogeneous* platforms, applications, and data exist.

Which brings us back to the issue of standardization, an issue that top-level executives can and should influence, providing strong and consistent IT leadership for their organizations. If users in the example had standardized the databases on either DB2 or Oracle (SQL Server 7.0 does not run on IBM mainframes or on Unix platforms), at least all the information would be integrated. If enabling technologies had been standardized, say on Java, the applications most probably would integrate. Standardizing those two crucial components of software infrastructure—enabling technologies and information management systems—would have taken the strain off the middleware technologies that glue them all together. Installing an update to the Win2K operating systems would probably not disrupt the integration of applications and information among the three platforms. (That is, unless Microsoft's update introduced a new feature that introduced new incompatibilities.)

In the best of all possible worlds, there would be no need for middleware technologies. In the best of all possible worlds, there would be no need for law enforcement agencies. We will never live in the best of all possible worlds, so we will need middleware and we will need police.

For two hours on February 4, 1999, and for another hour or so more the following day, E*TRADE.com's on-line trading site experienced a software glitch that disrupted service to all of its customers. This outage came during an extensive and effective TV advertising campaign that attracted many thousands of new customers to the E*TRADE site. It is not known whether any investors lost money because they could not buy or sell stocks during the outage, but a two- or three-hour outage of this sort could cost individual investors tens of thousands of dollars or more. Naturally, zealous legal guardians filed several lawsuits on behalf of E*TRADE customers. As a result of the software outage, and only two days after the first two-hour disruption, the New York State attorney general announced a formal investigation into the intricacies of on-line trading in general. Just as damaging for E*TRADE would be the loss of customer confidence in its capabilities. E*TRADE has not, as of this writing, revealed the exact cause of the software failure. Bloomberg News services on February 8 reported that E*TRADE Group, the Number 3 on-line broker, had four crashes lasting four and a half hours over three days, part of what the company said was new software that reacted badly to existing software. Probably something being connected by some sort of middleware technology hiccuped. I do not want to single out E*TRADE; Charles Schwabb's on-line trading services experienced similar outages just a few weeks after E*TRADE problems, and indications are that the causes of Schwabb's outages were similar to E*TRADE's.

The encouraging news is that middleware technologies are getting better and better. The cautionary news is that middleware is not bulletproof and needs constant attention from systems managers.

ENTERPRISE APPLICATION INTEGRATION SOFTWARE

Get ready for more enterprise application integration (EAI) software. Let us assume, for sake of illustration, that a company has just emerged from a three-year implementation and rollout of new ERP applications from SAP (or Baan or Oracle or PeopleSoft or someone else). After $100 million of software and consulting expense, it is finally up and running. And sales and marketing people now have that customer relationship management (CRM), also variously referred to as enterprise relationship management (ERM), from Siebel (or Clarify or Vantive or Epiphany or Oracle) with sales force automation, marketing automation, and customer call center management. And the web e-commerce site is up and churning on Netscape's Application Server. Do all of these applications talk with each other? No, not yet. Enterprise application integration software must make that happen.

We need not be discouraged. EAI software is available from several sound vendors, such as Active Software, Crossworlds, and a dozen or more emerging vendors, as well as from more traditional middleware providers like IBM, BEA Systems, Tivoli (IBM), and Computer Associates. And what is being generated is rather impressive. For one thing, these software providers are concentrating not only on achieving better integration among applications and data, but they are also alleviating that pesky problem of potentially disruptive application version changes. Standardized information management systems are a better solution, but users cannot always control which enabling technology an application provider chooses to use as the development environment.

So the news gets a bit better. Users still cannot just snap-in middleware, even with the newer generation of EAI software. It takes some planning, design, and people effort. But it is more streamlined, more predictable, and a bit less expensive overall. Executives still need to interview potential partners very carefully, separate promises from deliverables, and perform careful due diligence. With EAI as with IMS and enabling technologies, users need to select partners carefully and well, for they will be with users for a very long time, and success, or the lack thereof, is directly related to the choice of partners. And price should not be the overriding criteria. Just as with almost every area of technology, acquisition costs among various vendors are highly comparable.

That is not to say that every top-level executive will choose to be intimately involved in these decision cycles. Evaluations and recommendations should be centralized in the IS department where a chief information officer or a chief technology officer can be held accountable for establishing and enforcing organizational standards. But top-level executives, through specific directions or through even a nod or a frown, can communicate to their IS professionals what elements matter most among a variety of criteria. If that communication tells the IS staff to get the cheapest thing they can, that is what they will do. If, however, IS people are told to consider cost, but what matters most is integration, robustness, flexibility and whatever else is on the list of criteria, they will understand. Top-level executives must show that they are involved and that they understand the issues; if they do not, they must ask pertinent questions.

EXECUTIVE DECISION FACTORS

Decision factors surrounding middleware and integration technologies vary in different companies, because these decision factors are directly related to what users want to accomplish. That requires the participation of existing applications, data, and systems, none of which will be alike between any two organizations. If legacy systems and applications running on mainframes must be integrated, business executives need to understand the extent of their commitment to the integration endeavor, not just in terms of money, but in terms of time and human resources as well. In some cases, it is more expedient to scrap the existing systems and build new ones from the ground up. Even if the new applications come from several vendors, the new EAI software will integrate them more readily and will provide more than just a temporary fix. And just as important, that type of wholesale change affords an opportunity to standardize a number of software infrastructure components, especially the information management systems. IMS standardization in and of itself will deliver immediate and ongoing benefits to almost any organization.

Finally, think of middleware technologies not merely as the glue holding disparate systems and applications together but rather as *vision fulfillment* technologies. IT-savvy business executives will begin thinking of more and more ways to create value and wealth with information. Middleware technologies can help realize the new business visions devised by those IT-savvy business executives.

PART 2: APPLICATION SERVERS

Application servers are a kind of middleware that have emerged since the commercial viability of the Internet and Web. There are probably good arguments for treating application servers separately from other middleware technologies, but there is at least one strong argument for discussing them in close proximity. Applications servers are in a direct line of succession from the earliest mainframe middleware technologies. Before middleware concentrated on application and information integration, decades before the term "enterprise application integration" was coined, middleware usually focused on load-balancing among processors and systems in the mainframe and upper-end minicomputer worlds in data centers. Load-balancing simply shifts transaction processes to available computing resources. It is much like the queue in a bank or at an airline ticket counter, where everyone forms a single line and is assigned to the first available teller or ticket agent. The earliest types of middleware managed the processing queue, assigning transactions to available CPU cycles to be processed. These early middleware technologies took on a new and more sophisticated moniker, transaction processing monitors (TPM). About the same time, these TPMs took on responsibility for fail-over management, which is really pretty much an extension of load-balancing. As distributed computing evolved into networked computing, and with computing cycles becoming increasingly abundant and inexpensive, middleware's central focus began shifting to the system, information, and application capabilities discussed earlier in this chapter.

Now comes application servers, which integrate applications and information with the Web and include the functionality of most middleware technologies, such as transaction monitoring and application integration. So where middleware had largely been confined to a defined set of applications internal to an organization's IT infrastructure, or to a specific application shared by a consortium of organizations (e.g., bank ATM transactions), applications servers elevate and expand middleware services to the Internet and web. Web application servers permit an organization's applications to interconnect with the applications and information of other external organizations, customers, and constituents. In this role, application servers provide the essential technology for the formation of extranets and for more flexible and more easily enabled e-commerce activities. And it is precisely this e-commerce integration that will generate trillions of dollars for web-enabled businesses and that will transform the way public service organizations and even governments themselves serve their constituencies.

In a very strict and limited sense, application servers are the middle tier in three-tiered computing models. Recall the two-tiered client server model, where a large portion of an application's business logic is assigned to a "fat" client, generally a fully featured and robust Microsoft-powered and Intel-based PC. Then the shared resources, usually the data and some of the business logic, are assigned to a shared server. This two-tiered client-server model is based on the concept of local area networks, where a work group formed around common business or organizational interests share common resources.

The theoretical model for three-tiered client-server computing places the business logic on a middle-tier application server, with the data on the back-tier server. This delivers several important benefits. First, thin clients and fat clients can use the application, the business logic, since it is accessible through a browser. Not everyone needs to use a more expensive and cumbersome PC (fat client), but they may be able to use less expensive and simpler network devices (thin clients). The earlier three-tier models employed network computers (NCs), which had some intelligence (a good but inexpensive processor, a straight-forward operating, no local storage, a screen, mouse, keyboard, perhaps an optional printer or other output devices). These touted a business benefit of lower acquisition cost (NCs were introduced at under $1,000) and, more important, lower administrative and support costs (easier to set up and easier to maintain). The NCs' first benefit was pretty much obviated when PC manufacturers dramatically lowered their entry-level PC prices to within range of the early NCs. That, of course, did nothing to lessen the costs associated with the implementation and ongoing care and feeding of desktop PCs, nor did it lessen the complexity of using most PCs. But then, most buyers look only at the initial acquisition price tag, not the longer-term costs of ownership.

The debate over the validity and value of NCs persists, but it has become rather stale. Organizations are learning, some more slowly than others, that having a PC on every desk is not just costly but stupid, especially as we move further into Internet and Web-based systems. While certain knowledge workers do need the capabilities of fully configured PCs, just as certain knowledge workers need the capabilities of even more powerful workstations, many other information workers need only a browser and a screen. The paradigm of a fat client on every desk benefits ultimately only one company, Microsoft. The universal fat-client paradigm does nothing for most organizations, except to waste capital resources and to restrict their capabilities.

And keep in mind that just around the corner, so to speak, are highly capable voice-responsive technologies, built around powerful yet small and inexpensive 64-bit technologies. These will allow us to use thin clients we can talk to and that will talk back to us. Some forecasters project that in less than ten years, keyboards will be looked on as outmoded.

Which brings us to the more compelling benefits of three-tiered and *n*-tiered computing models: flexibility, scaleability, and openness. If all we need is a browser in order to access an Internet-harmonious network of applications (business logic) and information (databases), then employees, business partners, customers, and constituents can interact with and derive value from the organization with, say, a wristcomputer, or even through a very tiny microprocessor (a "nanobot") implanted in a human brain. In less than 10 years, we will be wearing computers disguised as jewelry that will have at least 100 times more processing power than the most powerful notebook PC on the market today—and they may cost one-tenth the price of today's notebook PC.

So why would anyone want to perpetuate a two-tiered fat-client/thin-server model of computing when it chiefly limits our choices and restricts our capabilities? Yet that is exactly what many organizations are doing at the end of the twentieth century.

Application servers enable *n*-tiered client-server models that reach out beyond local area networks to application and information resources almost anywhere on the World Wide Web. That is not to say that anyone can get to anything anywhere and anytime and do with it anything they like. Firewalls do work. Encryption capabilities and system security advances are and will continue to be one of the major efforts of the software and network technology industries.

WHAT IS IN AN APPLICATION SERVER?

Not all application servers are created equal. The following is a more or less complete parts list of an application server, which also illustrates the middleware heredity of applications severs:

- Web server (connection management)
- Network services (session management, client access, connection pooling, etc.)
- Object request broker (CORBA, COM/DCOM/ActiveX)
- Transaction processing monitor
- Load-balancing and fail-over
- Message-oriented middleware

- Security services
- Database connectivity
- Business/application logic

A good application server will take care of all of the plumbing tasks and let developers focus their efforts on the business and application logic. An application server has one overriding business benefit which does that: Developers can build and deploy business application on the Web faster, more reliably, and at a lower overall cost.

The differentiating factors between organizations that succeed and prevail in a networked information economy will be (1) the robustness, flexiblility, and openness of their IT infrastructures overall and especially of the software infrastructure and (2) the capability of the application servers that enable developers, whether internal or contracted, to build, deploy, and maintain those networked applications that engage customers and suppliers, partners and constituents.

While application server software technologies are relatively inexpensive to license, the selection of an application server requires very careful consideration. Organizations need to standardize on specific application server technology and be very comfortable with the vendor supplying and supporting that technology. Again, this is an area where top-level executives must exercise leadership.

KEY PLAYERS

At least a dozen companies provide mature application server technologies, including all of the major software companies: IBM, Microsoft, Oracle, Netscape, and Sun. Middleware providers offer application servers or links to application servers as well. Chosen well and wisely, the right application server could, over time, eliminate most of an organization's need for other types of middleware technologies.

There is a fundamental division between providers of application server technologies. On one side are the more or less open systems advocates who adhere to the Common Object Request Broker Architecture (CORBA) and Enterprise Java Beans (EJB). These include IBM, Oracle, Sun, Netscape/AOL, and the makers of just about every other application server technology. On the other side is Microsoft, which stands defiantly by its Distributed Common Object Model (DCOM) and ActiveX (DCOM for the Internet). DCOM traces its direct lineage to COM (Common Object Model), which originally was developed to allow users to move, say, a pie chart generated by an Excel spreadsheet into a Microsoft Word document or a PowerPoint presentation. DCOM allows users to do that in a local area network from one Microsoft application on desktop A to another Microsoft application on desktop B. Microsoft calls DCOM "COM with a long wire." ActiveX is an extension DCOM that allows users to move the pie chart from desktop A to desktop B over the Internet instead of just a "long wire." But that is not all. Microsoft bundles a variety of components, including Transaction Server and Internet Explorer Server, into NT Server, now Win2K Server, to give users application server functionality, or at least some that approximates it.

Why, when everyone else embraces open standards and builds robust, innovative, and competitive application server technologies, does Microsoft adamantly refuse to consider anything but its own proprietary technologies for this important *interconnectivity* technology?

Let us go back to that two-tiered "fat" client-server model. That model requires a fat Microsoft client on every desktop. And just because other PC manufacturers created a low-cost, entry-level PC to stave off the market penetration of thin clients (the Net PC) does not mean that Microsoft lowered prices for the Windows operating systems that power those lower-cost PCs, or for the Microsoft Office Suites of enabling technologies that go into just about every Microsoft-powered PC. They reconfigured their license pricing, but they really did not lower it.

Among the loyal opposition to Microsoft, Oracle currently has a significant lead. Even for a heterogeneous database environment, Oracle remains the leading IMS company for Internet and Web technologies, and its application server software can function as well with Sybase, DB2, Informix, and the rest as does with its own Oracle RDBMS. This is not an accident. Oracle developed the first networked databases with Digital's DECnet in the mid-1980s, which were perhaps the earliest client-server database configurations. Oracle has now released its Oracle8i server product, which integrates all of the application server functionality with Oracle's IMS capabilities. While Microsoft must focus the bulk of its energies and resources on delivering and stabilizing its Windows 2000 operating systems, Oracle remains free to focus its muscle on innovative Internet information capabilities and Web-enabled business applications.

Sun is a networking powerhouse and has, since its inception in the early 1980s, consistently propounded the idea that the network is the computer. Sun not only continues to adhere to this networking credo, but it also builds robust and reliable software. However, users without a major commitment to Sun platform technologies likely will not find Sun's Net-Dynamics application server to be a precise fit. More or less the same applies to IBM. For users heavily committed to IBM, and especially to Lotus Notes, IBM's WebSphere and Lotus Notes Domino should be at the top of the list for application server technologies. It is a bit too early to determine what the fate of Netscape's application server technology might be. Netscape originally acquired the technology from Kiva, and now Netscape has been acquired by America Online. The involvement of Sun in this new troika, with its own NetDynamics application server, makes the future of Netscape's application server unclear.

But what if an organization has some Unix, some IBM, and bunches of Microsoft as well? That is the way most of the world is, heterogeneous. Annrai O'Toole notes that "The world will never be all Java or all Microsoft/COM. . . . CORBA is the only way to address that."[1] Proprietary environments are viable only if we throw everything else out and build an entirely proprietary IT infrastructure, one that is completely reliant on a single software vendor who will provide competitive and stable technologies in a timely fashion. IBM and Digital came close to doing that during the 1970s and into the early 1980s, but today it is not very likely that anyone, even Microsoft, can deliver a complete IT infrastructure. In Internet time, technologies evolve rapidly and competitive conditions change swiftly. Business at the end of the 1990s moves at ten times or more the pace that it did in the 1970s and 1980s.

Finally, if users build flexible and robust IT infrastructures around open standards, starting with the Internet networking protocol, TCP/IP, and the World Wide Web, and if users enforce organizational standards, particularly for information management systems and enabling and application technologies, the dependence on middleware and application server technologies is minimized. Middleware and application servers will still be needed, but not as much, and firms will not expose customers and constituents to some of the frailties inherent in tying processes, applications, information, and systems together in a *posteriori* fashion. And firms will save loads of money, in the bargain.

PART 3: SYSTEMS MANAGEMENT TECHNOLOGIES

Systems management technology helps IS professionals keep all parts of the IT infrastructure, from networking and platforms to databases, applications, and middleware, running reliably, constantly, and securely. Systems and network management software locates and identifies devices on the networks; manages network, application, and data traffic; establishes and enforces security at all levels; detects and corrects potential network and even systems or platform problems before they occur or can do damage—in short, network and systems management technologies help ensure that everything works, all the time and the way it is meant to work.

Of all the technologies that go into making up the IT infrastructure, systems management and administration tools and technologies are perhaps the most esoteric and hidden. Top-level executives should not have to get involved in decisions concerning these technologies. Unlike all of the other software infrastructure components, systems management technologies do not enable business applications that create value for customers and constituents. What these management technologies do, however, is ensure that all the systems and software pieces fit together as they should, that they perform at optimum levels, and that they are secure and reliably available. In short, systems and network management technologies keep the whole thing running as it should. Top-level executives must be familiar with these technologies.

Let us set up a fundamental division between systems management and network management (areas that now overlap to such an extent that they are virtually inseparable). In many companies, traditional organizational structures still maintain a division between network management as a part of communication and telco management and systems management as fundamental functions of the IS department. In large part, that is why in large corporations and some government organizations there exists the relatively new position of chief technology officer (CTO). In theory, this person is responsible for all communications, networking, and computer systems—which would include telecommunications, PBX switches, and so on. An organization may have combined management oversight of networking and systems, or management responsibility may be separated.

Probably the most compelling issue for top-level executives that relates to systems and network management is how to organize internal management of these resources. There are no easy answers, and varying levels of political considerations are bound to be involved. One thing is certain. Top-level executives who understand the components and dynamics of their IT infrastructure are equipped to make informed decisions about the organizational structures supporting the various elements that compose the infrastructure.

Very broadly, systems and network management technologies fall into several functional categories:

- Systems availability, including the monitoring of systems resources, high availability, and fail-over, detecting and correcting systems and network problems before they occur—in general, keeping the systems and networks running
- Operational functions, including storage management (backup and recovery of data), load-balancing, remote desktop management, among other functions
- Systems integration services, including applications management, database management, email management
- Network management, including performance monitoring and optimization, network security management, and network traffic control
- Security, including password administration, role-base securities, and firewalls

Among these functions, which are not all inclusive, there are some echoes from previous IT infrastructure components. In fact, many modern operating systems integrate many of these functions into the platform technologies. Almost every platform provider also provides some sort of systems management package. Hewlett-Packard provides OpenView, IBM provides NetView, Sun provides Solstice, Compaq has Insight Manager, Intel has LanDesk, Microsoft has its Management Server, Oracle has its Enterprise Manager, and on and on.

Do these come automatically with the systems? Are they free? To be perfectly honest, platform vendors would like to charge for these, but in general, they are willing to give them away, or at least let them be used for extended trial periods, if users commit to purchasing their core products. Are they any good? Most of the limitations of these systems management packages relate to each vendor's product focus. H-P's systems management capabilities will work best in more nearly pure H-P platform environment. Microsoft's Management Server is not going to do anything for non-Microsoft platforms. IBM, Oracle, and Sun seem to have more open systems management environments with the broadest reach, but no more so than H-P's, and like H-P's, these systems management packages are informed by the particular vendor's priorities and concentrations, which may not coincide with the user's needs.

The two prevailing and more or less independent providers of systems management technologies are Computer Associates (CA) and Tivoli, even though Tivoli was acquired a few years ago by IBM. Both companies are leaders in a wide range of systems and network management software as well as in middleware. Fortune 1000 companies or global 2000-type organizations use a good deal of software from CA and/or Tivoli.

If the IT infrastructure has more than one type of platform technology, and especially if any of those platforms is either a mainframe or a high-end Unix server that supports what are called "seven-by-twenty-four" applications and operations or even business-critical "five-by-eight" environments, users probably want to consider the broader and more open range of technologies from Computer Associates and Tivoli. For a firm standardized on Oracle, its Enterprise Manager along with the system management tools from our platform technology providers—H-P or Sun or IBM or Compaq and others—should provide most of the needed functionality.

Also, increasingly some essential systems and network management functions are being "burned" into the system and network hardware itself. Oracle has partnered with several hardware providers, including H-P, Sun, IBM, Dell, and Compaq, to bundle its "Raw Iron" product on platforms that provide complete information management services on a network server that is, in effect, a snap-in database appliance. Cisco provides network traffic management capabilities burned into their new hardware network servers.

This is all part of a continuing effort by leading technology suppliers to make their parts of the IT infrastructure less costly and more efficient to manage and to make them more consistently reliable without operator intervention. That is not to say that the need for systems managers will disappear any time soon. Those responsibilities may shift, and the number of systems managers over time may decline, but someone will always have to watch these back-room operations. One day that "someone" probably will be a very intelligent robotics device, not quite a sentient being but probably close; however, that's several decades away.

Finally, as with other areas discussed, even if a vendor is willing to give supply systems management technology for free, that will not alleviate the need for or the cost of systems managers. Or as novelist Robert Heinlein tells us, "anything free costs twice as much in the long run or turns out to be worthless."[2]

NOTES

1. *Infoworld,* September 21, 1998.
2. Robert A. Heinlein, *The Moon Is a Harsh Mistress* (New York: Tor Books, 1966), chap. 11.

CHAPTER 13

Open Information Technology Infrastructure Directions

Our destiny exercises its influence over us even when,
as yet, we have not learned its nature: it is our future
that lays down the law of our today.

—Friedrich Nietzsche, 1878

JOURNEY'S END

We return to our IT infrastructure model a final time. (See Exhibit 13.1.) We started this journey of discovery with an allegory about an admiral's note card that read "port right, starboard left," and this is a good place to revisit that allegory. By now we should have a firm grasp of the IT infrastructure model, the major components that compose it, how these interrelate, and their relative importance to organizational missions. Everything else concerning IT issues can be directly related to the IT infrastructure model. If, during any discussion of IT issues, this model is kept in mind, usually people can understand where technology components and services fit and what their relationships are to the whole.

Readers should now be more comfortable with the issues surrounding IT and be better able to understand some of the nuances attending IT issues. Most of all, readers should now better appreciate the vital roles the IT infrastructure and its components play in the ability of business and public service organizations to fulfill their various missions.

Of all the trends and directions among information technologies, the expansion and further evolution of the Internet and web technologies

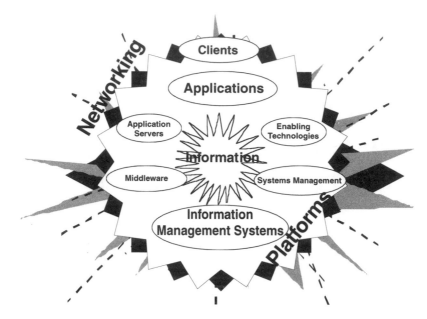

Exhibit 13.1   The Complete IT Infrastructure Model

will have the most impact on business and public sector organizations and their IT infrastructures. That is not a very profound statement, but it is one to keep in mind when dazzling technology predictions abound.

DECONSTRUCTING "OPEN"

The preceding chapters have discussed "open systems." The terrain of open systems is fraught with mine fields, and it is not so simple and straightforward to navigate as one would like. When it comes to information technologies, people bandy about the term "open" in almost every imaginable—and some unimaginable—contexts. IBM's AS400 computer series and its predecessors, the IBM Systems 32, 34, 36, and 38, are some of the most closed and proprietary systems sold during the last quarter century. Yet IBM sales literature and marketing campaign touted these as "open systems." This trick of rhetoric persists everywhere. Digital (now Compaq) has "Open VMS," a proprietary operating system that, for all intents and purposes, runs only on Digital VAX and Alpha hardware systems. Microsoft claims its operating systems are the most open in the world, yet every line of operating system code is proprietary and closed to outside developers.

Open systems, according to modern science, are "capable of ordering, structuring and regulating themselves," and "matter and/or energy is free to enter and to leave" these systems continually.[1] Open systems, in science, are living, growing, and self-organizing systems in which chaos is constantly tending toward order and which, when a state of equilibrium or ultimate order is achieved, dissipates again into chaos.

Open systems can take in new forms of energy and matter and evolve into new states. It is this continually evolving characteristic of open systems that defines them and allows them to endure. In nature these are *autopoietic structures* and "lie at the highly sophisticated end of nature's spectrum of 'open systems.'"[2] Think for a moment of the stock markets in terms of an autopoietic structure, an open system that is continually taking in new matter (capital) and energy (information) and is constantly on the verge of chaos but is always tending toward order.

Is it too much of a stretch to think of IT infrastructures as autopoietic? Well, maybe not too much of a stretch but perhaps a bit premature. Give the evolution of machine intelligence another two or three decades and we may just be there. But it is not premature to think of IT infrastructures as open systems, systems that are in a continual cycle of evolution, taking in and adapting to new technologies while delivering more power and capabilities to organizations and discarding older and obsolete technologies.

The lessons here are twofold. First, we should not think of an IT infrastructure as something we build once, then walk away from. The IT infrastructure for any organization is something that is continually evolving. Second, we should ensure that the IT infrastructure is built with open systems components that are capable of taking in and adapting to new technologies, which in turn allow it to evolve.

The good news is that, like anything else in business and public service organizations, IT infrastructures are by nature open systems that strive to evolve and adapt. The bad news is that, if we make decisions that limit an IT infrastructure's ability to evolve and adapt, we limit our organization's ability to evolve and adapt as well. So not only will the IT infrastructure reach a state of maximum entropy and begin to dissipate, but the organization's ability to create value for customers and constituents will also deteriorate, and the organization will extinguish itself or will undergo severe disruption that might lead it to transform again into an open system.

Very few technology providers will understand what we mean by open systems, using the definition borrowed from modern science. Top executives must, by their leadership and example, make certain everyone in the organization understands that the number-one priority is to ensure that the IT infrastructure is open and flexible, capable of integrating new technologies from high-tech companies that perhaps have not yet themselves been created. And IT infrastructures must be capable of scaling to the customer and constituent demands yet to imagine themselves.

Organizations do not buy open systems; they build them, and the building of open systems, including open IT infrastructures, is always a work in progress. Top-level executives must understand the need for open IT infrastructures and ensure that everyone at every level of the organization makes genuine open systems a cornerstone of the IT thinking.

MICROSOFT'S IT INFRASTRUCTURE OFFERING

Microsoft has been trying for several years to set up a fairly straightforward dichotomy: "You either get everything from us, or you can go elsewhere, and, oh, by the way, we're the ones who supply you with all those desktop PCs, so think about that before you decide to go elsewhere." And Microsoft can build a pretty compelling case, at least on Power-Point slides, although the outlook for Microsoft delivering a robust IT infrastructure anytime soon is very doubtful.

Microsoft claims it can supply almost the entire software infrastructure. All users need is Windows NT Server operating systems (now renamed Windows 2000 Server), Microsoft BackOffice, and Microsoft Office, plus some development tools like Visual Studio. That, Microsoft tells us, takes care of everything except the network infrastructure technologies, the hardware platforms (client and server hardware, which are both mainly Intel-based) and the business applications themselves. And Microsoft claims that going its way is much less expensive than going with alternatives or even creating mixed, heterogeneous IT infrastructures.

Sounds good in theory. Let us take a look at what Microsoft actually delivers. First, Windows 2000, BackOffice, and Office are closed and proprietary environments. For example, we can't use Microsoft SQL Server 7.0 on any other operating system except Windows. So if we choose to standardize our IMS—something that has real benefits for an

IT infrastructure—and we choose SQL Server 7.0, we must perforce run everything on Windows operating systems. But that is precisely what Microsoft has in mind: Standardize on any one of its offerings, and users then standardize on all of its offerings, giving it customer lock-in. Yet SQL Server 7.0 is the least capable—and least competitive—IMS available. All IMSs are not created equal, and those inequalities can directly determine an organization's competitive ability or even its ability to perform its mission at all.

Microsoft would also argue against the notion that its is a closed IT infrastructure. Microsoft would, in fact, argue that its infrastructure is more open than another type. It would say that users can get more applications and a wider variety of applications on Microsoft platforms than on any other platform. And that is right. But most of those are personal desktop applications, tools, and games. Almost everything that has any meaning for business and public service organizations of most sizes and that runs on Windows servers also runs on Unix servers.

Microsoft customers are locked into Microsoft and must keep buying its desktop software, which relates immediately to the major benefits of Microsoft's current monopoly of desktop operating systems and applications. That is shifting with the advent of three-tier and n-tier client-server models and with the widespread and rapid growth of Web and Internet environments. These are serious threats to Microsoft technology model and its business model as well. Therefore, Microsoft continues to try to commandeer the Internet, beginning with MSN, which is now little more than a minor competitor to AOL, and perhaps culminating with a Microsoft proprietary version of TCP/IP, if not a Microsoft proprietary version of the World Wide Web.

But that is not likely to happen. Why not? Currently there are roughly 100 million Microsoft desktops. The company itself is worried that it may have reached "desktop saturation" and is concerned that most of its revenues come from upgrades rather than from new users. And Microsoft's concern is justified. New users bring higher margins and expanding markets; selling upgrades does little to expand markets and customer base.

Even more important, those 100 million users represent only one-tenth of those who are projected to be using the Internet and Web in just four to five years. And it is very unlikely that the estimated 900 million new Web and Internet users will be gobbling up 900 million new fat Microsoft desktop platforms. Most will be using new generations of Net Computers (NCs), and dozens of other Web and Internet appliances. Fat

Microsoft desktops are just too bulky, awkward, and expensive, not only to buy but to maintain. And fat Microsoft desktops are no longer trendy, which may negatively impact PC sales more than most observers anticipate. In addition, it is doubtful that all the Compaqs, Dells, IBMs, and Gateways of the world could manufacture and distribute 900 million fat Microsoft PCs in five years. Nonetheless, it would be interesting to peek at some of the long-range forecasts of these companies and see for ourselves what their crystal balls are telling these PC manufacturers.

The Internet and World Wide Web are dynamic, open systems that are moving way too fast for Microsoft to appropriate, as it did the slower-developing desktop markets. Which brings us to the real liability of allowing any major IT infrastructure to rely too much on a closed, proprietary environment—closed IT infrastructures can and do debilitate organizations. Open IT infrastructures are dynamic, flexible, and robust. Closed, proprietary IT infrastructures are the opposite—static, rigid, and weak.

But what about the Microsoft's low cost? Doesn't that count? First, let us keep in mind that the real cost of the IT infrastructure components, especially the software components, are in the attendant people costs. Next, let me dispel this myth of low-cost acquisition. In Chapter 7, I discussed how the falling prices of PCs were almost entirely related to competition among PC hardware manufacturers and efficiencies realized by volume manufacturing, streamlined distribution, and lower cost of sales.

Microsoft's prices have not fallen. In fact, recent research by the Consumer Federation of America discovered that Microsoft last year overcharged its worldwide customers by as much as $10 billion while hardware prices were declining rapidly. The Gartner Group and others continually tell us that the annual cost of maintaining and supporting a single business PC is about $10,000—and that's an ongoing annual cost. That $10,000 annual cost for every business PC has never decreased even with the continual—and often dramatic—decline in PC hardware prices. Paul Strassmann, head of Software Testing Assurance Corp. and former vice president for strategic planning at Xerox Corp.—tells us that "Microsoft has caused an enormous escalation in support costs. The moment you put a PC on your desk you have inherited a tax."[3]

To its credit, Microsoft has forced many software providers to adopt commodity pricing structures for key software infrastructure components, and these companies and their customers are better off for it. Oracle was the first IMS provider to offer a "work-group" server version,

with work group pricing, of its flagship RDBMS. As a direct consequence, Oracle increased market share on Microsoft's NT servers from
less than 5 percent to almost 40 percent in just under a year, pulling ahead
of Microsoft's own market share for SQL Server and at the same time far
outdistancing IBM/DB2, Informix, and Sybase on Windows NT servers.

Software licenses of all types have undergone pricing adjustments as
a direct result of Microsoft's aggressive pricing for its NT Server software offerings. Of course, Microsoft's aggressive pricing tactics were
aimed at establishing the same kind of market dominance on the server
side that the company enjoyed on the desktop. That has not happened.
Windows NT server operating systems have enjoyed momentum, particularly in departmental and smaller business environments. However, no-
torious problems of Windows NT Server unreliability have slowed wider
deployment of Microsoft platform software into business-critical areas
of most organizations. And Windows NT Server continues to display a
limited ability to scale to increasing user and business application demands, all of which Microsoft promises will be alleviated with the release of Windows 2000 Data Server.

What Microsoft did manage to accomplish by forcing other software
providers to reduce and restructure prices seems to be backfiring. Almost every software vendor who offers products for Microsoft operating
systems offers better functionality and higher reliability and performance—overall better technology—than Microsoft and at about the
same price.

Many organizations that installed Oracle or IBM RDBMS on their
Windows NT servers already had purchased Microsoft BackOffice li-
censes for those same servers, which include Microsoft SQL Server
RDBMS. These organizations are not in the habit of spending money just
to spend money. And although Microsoft supporters truly believe that the
arrival of SQL Server 7.0 will obviate the need for other RDBMSs on
Windows NT Servers, the problems of scaleability and reliability persist.
In addition, SQL Server 7.0 only brings Microsoft's IMS offering up to
the functionality and performance that IMSs like Oracle, IBM/DB2, and
Informix were offering four and five years ago.

So why should top-level executives care about Microsoft's slow pace
for delivering new technologies? It has everything to do with shrinking
the gap between the availability of new software technologies that enable organizations themselves to innovate in their industries, to devise
new and more competitive ways of delivering new value to their customers and constituents. For example, if we are tied to Microsoft's SQL

Server IMS and our competitors are using the latest versions of Oracle or IBM/DB2 IMS technologies, our competitors have software capabilities that we will not have for perhaps another four or five years. Our competitors can do things with networked information that we cannot do, or that we cannot do as well as they can do. That is very likely to be a competitive disadvantage for us.

Not many top executives realize how critical this type of competitive disadvantage can be or how truly valuable this type of competitive advantage is.

Top-level executives need to understand that as they build and extend their IT infrastructures, they must partner well with the vendors who supply both components and services. The competitive viability and the flexibility and robustness of our IT infrastructures depend in very large part on the quality and character of our relationships among our partner providers. Enduring business partnerships and quality customer-supplier relationships are at best difficult to build and even more arduous to maintain. And even though the largest burden for establishing and maintaining these partnerships and relationships rests several levels below that of top executives, occupants of mahogany row must set the tone and monitor the well-being of their organization's relationships with key IT component and service providers. If we are dealing with a corporate culture that is at its base supercilious and derisive, there is not a good chance that our ongoing relationship will be harmonious or healthy.

Which brings us to the crux of dealing with Microsoft. The company insulates itself in the business world by channeling its products through distributors and value-added resellers, service and support companies, and third-party product providers. While this does give Microsoft a broader market reach than it otherwise might have, it also insulates Microsoft from its customers' realities and problems, placing that burden on the intervening companies.

The good news is that many Microsoft resellers and third-party service and support providers are genuinely upstanding businesspeople and deliver the kinds of supplier integrity most of us look for in business-to-business relationships. When estimating the viability of a relationship with Microsoft, focus carefully on the company that actually will be delivering products and services, not on the holder of the brand name. Excellent long-term relationships exist among hundreds and even thousands of Microsoft-specialized product, service, and support providers. Just do not expect to have that kind of relationship with Microsoft itself.

Microsoft has made some lasting contributions to both business and culture. It has spawned new innovation among start-up companies and independent software vendors, that in turn created a wealth of new products and services. But so far as transforming the world as we know it, Microsoft did little more than be in the right place at the right time and move aggressively in that place and at that time.

RAGTAG REBEL ALLIANCE

Some technology industry pundits point out that Microsoft is not, as others try to characterize it, the Evil Empire of George Lucas's *Star Wars*. And I must agree. Darth Vader and the Evil Empire have much better technology than Microsoft has.

The central players among the rebel alliance forces are Sun, Oracle, IBM, and the newly emerging America Online/Netscape. Soon to be joining the fray will be almost all the telecom and networking players, who mostly understand—and are concerned about—the frailties of Microsoft's technology in the fault-intolerant environments of global telephony and networking. Then there are the motley legions of Unix acolytes, with growing numbers of Linux developers and users swelling these ranks, and the just plain old "we-hate-Microsoft" contingents worldwide, some segments of which contain large numbers of the "we-love-our-Mac" fanatics. That's quite an opposition.

Among Microsoft's opposing forces, Sun has been the most defiant for the longest time, which is to be expected from a dedicated provider of Unix-based platforms. Scott McNealy has been consistently the most vociferous and the most engaging and entertaining critic of Microsoft's technological deficiencies and business conduct. And remember, Sun and McNealy are not attacking from positions of weakness. Sun has steadily risen among the ranks of platform providers. Along with IBM and Hewlett-Packard, it occupies the topmost rung of suppliers of true enterprise-class platform technologies. In addition, Sun's network computing model anticipated the commercialization of Internet technologies by almost a decade, giving Sun center stage among platform technology providers for networked information. Sun fully accepts that it is not an either/or world, that for at least another half decade or more heterogeneous environments, which integrate Unix and Windows platforms, will be the norm and not the exception in IT infrastructures, especially among global-2000 type organizations.

Microsoft would have no trouble taking on these companies one at a time. But together they make a worthy and formidable foe. When the telecom forces jump in, which they are likely to do once Microsoft starts screwing around with TCP/IP and offers a propriety Microsoft protocol in its place, Microsoft could be in very deep soup indeed.

However, Gates and company may just decide to go for it all. And why not? Trample the telcos, own the access to all of the world's communication services, set up the über Microsoft portal for everything—not just PCs and Web sites but for TV broadcast and cable, for telephones, for public services, for *everything!* And don't think that the folks in Redmond have not thought about just that sort of scenario. Since their earliest strategy meetings about the Internet, which very nearly passed them by, Microsoft's top managers have been concerned about ways of extracting their "vig" from Internet users. And "vig" is the word Microsofties use, adopting the underworld's slang for the exorbitant interest rates charged by loan sharks. If Microsoft could defeat the rebel alliance forces, especially the telcos, it could become the toll-taker on the global information superhighway, and Mr. Gates's worth would easily quadruple or quintuple.

Of course, Microsoft also has announced products to facilitate integration of Windows platforms with Unix environments, but few observers expect to see any truly meaningful products appear. Most high-tech observers anticipate that the few Unix integration products that actually ship from Redmond are likely to be either token offerings or Trojan horses.

A dozen or so miles north of Sun Microsystems on U.S. Highway 101 stand the gleaming glass towers of Larry Ellison's Oracle Corp., the second largest software company in the world, after Microsoft. Ellison has always been a harsh critic of Microsoft's technologies and business tactics. And, much more so than McNealy, Ellison sometimes seems to frame those criticisms in a personal context. Ellison genuinely admires and respects Bill Gates, but he also seems sometimes to see himself and Gates as personal rivals. The Oracle initial public offering (IPO) was made on March 12, 1986, opening at the then common IPO price of $15 per share. When it closed at $21.75 that first day, it made Ellison a paper millionaire

93 times over. Microsoft's IPO opened the very next day at $21 per share and closed at $28, making Gates a paper millionaire 300 times over. Of course, that all seems like chump change at the end of the twentieth century with Ellison's net worth climbing above $10 billion and Gates's estimated worth hovering somewhere above $80 billion.

IBM is still smarting from the trashing it has taken over the last decade and a half from what some think were below-the-belt Microsoft blows, particularly surrounding joint IBM-Microsoft OS/2 operating system effort. At the time, many observers likened Microsoft's duplicity to a case of the dog biting the hand that feeds it. Lou Gestner was not at IBM's helm then, but the IBM culture still bears a cross of humility and, one must assume, would delight over any Microsoft misfortune to which IBM could contribute. IBM and Gestner have done an outstanding job resurrecting Big Blue's fortunes and stature, especially among Global 2000-type organizations, and IBM has balanced its efforts well among Windows PCs, Windows NT Servers, Unix platforms, and mainframes. And people tend to forget that if IBM were to separate its software license and services revenues from its overall business, IBM comes out far and away to be the largest software company in the world, probably about the size of Microsoft and Oracle combined.

Two interests hold these three leaders of the opposing alliance together: first, Microsoft's intention to dominate the enterprise IT infrastructure with Windows 2000 clients and servers is a direct threat to each of these company's core businesses; so for Sun, Oracle, and IBM, Microsoft becomes a mutually regarded and menacing competitor. So long as Microsoft stayed on the desktop and in smaller work groups, none of these three really felt much threat from Redmond. But when Microsoft made moves to reach beyond the desktop and the local work group into department, line-of-business, and enterprise spaces, the mutual interests of Sun, Oracle and IBM began coalescing in opposition to Microsoft.

This is not a business conspiracy. It is doubtful that executives from IBM, Sun, and Oracle ever met in one place to discuss a Microsoft threat, or that e-mails were exchanged or phone calls made. It is simply that Microsoft so positioned itself as to present an almost identical threat to each of these three companies' core businesses.

The second interest holding Sun, Oracle, and IBM together is that these three combine into the most formidable software consortium imaginable. Together they employ tens of thousands of many of the best software engineers in the world. And they are all experienced in providing high-quality, bulletproof platform and software infrastructure components for the world's largest and most mission-critical networked information environments, something Microsoft's software developers have very little experience doing. IBM, Oracle, and Sun have toiled long and hard with large business and government organizations around the globe, and they each have a keen sense of protecting not just their core business but their customers as well.

Finally, Sun, Oracle, and IBM have coalesced around one of the most portentous technologies to emerge since the commercialization of the Internet and World Wide Web, a technology designed specifically to enlarge and enrich networked information and networked applications: Java and its progeny. Both Oracle and IBM are firmly committed to Sun's Java standards, making this troika, if their alliance holds firm, an uncommonly formidable force.

Java is an enabling technology for the Internet. IBM, Oracle, and Sun are experienced in networked information and network computing architectures and technologies. Their strengths are in enterprise-level environments as well as in departments and work groups. They are proponents of *n*-tiered client-server architectures. They provide open, flexible, scaleable, reliable, and robust IT infrastructure components. Microsoft would like to perpetuate fat-client two-tiered architectures to extend its desktop revenue model. Its technologies are closed, rigid, less than reliable, and not particularly scaleable or robust.

Now into the mix is thrown America Online/Netscape, which also has an alliance with Sun, where both Java and *n*-tiered client-server architectures come into play. This newly combined company led by Steve Case is decidedly Internet and Web-centric. The only tie to Microsoft of any consequence is the presence of AOL's icon on Microsoft Windows 98 desktop screen. Other than that, AOL/Netscape is about browsers, e-commerce, and Internet and Web services and content; it has very little stake in fat clients or two-tiered client-server architecture. With Microsoft's business practices under the U.S. Department of Justice's and the U.S. federal court's antitrust microscopes, it is unlikely that Microsoft will do anything to change Windows 98 desktop to remove AOL. However, do not be surprised to see AOL's icon missing from future Microsoft desktops releases.

With AOL/Netscape in the mix, there is now a truly strong, well-armed contingent of e-commerce providers for organizations of all types and sizes to turn to for robust, scaleable, open, and flexible platform and software infrastructure technologies. Not only that, but IBM, Oracle, and Sun have what Microsoft has never had, mature professional sales and support cadres that can build and maintain business partnerships with enterprise customers. Microsoft seems more and more ill-equipped going into this serious competition for enterprise e-commerce environments and applications and the IT infrastructures that support the world's largest organizations.

Interestingly enough, some of Microsoft's traditionally strong supporters are sitting on the sidelines, at least during the early stages of this confrontation. Hewlett-Packard maintains its dual-platform strategy. Compaq, digesting and adapting to customers and products that came with its acquisitions of Digital and Tandem, has room to hedge its bets. Intel seems now worried more about finding platform technologies that can take advantage of its scaleable architectures and upcoming 64-bit technologies, neither of which Microsoft can do very soon or very well. Even Dell seems to be broadening its vision, taking on products like Oracle's Raw Iron snap-in database server. For all its muscle, Microsoft seems standing oddly alone. Its armies of cheerleaders keep on cheering, but cheerleaders usually do not get out on the field of competition.

Technology observers and analysts are rapidly cooling toward Microsoft's ability to deliver the necessary technologies and services that will take it beyond its initial successes with Windows NT. While Windows 2000 clients, especially the professional client, should enjoy immediate success among serious business users, its server products need to arrive on time, fully featured, and darn near bulletproof, something Microsoft has never pulled off before, or the enterprise solution train will leave the station without Bill Gates and company onboard. Consultants and integration services providers also seem to be expressing a much less enthusiastic attitude about Microsoft's ability to deliver real business-critical IT infrastructures totally built on proprietary technologies.

"WHAT ROUGH BEAST . . ."

One of the real challenges for top-level executives is ensuring that what their organizations do today works well for tomorrow. It is that strategic thing. But when it comes to technology, there are lots of arrows pointing in different directions, lots of claims and cloudy visions, and most come from the technology vendors themselves or from consultants and service providers.

This speaks directly to points discussed earlier about top-level executives needing to ensure that their organizations are not merely looking at technologies made available to them by vendors but that there is a constant and consistent effort throughout organizations to understand how both existing and emerging technologies can be used to create new value and wealth.

As mentioned, technology providers will habitually build and sell products and services that do not necessarily fit the needs of their customers but rather fulfill their own self-interests. Top-level executives must understand and control this vendor propensity and make certain that what is delivered is in alignment with the needs of the business, society, and culture.

That sounds like a tall order, but it is really not that arduous a task. Directly influencing the alignment of IT with organizational directions and requirements requires a broad understanding of IT issues, where they fit and what they can do in relation to an organization's endeavors and missions.

With the Internet and Web we have reached a new plateau, and we are still exploring and settling into it, what I have been calling networked information. That will last for some time. Almost everything that has transpired over the past 50 years of commerical computing has prepared us for this point. And almost everything we hear from every sector takes its expression from the emerging phenomena of networked information. There is no clear or even vague sense of what the plateau after this one might bring. But there is really nothing dramatic and paradigm-shattering to anticipate just yet. For the present, tremendous strides can be expected in developing and refining the networked information paradigms we have only just begun to explore.

If we look to the heavens—quite literally—we see some of the strides made. The International Space Station presents some very new challenges that our best and brightest scientists and engineers will be confronting and overcoming during the first decade of the twenty-first century. I believe that, among other things, there will be more strides in battery and power supply technologies. It is all well and good to forecast a future that includes tiny networked appliances that are worn embedded in jewelry and clothing, or even surgically implanted network applicances, but what about the batteries for these. Where will the electricity come from? Or, better yet, when will we move beyond electricity as we know it? Ultimately, the power to drive hardware probably will come from solar power conversion, but these energy sources will need to be incredibly tiny and durable. And where are we going to put those personal solar panels in the first place?

Finally, keep in mind that the human impulse that drives every significant breakthrough in technology through history is connectedness, humankind's irresistible compulsion to reach out and extend its contact with others of our species and, especially, to find new ways of extending and enhancing our points-of-value contact and interchange. Ultimately, this compulsion is an innate tendency of nature, of life itself. What we may well learn from this age of networked information that we are now entering is a way to get back in sync with what Fritjof Capra calls the "Web of Life." And that just might help us save our planet's ecosystem from impending disasters, which in turn will save our species from extinction. And I am bold enough to assign that responsibility to the institutions of commerce and to their leaders, if only they can understand the paradigms of networked information on which all of nature seems to be based.

NOTES

1. Ian Marshall and Danah Zohar, *Who's Afraid of Schrodinger's Cat: All the New Science Ideas You Need to Keep Up with the New Thinking* (New York: Wm. Morrow, 1997), p. 255.
2. John Briggs and David Peat, *Turbulent Mirror: An Illustrated Guide to Chaos Theory and the Science of Wholeness* (New York: Harper Collins, 1989), p. 154.
3. Quoted in *Upside* (June 1998), p. 134.

CHAPTER 14

Summary and Suggestions

*This last century has seen enormous technological change and the
social upheavals that go along with it, which few pundits circa
1899 foresaw. The pace of change is accelerating. . . . The result
will be far greater transformations in the first two decades of the
twenty-first century than we saw in the entire twentieth century.*
— RAY KURZWEIL, *The Age of the Smart Machine,* 1999

LIVING INFORMATION TECHNOLOGY INFRASTRUCTURES

I must caution executives one last time against viewing IT infrastructures as being static once built. In fact, IT infrastructures are in constant states of maintenance, rebuilding, expansion, and enhancement. IT infrastructures endure an increase in user traffic on a monthly basis that would drive even a Los Angeles highway engineer to strong drink well before lunch. Exponential demands are placed on IT infrastructures. And every time a new business application runs well, the number of users initially anticipated doubles or triples within just weeks. Word spreads fast, and both internal organizational users and external business partners and even customers seem to have a sixth sense that draws them toward new value created by networked information.

For example, let us look briefly at the now infamous case of America Online. With massive marketing campaigns in the mid- and late 1990s, AOL gave away diskettes and CD-ROMs containing a trial copy of its software. The campaign worked well, almost too well. AOL experienced agonizing outages and excruciatingly slow response times when a flood of users began subscribing to AOL's services. AOL's IT infrastructure planners had not accurately anticipated the sheer numbers of users that the inordinately successful marketing campaigns were attracting. Fortunately, Steve Case and his IS mechanics were able to shore up and expand their IT infrastructure before they lost too many of their new customers. Unfortunately, in line with the universal 80/20 rule, a good number of the users that AOL did lose were some of their oldest and most profitable customers.

Even Amazon.com's well-planned and almost innately scaleable IT infrastructures were hit early on by some slow response times and even a few planned outages when customer demand exceeded capacity. In fact, the only time this writer ever bought a book over the Net from one of Amazon.com's online competitors was one Sunday morning when Amazon.com's site was down for upgrade and maintenance. A couple of mouse points and clicks, and there I was at Barnes and Noble's new online bookstore.

The real lesson for top executives is that an organization's IT infrastructure is in a constant state of transformation and expansion, always responding to new conditions and new demands. And IT infrastructures must be versatile and agile, to expand and adapt to new business opportunities and new technologies, to extend and enlarge the points-of-value interchange. IT infrastructures that are static and rigid, closed, and proprietary come close to something that scientists might call a state of maximum entropy, that point where they are so tightly ordered that they become inert and begin to dissipate. A "dissipative" IT infrastructure can result only in a deterioration of an organization's ability to fulfill its mission, to deliver value to its customers and constituents.

Top-level executives need to keep one thing in mind about their IT infrastructures: These are almost living entities. They are alive 24 hours a day, seven days a week, conducting business transactions, providing information and entertainment, and generally making life happen. IT infrastructures need constantly to grow and to transform and adapt—to new technologies, to new economic and business conditions, and to constantly increasing demands, from internal users, external business partners, and customers and constituents.

Top-level executives should have a discussion item on every formal executive committee and board-level meeting on the state and well-being of the organization's IT infrastructure. This is the one thing that executives can do to both focus executive management on a core asset of the organization—information and the technologies that support it—and to perpetuate a comfort and control level with IT among the organization's business leadership.

SUGGESTIONS: SOME DOS AND SOME DON'TS

Keep in mind that power is not necessarily effectively exercised through authority edict. The people most directly responsible for carrying out an organization's strategies are not poorly educated factory workers. Factory workers are still a part of the scheme, but they are likely to be half a world away in a third-world country, or they are highly unionized. The workers most directly responsible for an organization's success, or for its lack thereof, are highly paid, very well educated, and very mobile knowledge workers.

And the network paradigms function well for knowledge workers. Power in networks comes not from authority or edict but from influence, the kind of influence characteristic of the best leaders.

Here are some suggestions on providing leadership and influence surrounding the critical IT issues. This is not a definitive list. Executives should add to it as they move forward in their comprehension of and influence on their organization's IT capabilities. We will start with a list, then move into some discussions of each item.

Don'ts

1. Don't make cost of acquisition a primary or even secondary criteria for any component in the IT infrastructure.
2. Don't underestimate the people costs of an IT infrastructure.
3. Don't hesitate to ask questions about even the slightest unclear element in an IT discussion.
4. Don't be a passive receptor of technologies as they are offered by technology suppliers.
5. Don't become entangled in the visions of technology suppliers.

Dos

1. Do lead standardization efforts that make sense.
2. Do establish executive relationships with the three or four most crucial providers of components and services for the organization's IT infrastructure.

3. Do encourage experimentation with new technologies both inside IS organizations and among business units and departments.

4. Do make learning about IT and its roles a priority for all nontechnical executives, managers, and professionals.

5. Do bookmark technology news sites, such as cnews.com and techweb.com, and glance at their headlines several times a week to gain and maintain a business feel for what is happening in high tech.

Let us go through these in a bit more detail.

1. *Don't make cost of acquisition a primary or even secondary criteria for any component in the IT infrastructure.* Dr. W. Edwards Deming, the grand master of the quality movement during the last half of the twentieth century, offered a 14-point management methodology; the fourth point of the Deming Management Method calls for an end of the practice of awarding business on price tag alone.[1] The practice of awarding business to the lowest-price provider has several important drawbacks. First, it leads to a proliferation of suppliers. Second, "it causes buyers to jump from vendor to vendor"; and, third, it creates a reliance on specifications, "which become barriers to continuous improvements." Deming notes that a price tag "is unambiguous and therefore appealing. Determining quality is another matter entirely, and it requires some degree of knowledge and skill."

Deming's comments, coming from interviews with Mary Walton during the mid-1980s, are framed in the context of manufacturing and quality issues surrounding manufacturing. But his words are just as applicable today to IT infrastructures.

Today, the fundamental raw material for creating value and wealth is information. We will return to the issue of standardization, and the roles top executives should play in those efforts, later. But for now, keep in mind that Deming stresses that a purely quantitative emphasis on selecting components and suppliers is detrimental to an organization's quest for quality. We simply take this one step further and apply it to modern business's most vital asset, information and the technologies that support information.

It is also important to recall that the major ongoing IT investment is in people expenses related to development, implementation, deployment, and ongoing management and support. Some of an organization's most valuable assets are information itself and the knowledge workers who use that information as raw material in the creation of value and wealth. Finally, keep in mind that the IT infrastructure is a growing, expanding, and adapting—if not a living—thing. What we invest in today, we want to work for at least a few years. Rarely, if ever, does buying cheap components result in a robust infrastructure.

Top executives need to communicate clearly and consistently to other executives and through them to their managers and staffs that cost of acquisition is *not* a primary or secondary criteria. The entire organization needs to know that while total cost of ownership is a consideration and must be watched carefully, the real goal is to build, extend, and maintain a flexible, open, and robust IT infrastructure that serves the organization today and that can grow and adapt well into the future. Quick fixes may sometimes be necessary, but what users really want is an IT infrastructure that will continually help the organization create new value for customers and constituents and help it compete well both immediately and for the long term. Communicate those messages throughout the organization. If managers and staff know top management wants quality information technology at the best—not the cheapest—costs, that is also what they will deliver.

Finally, we need to look with continual skepticism on the claims of any technology supplier that their low acquisition cost is a distinguishing virtue vis-à-vis their competition. Remember, at component levels, cost of acquisition falls within pricing bands that make one vendor's unit price barely distinguishable from another's. Product or services bundling may mask some of these similarities, creating a deceptive price distinction, but in the highly competitive arena of IT, pricing practices are usually tit for tat. As in any other area of business—or for that matter, in life in general—if the deal seems too good to be true, it is probably neither good nor true.

2. *Do not underestimate the people cost of IT.* The human costs of building, maintaining, and expanding IT infrastructures represent a larger overall cost of ownership than do just the technology components themselves. And technology suppliers are making decent strides in building many of the administrative and management tasks into the technologies themselves, thereby automating some previously people-intensive technology management tasks. But the sheer expansion of demands being made on IT infrastructures and the rapid evolution of the individual technologies pretty much ensures that people costs will not recede any time

soon. The biggest problem IS managers face is just *finding,* and then retaining, qualified IS professionals at every level.

Top-level executives need to appreciate not only the impact of people
costs on the overall cost of IT ownership but also the importance of
building cultures that attract and retain competent IS professionals,
again at every level. That does not mean relaxation of dress codes at the
midtown Manhattan corporate headquarters building or duplicating a
free-wheeling Silicon Valley campus for eccentric programmers. But it
does mean sincerely understanding and expressing personal appreciation for the roles IS personnel play in the larger organizational missions.
If IS professionals know that top-level executives actually understand
what IS does and appreciate its contributions to corporate goals, IS
managers will not have as much difficulty recruiting or retaining competent professionals. An informed pat on the back contributes as much
or more to increasing employee job satisfaction than almost anything
else a manager can do.

3. *Do not hesitate to ask questions about even the slightest unclear
element in any IT discussion.* That may seem even a bit too obvious to
state. But think about the times when someone used a technology term
or acronym and we let these slip by, usually out of a need to avoid em-
barrassment that would result from admitting we do not know what the
person is talking about. Technology professionals use jargon on purpose.
It is a fraternal language. Those who know the terminology, concepts,
and, most especially, the acronyms are members of the fraternity and
are granted all the rights and privileges that pertain therein. Those who
do not know the terminology, concepts, and acronyms are part of the
great unwashed and consequently have neither rights nor privileges.
How do we move into the fraternity?

First, top-level executives who have read this volume should have a
firm grasp of and comfort with the concepts of information technologies
and of the roles they play in a larger IT infrastructure and how they affect an organization's ability to create value and wealth.

We will learn by asking questions in context. And because we refuse to let our technologists slide by without clearly explaining terms,
we not only learn things about ourselves but the technologist learns
something about us as well. As Will Rogers once said, "Everybody is
ignorant, only on different subjects." The technologist learns we can

ask pointed questions. And last but not least, we have broken the code. So ask questions about technology.

4. *Don't be a passive receptor of technologies as they are offered by technology vendors.* This "don't" speaks to one of the dimensions in shrinking the gap between the emergence of new or improved technologies and our use of those technologies to create value and wealth. If we have a technology, how can we use it to create new value and wealth? First we need to be constantly aware of the progress of technologies, which means not just observing the development of technologies but also understanding how each fits with other technologies in our organizational and commercial contexts. After reading this book, our comprehension of the IT infrastructure models help us to do just that, to determine where a given technology might fit and how it might contribute to new value creation. Next we must match the technologies, sometimes in new arrays, to a new business opportunity or, for public service organizations, to new ways of delivering better, more effective, and efficient services to constituents.

All of this means devising new organizational strategies, based both on knowledge of the new and emerging technologies, on aggregate professional and business knowledge, and on informed comprehension of (and gut feel for) what sorts of new or improved products and services customers and constituents will find valuable. That is sometimes difficult to grasp in the abstract, but that's how Jeff Bezos came up with Amazon.com and became a billionaire.

Modern top executives and their organizations must pay continual and close attention to the advancements among information technologies and also must innovate new strategies that combine new technologies and organizational abilities in new ways, which can create new value without having to wait on or rely on an intervening technology company. Exhibit 14.1 provides another look at how new and emerging technologies normally find their way into organizations that use them in their own business or public service efforts.

This type of dependence on technology vendors as the middleman works well for common and undifferentiated components, but such components rarely give organizations a competitive edge or enable a business to streak ahead of its competition. "Off-the-shelf" applications are very much the same as those our competitors are using. There is no competitive edge in that.

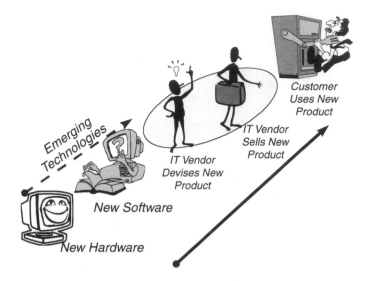

Exhibit 14.1   Common Migration of Technology to Business

In order to create new business and organization value, top executives must lead organizations that themselves are constantly aware of innovations in technologies that they can apply uniquely and strategically to creating new value for customers and constituents. That may involve automated processes and transactions, and it should integrate existing IT infrastructure components, especially business applications and information management systems. The new value is created not from automating existing processes and transactions but from innovating new processes, which drive new transactions. It is about creating new value. Although technology providers can supply components, services, tools, and building blocks, they cannot create new value for their customers. Exhibit 14.2 indicates how top executives need to be responsible for driving that effort.

Unfortunately, most top-level executives are just taking whatever the technology suppliers give them. That will not put them ahead of our competition, or open new areas of value creation for us. Jeff Bezos's background in computer science and electrical engineering gave him an understanding of the bits and pieces, which then enabled his vision of Web commerce and now results in Amazon.com and a transformation of an entire segment of the retail industry. And most of the entrepreneurs who are innovating new business directions with Internet and

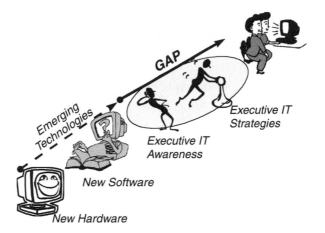

Exhibit 14.2   New Business Application Creates New Customer Value

Web technologies have backgrounds in technology. They know how to pick up the ball and run with it.

Top-level executives in all types of organizations must do the same thing. As indicated in Exhibit 14.2, each executive must assume the responsibility of "shrinking the gap" between the emergence of new or improved technologies and his or her organization's successful implementation of those emerging technologies in the creation of value and wealth.

5. *Don't become entangled in the visions of technology suppliers.* Technology suppliers are businesspeople, first, last, and always. Their priority is to create wealth for their shareholders. Most technology providers are willing, even eager, to understand where we are coming from and where we would like to go. Unfortunately, most IS managers, with whom technology providers primarily deal, are not very good at articulating the business visions of our organizations to IT suppliers. So technology providers articulate their own visions as points of departure, selling us on where they want to go rather than understanding where we want technology to take our organization and our customers and constituents.

The most outstanding example of this is Bill Gates's book, *The Road Ahead.*[2] The publishers even managed to make Gates look like a Pied Piper on the cover photograph. That book is one technology provider's vision of what the future may hold. I believe it is not the vision any top-level executive should adopt or perhaps even integrate. Yet if we do not have a sound and integrated IT vision and strategy for our own business, we are pretty much at the mercy of other people's visions and their self-interests.

There are probably another dozen or more "don'ts" for top-level executives who should keep their minds open, asking questions, listening and learning, and adding more "don'ts" to the list. But these are five to start with, as are the "dos." Enlist the aid of IS professionals and fellow executives and add to these lists. It is among the "dos" that we find cornerstones for new behaviors, new organizational cultures, and new ways to extend IT infrastructure investments into the creation of new value and expanded wealth.

    1. *Do lead standardization efforts that make sense.* There are a couple of compelling reasons for top-level executives to do this. First, it is relatively easy for them to tell their IS and operational executives that the organization would benefit from standardizing certain fundamental components of the IT infrastructure—specifically, networking technologies, information management systems, groupware and professional productivity tools, and middleware and application servers, and for IS to start moving toward standardization in these areas. Top executives then should monitor the standardization processes through status reports from IS executives at monthly management committee meetings (one of those that IT agenda items touched on earlier).

    Top-level executives should look for and expect two principal benefits from standardization among IT infrastructure components. First, there should be an overall cost reduction among people who must manage and maintain parts of the IT infrastructure. IMSs and networking are two areas that stand out here. If, for example, we have several IMSs installed, as many organizations do, we need our IS staff trained and experienced database administrators (DBAs) *for each of these.* By standardizing on one platform, we reduce the number of DBAs needed.

    The second compelling advantage comes again from Dr. W. Edwards Deming, who urges organizations to select carefully sole-source suppliers especially for core components and not to award contracts for these components on the basis of low price. According to Deming: "Two or more suppliers of the same item will multiply the evils that are necessarily inherent and bad enough with any one supplier."[3] Driving component selection by emphasizing pricing results in a mechanistic reliance

> Southwest Airlines uses only one type of aircraft in its fleet, the Boeing 737 airliner. What benefit does the company derive from using only one type of aircraft? Herb Keller, Southwest's CEO, would tell us that he does not need as many differently trained and experienced mechanics and avionics technicians, and it also reduces the costs of spare parts inventories. In turn, Southwest has fewer mechanical delays and better on-time performance than any other airline in the United States. As a direct result of standardization of core infrastructure components, Southwest Airlines probably also enjoys lower overall maintenance costs per passenger mile than other airlines—all of which results in better customer value (lower fares, better on-time performance) and higher profits for Southwest's shareholders.

on specifications and does nothing to engender continuing improvement. So it is much more preferable, according to Deming, to establish long-term relationships "of trust" with core component suppliers.

> There must be a long-term management arrangement—a "gentleman's agreement." There is no legal definition of long. The one thing it is not is an annual contract based on price tag. It is more powerful. With a gentleman's agreement, you're on your own and so is he. It is far stronger than a legal agreement, which your lawyers can always help you get out of.[4]

Top-level executives must lead organizational efforts that standardize some of the core components of their IT infrastructures and focus on long-term relationships with suppliers of those components. Mark Twain was first to tell us, "Put all your eggs in one basket and—WATCH THAT BASKET."[5] Deming is telling us much the same thing. Deming also tells us to "Ask people who do it this way. They would have it no other way."[6]

Most contemporary top-level executives have been isolated from IT issues partly because of their own lack of acquaintance and comfort with those IT issues and partly because, in most organizations, top executives are isolated from even minimal involvement in these types of relationships.

Only top-level executives can lead any initiatives to standardize core IT infrastructure components. Such efforts will result not only in overall cost reductions but in a better, more robust, and more open, flexible, and scaleable IT infrastructure. That, in turn, will improve an organization's overall ability to create new and ongoing value for its customers and constituents in the networked information economy.

Standardization of information management systems can greatly reduce costs and increase overall capabilities of an IT infrastructure. The current shelf life of business applications is roughly three to five years, perhaps less. The current shelf life of databases is roughly ten years or so, and the shelf life of information contained therein very often is even longer. New applications must be integrated with existing applications, which affects both applications and the data and information these applications use and share. And all of these directly impact every aspect of an organization's efforts. The key role of middleware technologies is the integration of applications and data. If we standardize our data and information management systems, we need only to integrate the applications; the information is already "normalized" and can be used in any application.

Networking technologies are another core IT infrastructure component that calls for executive attention and leadership for standardization. The good news about networking technologies is that, because of the International Standards Organizations (ISO) and its communications model, the telecom and networking industries are already more standardized than other IT hardware and software components. Here the driving reason for selecting a single dominant supplier is principally that of establishing a long-term relationship, making networking and telecom providers key partners in our enterprise, not just low-bid suppliers of services or components. As with hardware and software, networking technologies are fiercely competitive, so prices between one supplier or another should not differ widely. Having a network and telecom technology provider who is a real partner in our enterprise, who understands where we want to go and is eager to help us get there, is infinitely more valuable than saving a few cents on long-distance services. There is much, much more at stake in a networked information economy than marginal difference in long-distance phone bills.

2. *Do establish relationships with top-level operational executives from several of the most important component suppliers to the IT infrastructure.* Standardization of core components puts an organization in the position to establish and leverage relationships between that organization's executives and executives from technology provider organizations. Few top-level executives make such relationships a permanent process, part of their own monthly and quarterly agendas. Many of the best technology and service providers do make strong and continual efforts to establish and nurture such executive relationships, but too often they are delegated to IS executives. Now that top-level executives understand and are comfortable with IT issues, they should have less reason to avoid their responsibilities of engaging in valuable relationships with technology executives.

Which technology executives should these key relationships be established with? The chief executive officer? Maybe. The chief operating officer? Probably. The senior vice president of Sales and Marketing? Definitely. There is a direct correlation among the size of our respective organizations, the amount of strategic and fiscal commitment, the geographical proximity of headquarters locations, and any number of other factors. As a general rule, executives should have solid personal relationships with those who are most responsible for our business, whose own performance is measured in large part on the health of our relationship and on our continued and expanded successful use of their technologies and services. It does not necessarily need to be the technology provider's CEO. In fact, in many technology companies the CEO is more highly technology oriented and less likely to understand and become engaged with our own organizational priorities and requirements. The real rule of thumb is to consider the relationship carefully and to make these valuable relationships a part of the executive routine.

3. *Do encourage experimentation with new technologies both inside IS organizations and among business units and departments.* This sort of experimentation is an investment both in the future directions of the IT infrastructure and in their capabilities to expand and enhance the value offered to customers and constituents. Top-level executives need to establish and communicate as part of their organization's cultural fiber a true environment of experimentation and exploration surrounding IT. Such a culture will result in innovative uses for IT and in expanded capabilities for the IT infrastructure. Experimentation should involve new uses of existing technologies as well as the application of new and emerging technologies to new processes, to new means of creating value and wealth. Executive lead in the standardization of core IT infrastructure technologies further facilitates both kinds of experimentation and ensures that successful pilot projects will integrate more easily into the IT infrastructure.

Processes for experimentation need to be established and monitored, and there will be some costs associated with both. There is also the cost of the people who are involved directly and indirectly in these kinds of projects. But it is here, by encouraging an organizational culture of IT experimentation, that top-level executives will find ways to shrink the gap between the ever-evolving capabilities of IT and their own organization's ability to implement new or improved technologies in the creation of value. And shrinking that gap is one of the most powerful competitive advantages at the fingertips of most executives today. Experimentation requires management and process oversight, but most of all it requires top-level executive vision, leadership, and commitment. If we must, we can look on it as an elaborate IT suggestion box. Properly initiated and executed, the IT suggestion box should yield our next major competitive advantage by offering up new ways of creating value with our IT infrastructure and its component technologies.

4. *Do make learning about IT and its roles a priority for all nontechnical executives, managers, and professionals.* Again, this is a priority requiring the leadership and commitment of top-level executives. First, it means reading books like this one, participating in appropriate executive seminars and workshops (of which there are few), even taking a few hours to walk around a trade show exhibit of a technology conference. But best of all it means questioning the IS staff on things executives may be uncertain or unclear about. The absolute best single thing that a top-level executive can do in this regard is to visit his or her IS executives on a regular (monthly) and informal basis in the IS executive's office, just to ask questions, learn, and get an increasingly better feel for and comfort level with IT issues in general. Encourage people to draw diagrams while they explain answers.

One of the best things readers of this book can do is to draw a free-hand depiction of the IT infrastructure model built in this book from memory until they are comfortable enough to draw it in front of staff or peers during a meeting. Then think about the organization's IT infrastructure specifically. What kinds of networking are there? What kinds of platform technologies? What IMS, what tools, what middleware, what applications? Ask IS executives and staff to help identify these and place them into the IT infrastructure model.

The model in this book is not applicable to every IT infrastructure. It *is* all-encompassing, in that the components discussed will be consistently present in one form or another. The basic relationships among the components will persist as well. But the details of construction and capabilities can vary widely.

If someone, probably an IS staff person, questions the veracity of the model, hand him or her the marker and ask him or her to draw an IT infrastructure. And pay close attention. The person is very likely to come up with new insights and expand comprehension not just of the model itself but how it works in a specific organizational environment.

These informal learning sessions not only expand top executives' comprehension of IT issues but show IS professionals that the executive leadership is curious and eager to learn about IT and that IT occupies a central role in the larger organization. Executives in turn should teach IS managers and staff about the larger organization's missions and strategies and how IS fits into that larger picture, about organizational priorities, and about the creation of value and wealth.

The bottom line is that executives must get closer to the IS organization through informal but regular and consistent get-togethers on their turf. Avoid formal meetings. It is okay to have an agenda sketched out of topics to cover, but keep it free flowing. The best of these get-togethers are shirt-sleeve sessions over sandwiches.

Also do not hesitate to ask IS staff members about their jobs, what they work on, where they went to college, and so on. If they mention something of keen interest, ask them to explain more. Schedule an extra half hour or more between the regular informal session just to meander around the IS shop. Executives who do so not only learn a great deal about IT but seem to look forward to these informal sessions.

5. Finally, *do subscribe to one or two IT industry periodicals or online news services.* Cnews.com and techweb.com are excellent places to start. It is relatively easy and quick to scan the daily or weekly headlines, get a feel for what is in the high-tech news, and click on selected articles. Information offered by these and similar websites is also valuable to anyone who invests in technology stocks. Many of these will "push" summary news to an email address almost daily, with very short summaries of new items including the URL for immediate access to full story on the Web. Reviewing this information can take as little as a few minutes every day, but it pays off in much the same way regular exercise pays off. It improves cognition and maintains and expands the knowledge base itself.

NOTES

1. See Mary Walton, *The Deming Management Method* (New York: Perigee/ Putnam, 1986), chap. 8 for a discussion of Deming's concepts here.
2. Bill Gates with Nathan Myhrvold and Peter Rinearson, *The Road Ahead* (New York: Viking, 1995).
3. Quoted by Walton, *The Deming Management Method*, p. 62.
4. *Ibid.,* p. 64.
5. Mark Twain, *Pudd'n head Wilson* (New York: Simon & Schuster, 1998), chap. 15.
6. Walton, *The Deming Management Method,* p. 65.

Glossary[1]

API See *application programming interface.*

Application integration The task or effort of making different business applications, typically using different information resources, work together so that users can access both data and application functionality transparently from all applications inside an enterprise. Also see *enterprise application integration* and *middleware.*

Application programming interface (API) Programs attached normally to an operating system that define for software developers how their applications can interact with services and resources of the operating system and the computer itself.

Application server (a) A server attached to a network that provides clients with business applications so that business logic is shared among users and not isolated on individual desktops; (b) a category of middleware server which Web enables business applications making them accessible through browser technology over the Internet, intranets, or extranets.

Advanced Research Projects Agency See *Defense Advanced Research Projects Agency.*

Bandwidth The capacity of a network to process and transmit information. Bandwidth is limited by a network's narrowest link, frequently the modem.

Batch processing Refers to early business applications where similar transactions (e.g., customer billing) were gathered together according to defined periods (e.g., daily, weekly, monthly), keypunched and verified, then processed in one computer run. Compare *on-line transaction processing.*

Bit, bytes   *Bits* are the primary unit of instruction for computers; they are either "1" or "0," indicating an on or an off state for electricity flowing through hardware circuits. *Bytes* consist of a group of *bits,* usually either 16, 32, or 64 bits, that form a higher order of information, normally an alphanumeric character (e.g., "a," "3," "&," etc.). The greater the number of bits composing a byte, the more computer instructions are contained within a unit of information, allowing the computer to perform more operations faster.

Blue screen   What a system operator sees when the Windows NT server operating system encounters an error (see *bug*). The *blue screen* usually displays an error message and frequently requires the system to be shut down and restarted. (See *reboot.*)

Boot, boot-up   The act of starting up the operating system during initial power up of the computer hardware. With most computers today, this happens automatically as soon as power is turned on.

Boot-up   See *Boot, boot-up.*

Bridges, routers, gateways, hubs   All key networking technologies that connect users and networks to each other, locally and over long distances. *Bridges* connect local area networks (LANs), normally locally, that use the same protocol (speak the same networking language). *Routers* link LANs that use different protocols and link LANs to wide area networks (WANs). *Gateways* examine the content of messages being transported and route them to their proper destination according to content and type, for example, emails. *Hubs* in general manage the physical connectivity and wiring of networks within a given physical location.

Browser   Client software that allows a user to navigate the *World Wide Web* and access, retrieve, and interact with information and applications residing on remote servers virtually anywhere on the Internet. Netscape's Navigator and Microsoft's Internet Explorer are the two most widely user browser technologies. Browser technologies bestow "Netizenship" on everyone. Anyone who has a PC with a modem and a browser or a Network Computer or Network Appliance (which have embedded modems and browser technologies) can be a part of the Internet.

Bug   A system or software error that may freeze a process, sometimes requiring the system to be completely shut down and restarted, or introduce into business processes barely detectable errors that can result in inaccurate results.

Business intelligence systems (BISs)   Business tools and applications that enable the extraction and analysis of information for strategic and tactical business planning purposes. Also called *decision support systems*. They usually involve *data warehouse* technologies.

Byte   See *bits, bytes.*

Chief information officer (CIO)   The executive responsible for an organization's information systems (IS) operations, usually at the corporate enterprise level. Some CIOs report to the chief executive officer (CEO); others report to the chief financial officer (CFO) or, more recently, to the *chief technology officer (CTO).*

Chief technology officer (CTO)   The executive responsible for all information systems, networking, and telecommunications in an organization at the corporate enterprise level. The CTO reports to the chief executive officer (CEO). Either the chief information officer (CIO) or vice president of information systems (IS) may report directly to the CTO.

CIO   See *chief information officer.*

Client-server architectures   These define how clients and servers interact with each other, usually in an application environment, and which platforms are responsible for supporting the interface logic (see *graphical user interface*), the business logic (the application), and the information (the database). These are normally "two-tiered" (interface and business logic on the client; database on the server); "three-tiered" (interface logic on the client; business logic on an *application server;* data on a *data server*); or "*n*-tiered" (an expansion of "three-tiered" where any number of different application and data servers are available to many different types of clients over networks).

Clients   Platform technologies (hardware and operating systems) through which users access information and applications. "Fat clients" are self-contained, accessing and using information contained inside their own hardware but also capable of accessing external application and information through networks. "Thin clients" (sometimes called Network Computers) have minimal hardware (screen, mouse, keyboard, processor, memory) and a compact operating systems but normally no

Enterprise resource planning (ERP) Evolves from manufacturing resource planning (MRP), which originally referred to all the applications and processes that made up a complete manufacturing cycle, from computer-aided design (CAD), to product data management (PDM), to computer-integrated manufacturing (CIM). ERP adds financial, human resource, inventory, and shipping applications, among others, to MRP, all of which are "back-office" applications.

ERM See *enterprise relationship management.*

Extranet Extension of the term *Intranet* to describe the use of Internet and Web technologies to form specific networks among two or more independent organizations that require the interchange of information and the use of common applications. For example, a manufacturer and its suppliers, or a distributor and its product suppliers.

Gateways See *bridges, routers, gateways, hubs.*

Graphical user interface (GUI) The screen-based interface common to Microsoft Windows or Apple Macintosh operating systems or the interface environment supplied for a specific application (e.g., medical resonance imaging). GUIs are the technology through which most users access and interact with information and applications. Soon to be largely augmented and later replaced by voice-recognition and voice-responsive interfaces.

Groupware Enabling technologies that facilitate collaboration and group productivity (e.g., workflow, project management). For example, Lotus 1-2-3 is a personal productivity tool, enabling spreadsheet users to become individually more productive, whereas Lotus Notes is a group productivity tool enabling more productive collaboration among a group of individuals, the work group.

GUI See *graphical user interface.*

Hubs See *bridges, routers, gateways, hubs.*

Information management systems (IMSs) The combination of database technology with information management tools and technologies commonly bundled together by IMS providers such as IBM, Informix, Microsoft, Oracle, and Sybase. Although the relational database technology from each of these suppliers can be relatively similar and has become more or less a commodity, what each vendor includes in its total IMS package can different radically and deserves close scrutiny.

Information systems (ISs)   Normally applied to departmental organizations and professionals whose chief responsibility is managing information technology (IT) resources and providing information services for enterprise-level organizations.

Information technology (IT)   Refers to the broad range of hardware and software technologies, including networking technologies, that make up the IT infrastructure.

Integration   The effort and ability to make separate and often disparate systems, applications, and information work together so that users access all resources transparently.

Internet   Not a physical network but a set of standards and technologies that creates a virtual network of thousands of separate networks, so that a user attached to one network can access the information and resources residing on any other network.

Intranet   A network that uses Internet standards and technologies, normally internal to an organization and set up around a community of interest or practice or a work group whose members are geographically remote from one another. Compare *extranet.*

IS   See *information systems.*

IT   See *information technology.*

Java   A set of enabling software technologies designed by Sun Microsystems to build Internet and intranet/extranet business applications. Java applications can be developed and deployed quickly and at lower cost than can applications developed with traditional tools, such as fourth-generation languages, and can run transparently over Internet-harmonious networks without regard to operating systems or hardware platforms, either clients or servers.

Knowledge   See *data, information, knowledge.*

LAN   See *local area network.*

Legacy   Applications or information on existing systems that cannot be replaced efficiently. Legacy applications are frequently written in third-generation languages (normally COBOL) and are housed on proprietary mainframe or minicomputers. Legacy data are frequently contained in hierarchical ("flat-file") databases (e.g., IBM's older information management system).

Linux   A widely used Unix-like operating system that can be used commercially without paying any licensing or royalty fees. Originally developed by Linus Torvalds, a computer science student in Finland, Linux conforms to all standards for Unix-like operating systems and can run most existing Unix-based applications with little or no alteration to the application. Linux provides both 32-bit and 64-bit hardware support and supports all standard Unix and Internet protocols. A growing community of system and software vendors have initiated support for Linux, including Intel, Hewlett-Packard, IBM, as well as nearly all major information management systems providers. Linux is emerging as the major alternative to Microsoft's Windows 2000 server operating system and is sufficiently robust, scaleable, and reliable to support large enterprise and networking applications.

Local area network (LAN)   A collection of PCs connected to a PC server that enables the sharing of devices (usually printers and modems) and commonly used files (database or application files). LANs have grown in sophistication over the past two decades but are still generally limited by their physical wiring constraints.

Middleware   A group of technologies traditionally used to direct processes to appropriate and available resources, to monitor transactions, and to provide fail-over capability among computing resources. Modern middleware technologies also focus on *application integration* (see also *enterprise application integration*) and enabling business applications to be accessed through Web and Internet technologies (See *application server*). See also *Unix*.

Network   Telecommunications technologies that enable the interchange of information among a variety of applications and users.

Network appliance   Normally a device that can access Internet-based information and application resources and designed for a specific set of predetermined functions. It belongs to the category of "thin clients." Also referred to as "Internet appliance."

Network computers   A client platform designed to access information and applications through a browser and on the Internet (and intranets/extranets). Like network appliances, one of the class of "thin clients."

Network operating system (NOS)   Similar to operating systems but dedicated to networking tasks among client and server platform technologies.

NOS   See *network operating system.*

OLTP   See *on-line transaction processing.*

On-line transaction processing (OLTP)   The processing of transactions as they occur with little lag time between the transaction event, the processing of transaction, updating of computer records, and output. Airline reservation and ticketing and point of sale transactions are two examples of OLTP. Supersedes *batch processing.*

Open systems   Hardware and software technologies that conform to standards that are normally established and maintained (if not enforced) by standards organizations such as the Institute of Electrical and Electronic Engineers (IEEE), the Consultative Committee for International Telephony and Telegraphy (CCITT), or the Open Group. Standards do not belong to an individual technology provider (e.g., Microsoft); however, vendors may commit to open systems by ensuring that their products are compatible with and run on the widest range of available technologies, for example, Java and Oracle.

Operating systems   A set of software that manages the functions of platform hardware (processor, memory, storage, input, and output) and coordinates and controls the use of system resources by application programs.

PC   See *personal computer.*

Personal computer (PC)   Normally, a stand-alone device consisting of a processor (e.g., Intel Pentium), storage devices (normally a hard disk and a CD-ROM or diskette), memory (16MB or more), an operating system (Mircosoft Windows or Apple Macintosh), input devices (keyboard and mouse), and output devices (at least a screen and commonly today audio speakers). PCs serve only one user at a time, although they may perform several tasks simultaneously. PCs include desktops, laptops, and notebooks.

Proprietary   Any platform product, hardware or software, that is the exclusive technology of a single vendor and is not transportable to other technologies in its same class. The opposite of *open systems.*

Protocol   A set of instructions that defines the way in which data packets are assembled, transmitted over networks, and reassembled at their destination back into their original form. Also see *Transmission Control Protocol/Internet Protocol.*

RDBMS   See *relational database management system.*

Reboot   The process of restarting an operating system and the applications running on the operating system. Normally called for when an operating system encounters a *bug,* which results in freezing all processes or displays an error message that cannot be overridden. See also *bluescreen.*

Relational database management system (RDBMS)   The organization of data into rows and columns and the ability to define and manipulate data and to perform ad hoc queries on the database using a Structured Query Language (SQL). See also *information management systems.*

Routers   See *bridges, routers, gateways, hubs.*

Scaleability   The ability of a system to expand in order to meet increased numbers of users and increased demands by users. Normally applies to major software components like *operating systems, information management systems,* and applications, but can apply to hardware, network capacity, and even tools and *middleware.*

Server   Platform technologies combining hardware and operating systems that provide information, applications, and network services to clients and users.

Standards   See *open systems.*

TCP/IP   See *Transmission Control Protocol/Internet Protocol.*

Transmission Control Protocol/Internet Protocol (TCP/IP)   The predominant Internet technology that allows different types of information to flow between different computers regardless of operating system, hardware, or application types. Originally TCP in the early 1970s, later split into TCP/IP, with TCP taking care of the packets and IP taking care of the addressing and forwarding services. Integrated in the Unix operating system at UC Berkeley under the sponsorship of the *Defense Advanced Research Projects Agency* (DARPA), making Unix and TCP/IP the bedrock of the Internet. Also historically the first use of the term "Internet" for the "inter-networking of networks."

Thin client   A client device that is dependent on a network for access to information and application resources. See also *network appliance* and *network computer.*

Universal resource locator (URL)   Introduced by Tim Berners-Lee. (See *Web.*) In simple terms, a pointer used on the Web to access an object, which might be a file (text, graphic, video, audio), a directory, or a website (e.g., Amazon.com). Normally seen, for example, as http://www.cnn.com/weather/html, which would be the URL for CNN's weather page, which is an html file. URLs can take a Web user to a site, such as this one does, or to a specific document within a website, like this one: http://interactive.wsj.com/articles /SB91945111740479000.htm, which would take us to an article in the February 19, 1999, *Wall Street Journal* about Olivetti's bid to acquire Telecom Italia.

Unix   Refers to a class of open, standards-based operating systems normally although not exclusively used as a server operating system242

. Unix is both multitasking and multiuser. First developed by Bell Labs in the late 1960s and early 1970s, written in C (a third-generation language), also developed initially by Bell Labs, and integrated with TCP/IP, Unix forms a large part of the Internet's backbone. Originally used by scientists and engineers, Unix began commercial adoption in the early 1980s and provides a reliable, robust, and scaleable platform for any size business application. Unix is widely used to support large enterprise-class applications in business and in government. Although versions of Unix differ among various suppliers, all are so similar that information management system and application providers, such as Oracle or SAP, have little troubling transporting their software to run on different versions of Unix. See also *Linux.*

URL   See *universal resource locator.*

Web   Refers to the World Wide Web, a part of the Internet that uses an established standard for organizing, locating, retrieving, and displaying any type of information residing on any server in any network. First developed by Tim Berners-Lee, a British physicist working at Conseil European pour la Research Nucleaire (CERN) in Switzerland, the Web was aimed at allowing access to a wide variety of information residing on different computers. The Web consists of three primary components, initially developed by Berners-Lee: hypertext markup language (HTML), hypertext transfer protocol (HTTP), and universal resource locators (URLs).

Wide area network (WAN)   A network internal to an organization that links geographically remote offices over most types of long-distance communications. Unlike *local area networks* (LANs), which allow only one transmission to occur at a time, WANs are designed to accommodate multiple transmissions from multiple users. Notoriously expensive and slow, WANs are being superseded by intranets for networking within an organization and by extranets for networking among individual organizations (e.g., between a manufacturer and supplier).

Windows NT   Microsoft's flagship proprietary operating system, which currently comes in two 32-bit versions, one for PCs (Intel-based desktops, notebooks, etc.) and one for servers (either Intel-based or Digital/Compaq Alpha servers). The next release will be called Windows 2000, either for clients or for servers, and each will have several variations, for personal users, professional users, and enterprise environments. The client operating systems will replace Windows 95 and Windows 98. The top-end server, Windows 2000 Data Server, will be Microsoft's product offering for large-enterprise applications, such as ERP, and is intended to compete with Unix-based platforms from IBM, Hewlett-Packard, Sun Microsystems, and others. See also *Linux* and *Unix.*

NOTE

1. For more detailed definitions and discussions of most of these terms and concepts, see:

   Keen, Peter G. W. *Every Manager's Guide to Information Technology: A Glossary of Key Terms and Concepts for Today's Business Leaders.* Cambridge, Mass.: Harvard Business School Press, 1995. First published in 1991 and expanded in 1995, Keen's glossary is slightly dated.

   Keen, Peter G. W., Walid Mougayar, and Tracy Torregrossa. *The Business Internet and Intranets: A Manager's Guide to Key Terms and Concepts.* Cambridge, Mass.: Harvard Business School Press, 1998. Roughly 60 percent of the nearly 300 pages are glossary and cover the newer, more Internet-related concepts and terms that have emerged since Keen's last glossary.

   Sheldon, Tom. *Encyclopedia of Networking.* New York: McGraw-Hill, 1998. An in-depth technical compendium of networking terms and concepts.

Index